C000257741

A Companion to Common Worship

Volume 2

Founded in 1897, the Alcuin Club seeks to promote the study of Christian liturgy and worship in general, with special reference to worship in the Anglican Communion. The Club has published a series of annual Collections, including *A Companion to Common Worship*, volumes 1 and 2, edited by Paul F. Bradshaw, and most recently, *Christian Prayer through the Centuries* (SPCK, 2007) by Joseph A. Jungmann. The Alcuin Liturgy Guide series aims to address the theology and practice of worship, and the most recent in the series is *The Use of Symbols in Worship*, edited by Christopher Irvine. Two forthcoming titles, written by Benjamin Gordon-Taylor and Simon Jones, will cover the celebration of the Christian year. The Club works in partnership with GROW in the publication of the Joint Liturgical Studies series, with two studies being published each year.

Members of the Club receive publications of the current year free and others at a reduced price. The President of the Alcuin Club is the Rt Revd Michael Perham, and its Chairman is the Revd Canon Dr Donald Gray CBE. For details regarding membership, the annual subscription and lists of publications, contact the Secretary, Mr Jack Ryding, 'Ty Nant', 6 Parc Bach, Trefnant, Denbighshire LL16 4YE; email alcuinclub@gmail.com

Visit the Alcuin Club website at: **www.alcuinclub.org.uk**

A Companion to
Common Worship

Edited by
Paul Bradshaw

Volume 2

Alcuin Club Collections 81

First published in Great Britain in 2006

Society for Promoting Christian Knowledge
36 Causton Street
London SW1P 4ST

Copyright © Paul Bradshaw 2006

All rights reserved. No part of this book may be reproduced or transmitted in any form or by any means, electronic or mechanical, including photocopying, recording, or by any information storage and retrieval system, without permission in writing from the publisher.

SPCK does not necessarily endorse the individual views contained in its publications.

British Library Cataloguing-in-Publication Data
A catalogue record for this book is available from the British Library

ISBN 978–0–281–05778–8

10 9 8 7 6 5 4 3 2

Designed and typeset by Kenneth Burnley, Wirral, Cheshire
Printed in Great Britain by Ashford Colour Press

Produced on paper from sustainable forests

Contents

Contributors

The Revd Dr **Paul Bradshaw** is Professor of Liturgy at the University of Notre Dame, and a member of the Church of England Liturgical Commission.

The Revd Canon Dr **Anne Dawtry** is Course Director of South North-West Training Partnership in the Diocese of Manchester and Assistant Priest in the Chorlton Team Ministry.

Ms **Dana Delap** is a prison chaplain and a member of the Church of England General Synod and of the Liturgical Commission.

The Revd **Harry Everett** is Vicar of All Saints', Reading.

The Revd **Gordon Giles** is Vicar of St Mary Magdalene's, Enfield, in the Diocese of London, and was formerly Succentor of St Paul's Cathedral.

The Revd **Benjamin Gordon-Taylor** lectures in liturgy and ecclesiology at the College of the Resurrection, Mirfield.

The Revd **Carolyn Headley** is a hospital chaplain for Portsmouth Hospitals NHS Trust and a former Tutor in Liturgy and Spirituality at Wycliffe Hall, Oxford.

The Revd Dr **Simon Jones** is Chaplain and Fellow of Merton College, Oxford, and teaches liturgy at the Faculty of Theology in the University of Oxford and at St Stephen's House, Oxford.

The Ven. **Trevor Lloyd** was formerly Archdeacon of Barnstaple and a member of the Church of England Liturgical Commission.

Dr **Bridget Nichols** is Lay Chaplain and Research Assistant to the Bishop of Ely.

The Revd Dr **Paul Roberts** is Vicar of St Saviour with St Mary, Cotham and St Paul, Clifton in Bristol. He was formerly Chair of the General Synod Steering Committee for the Additional Collects.

The Revd Dr **Phillip Tovey** is Director of Reader Training in the Diocese of Oxford and Lecturer in Liturgy at Ripon College, Cuddesdon.

Abbreviations

ASB	*The Alternative Service Book 1980*
BAS	The Anglican Church of Canada, *Book of Alternative Services*, Anglican Book Centre, Toronto, 1985
BCP	*Book of Common Prayer*
CCP	Society of St Francis, *Celebrating Common Prayer*, Mowbray, London, 1992
CW	*Common Worship*
CWPE	*Common Worship: President's Edition*
DP	*Common Worship: Daily Prayer*, 2005
ECUSA	The Episcopal Church in the United States of America
ECY	Michael Perham (ed.), *Enriching the Christian Year*, SPCK, London, 1993
LHWE	The Church of England, *Lent, Holy Week and Easter*, Church House Publishing, London, 1986
NPFW	The Church of England, *New Patterns for Worship*, Church House Publishing, London, 2004
PFW	The Church of England, *Patterns for Worship*, Church House Publishing, London, 1995
PHG	The Church of England, *The Promise of His Glory*, Church House Publishing, London, 1991
RCIA	The Roman Catholic Church, Rite of Christian Initiation of Adults
Silk, *PUAS*	David Silk, *Prayers for Use at the Alternative Services*, Mowbray, London, 1980
TS	*Common Worship* Times and Seasons

Chapter 12 includes material adapted from *Common Worship: Ordinal. Report by the Liturgical Commission* (GS 1535), which is copyright © The Archbishops' Council 2004 and is reproduced by permission.

Acknowledgements

On page 121, the Collect for the Second Sunday in Advent, in *Common Worship: Services and Prayers for the Church of England*, is adapted from the Book of Common Prayer, the rights in which are vested in the Crown, and is reproduced by permission of the Crown's Patentee, Cambridge University Press.

On page 123, the Collects for the Third Sunday of Lent and the Feast of the Epiphany are copyright material taken from *A New Zealand Prayer Book – He Karakia Mihinare o Aotearoa* and are used with permission.

On page 126, the Collects for the Fourth Sunday in Advent are copyright © The Archbishops' Council and are reproduced by permission.

Chapter 1

Daily Prayer

A. HISTORY

Jewish and Early Christian Practice

Most modern Jewish scholars are convinced that no general obligation to observe regular times of prayer every day existed in Judaism until after the destruction of the Temple and the transformation of the faith that resulted from that catastrophe. Prior to that event daily prayer would probably have been the custom only of certain pious groups. It appears that some people recited the *Shema* (Deuteronomy 6.4–9; 11.13–21; Numbers 15.37–41) twice a day, morning and evening; although strictly speaking a creed rather than a prayer, it was in later times accompanied by brief prayers before and after, and something like this may well have been the case in the first century. Others apparently followed a tradition of prayer three times a day, first mentioned in Daniel 6.10. In later centuries these two patterns were combined to form the expected norm for all Jews. While these daily devotions might on occasion have been performed corporately, more often than not the practice would have been an individual one.

Although earlier generations of scholars supposed that the oldest Christian practice was prayer twice a day, morning and evening, and that this would usually have been done in corporate gatherings rather than as an individual action, those assumptions have been challenged by more recent research. It now appears that prayer three times a day may have been the more common practice. This pattern is first mentioned in the *Didache*, a church order probably dating from the late first or early second century, and recurs in other Christian texts from the second and third centuries, which also include prayer in the middle of the night as part of the regular daily cycle. While in rural communities the timing of the thrice-daily prayer would have been regulated by the movement of the sun (sunrise, noon and sunset), in urban settings it seems to have been co-ordinated with the major divisions of the Roman day, which would have been publicly announced: the third hour (about 9 a.m.), the sixth hour (about noon) and the ninth hour (about 3 p.m). By the middle of the third century there is evidence from Cyprian in North Africa that it was the custom there to combine the two cycles into a composite pattern of prayer five times a day (morning, third, sixth and ninth hours, and evening) and once again in the middle of the night.

While there are signs that married couples, whole families and groups of Christian friends may have prayed together at these times, yet for many Christians, as for many Jews, this must in general have been an individual activity. It is important not to assume from this, however, that what was done was thought of as private prayer. Christians understood themselves to be members of the body of Christ, and their prayers to be united with one another, whether they happened to be praying alone or with others.

We have no detailed knowledge of the content of these times of daily prayer, but from the clues that do exist we may reasonably assume that they were largely extemporized and composed chiefly of praise and intercession. The singing of psalms and hymns seems originally to have been associated with Christian community meals, but Tertullian, writing in North Africa at the beginning of the third century, tells us that the 'more pious' there were accustomed to include in their daily prayers psalms that have an 'Alleluia' in the biblical text, so that those present may use it as a response. Presumably others were not yet doing so.

Fourth-Century Developments

After the cessation of persecution in the fourth century allowed church buildings to become more common, the public celebration of the daily hours of prayer became an established practice. Because assembling together was only a practical possibility for ordinary folk at the beginning and end of their working day, and not during the day or in the middle of the night, morning and evening prayer were usually the sole hours that were prayed in many churches. However, in major cities other times might also have formed part of the publicly celebrated cycle. The pre-eminence of morning and evening over the other traditional hours of daily prayer was given a theological rationale by the claim that they constituted the true fulfilment of the morning and evening sacrifices of the Old Testament (earlier generations of Christians had seen those sacrifices as finding their fulfilment in the ceaseless praise and prayer offered by believers in every place).

These daily services were composed of two principal elements – praise for God's creation and redemption, and intercession for the needs of the world. The core of morning prayer everywhere seems to have been Psalms 148–150, repeated every day. In many places, especially in the East, this was followed by the canticle, *Gloria in excelsis*, and preceded by Psalm 63, because its first verse was (mis)translated in Greek as referring to the morning. Psalm 51 often formed a penitential introduction to the service. Only on Sundays and festivals was there any variation in this daily pattern. Evening prayer seems to have been less standardized. There was no equivalent of Psalms 148–150, but in Eastern practice Psalm 141 seems to have been the counterpart to Psalm 63, because of its reference to the offering of the evening sacrifice in verse 2, and the hymn *Phos hilaron*, 'Hail, gladdening light', was sung at the beginning as the evening lamp was ceremonially lit, a traditional domestic custom now taken over into ecclesiastical practice. Intercession was often in the form of a litany, with its petitions varying according to the needs perceived by the local church. Modern scholars have given the name 'cathedral office' to this pattern of prayer. Neither morning nor evening prayer usually included any Bible readings, which belonged instead to distinct services of the word. These were held on Sundays, as part of the eucharistic rite, and on Wednesdays and Fridays, the standard days of fasting each week, generally at the conclusion of the fast at the ninth hour, and often on a daily basis during the season of Lent.

While congregations were still being urged by preachers to observe all the other daily times of prayer wherever they happened to be, few did so, and those hours came to be thought of as the preserve of the especially devout and of the new religious communities that were emerging in towns and cities throughout the Christian world. Some of these groups joined in whatever hours were being celebrated in their local church or cathedral and then completed the rest of the daily cycle in their own communities, while others kept the entire daily round within their community. This pattern of prayer has been described by modern scholars as the 'urban monastic office'.

Long before the fourth century dawned there had been some Christians who had not been content merely with frequent times of prayer each day, but wanted to fulfil the apostolic injunction to 'pray without ceasing' (1 Thessalonians 5.17) rather more literally, keeping up a constant vigil of praise and prayer throughout their waking hours while they toiled at their daily tasks. This vision of ceaseless prayer was taken up by the hermits and ascetics who took to the deserts of Egypt and Syria in the early part of the fourth century. Dissatisfied by what they regarded as the laxity of the lifestyle of the majority of members of the Church in the post-persecution era, they withdrew from society and devoted their lives to engaging in spiritual combat with the devil in the isolation of these regions. Their constant prayer was interrupted only by the minimal breaks for food and sleep. Once they had risen for prayer during the night, they did not return to bed but immediately embarked upon their daily vigil of prayer, continuing until daylight enabled them to start work, which they then did to the accompaniment of their praying.

The content of their prayer was significantly different from that of their contemporaries back in the towns and cities. Instead of praise and intercession, their focus was on perpetual meditation on the word of God. They would recite to themselves passages from Scripture they had learned by heart, alternating this with silent reflection on its meaning, intent on fostering their own spiritual growth towards perfection. We may thus describe their prayer as inward looking, in comparison with the more outward orientation towards the world seen in the prayer of the Church at large. As communities of monks were gradually formed in the deserts, they too adopted a similar spirituality and pattern of praying. The Pachomian communities of Upper Egypt seem to have assembled together twice each day, morning and evening, and to have practised in those gatherings the same sort of praying as they would maintain individually in the rest of the day: different members of the community in turn would read aloud a passage of Scripture, with a period for silent meditation in between. In Lower Egypt, however, the monks would mostly pray alone in their cells, and here the preferred texts as the basis for their meditation were the canonical psalms. Since they were thought by early Christians to have been written by King David under the inspiration of the Holy Spirit, and to have been prophetic in character, referring to the Messiah who was to come, they seemed the natural choice for those who wanted to form their own lives after the pattern of Christ. Each psalm was interpreted as either being addressed to Christ or to be about Christ or to be Christ speaking. Unlike the selected psalms of praise in the 'cathedral office', these communities used the whole Psalter, learning it by heart and reciting it in its biblical order with silence for meditation after each psalm. This distinctive pattern of praying is termed the 'desert monastic office' by modern scholars.

Cross-Fertilization: The Traditions Combined

It is hardly surprising to find that, as time went by, the thoroughgoing asceticism of the desert monks began to influence the spirituality of urban monastic communities, including their patterns of worship. The first signs of this are already evident in the fourth-century sources with the emergence of a nightly vigil in urban monasticism, joining the ancient time of prayer in the middle of the night to morning prayer with a service of alternating psalms and silent prayer, the psalms being sung in their biblical order. This shortening of the period of sleep led in some cases to monks going back to bed once morning prayer was over, and to the consequent emergence in many monastic rules of an additional time of prayer after the morning office at the first hour of the day (and therefore called 'Prime' in the West) to put an end to this 'second sleep', as it was known. Together with prayer at bedtime (known as 'Compline' in the West), the urban monastic round in most places now consisted of a total of seven daily services, in addition to the long night office (given varying names in different traditions, such as Nocturns or Vigils, and later Mattins, because it was the first service of the day): morning prayer (usually called 'Lauds' in the West, because its core was the *Laudate* Psalms 148–150); the first hour ('Prime'), the third, sixth and ninth hours ('Terce', 'Sext' and 'None'), evening prayer (often called 'Vespers' in the West) and Compline.

As time went by, Western monastic traditions were more profoundly affected by the ideal of the Egyptian desert monks, and the practice of using the whole Psalter began to supplant the older tradition of using only certain psalms selected for their appropriateness as hymns of praise at every service of the day. The Rule of Benedict, for example, aimed to complete all 150 psalms in the services each week, with only a few of them being repeated daily. Intercession disappeared almost entirely from the offices, and even the silences for meditation between the psalms were reduced in length, and eventually eliminated altogether, as the psalms themselves came to be thought of as being the praise of the Church (in accordance with the 'cathedral' tradition) and no longer as the food for individual meditation going on between them (as in the 'desert' monastic tradition), even though not all of them were explicitly songs of praise. The tradition of also interpreting them christologically, however, continued to linger on. Bible reading too now became a feature of the daily services, usually just brief passages at the daytime hours but more substantial readings along with the psalms during the long night office.

It was not simply in monastic communities that the earlier distinct traditions were mingled. Often under the influence of bishops who either had themselves been monks or had been attracted by the monastic ideal, the 'cathedral' tradition itself began to adopt more of the monastic hours of daily prayer and to incorporate a wider range of psalmody. While in Eastern rites the distinction between what had originally been 'cathedral' elements and those that were 'monastic' tended to remain visible in these hybrid offices, this was not so in the West. Not least as a result of the practice in Rome and other major cities of some monastic communities being given the responsibility for maintaining the prayer and sacramental life of certain city churches, and therefore using an 'urban monastic' form of daily office, even if it was still with a 'cathedral' understanding of what they were doing, 'cathedral' features gradually diminished in all types of daily prayer and 'monastic' forms took over. Selected psalms and canticles decreased in frequency, being largely supplanted by a pattern involving the use of all 150 psalms within a given period of time, and intercession virtually disappeared from the services.

The clergy were also increasingly pressed to be present at every one of these daily offices in their churches, especially as the distinction between the monastic and clerical vocations was becoming blurred. The ordinary people, however, generally continued to adhere to their traditional custom of attending only morning and evening prayer, but because the chanting became more elaborate and the range of psalms greater, and they themselves were illiterate and in any case unable to understand the Latin language used for worship, they became passive spectators at the praise and prayer being offered by others. In the course of time their attendance at morning and evening prayer tended to be limited to Sundays and major feasts.

The Middle Ages

Although prayer seven times a day together with a lengthy night vigil might seem enough for any Christian, even for those monastic communities dedicated to a life of prayer, the services were gradually enlarged in the course of the Middle Ages in the West by the addition of a number of secondary elements. Chief among these were the 'little hours'. These were miniature versions of the main offices, made up of selected psalmody and prayers and usually honouring one of the saints or one of the mysteries of salvation, which were appended to each of the daily times of prayer. Different communities had different devotional preferences, but the most popular choices were the little office of the

Blessed Virgin Mary and the Office of the Dead, the latter being seen as intercession rather than praise. Thus more and more time each day was taken up
with prayer.

While singing these offices every day came to present something of a burden
even to monastic communities, it proved an intolerable load for those like the
Franciscans, whose way of life was itinerant, and above all for the ordinary
clergy engaged in pastoral work or in study at the universities springing up
throughout Europe in the later Middle Ages. They were required to maintain
exactly the same round of prayer as their monastic counterparts. On the other
hand, because small communities and individuals could not be expected to
possess all the books required for a full celebration of the office, it tended to be
abbreviated in part so that everything necessary could be contained within a
single large volume, known therefore as the Breviary. Nevertheless, the result
was that for these people the daily office ceased to be a communal celebration
and became instead something to be recited individually on most occasions,
and frequently not at the specified hour. There was a common tendency to
group the eight times of prayer into two major blocks each day, morning and
evening, in order to accommodate them within an active rather than contem-
plative way of life. Sometimes even that did not work, and clergy and others
found themselves slipping behind in finding time to recite their offices
by several days – or even longer. The most famous instance is that of the
Augustinian canon, Martin Luther:

> When I was a monk I was unwilling to omit any of the prayers, but when
> I was busy with public lecturing and writing I often accumulated my
> appointed prayers for a whole week, or even two or three weeks. Then I
> would take a Saturday off, or shut myself in for as long as three days
> without food and drink, until I had said the prescribed prayers. This
> made my head split, and as a consequence I couldn't close my eyes for five
> nights, lay sick unto death, and went out of my senses. (*Table Talk*, 495;
> English translation from Theodore G. Tappert (ed.), *Luther's Works* 54,
> Fortress Press, Philadelphia, 1967, p. 85)

He eventually fell three months behind and gave up altogether.

Another major factor that affected the form of the daily office in the Middle
Ages was the considerable expansion of the liturgical year with the multiplication of saints' days and other festivals. Rather than simply continuing with the
regular cycle of psalms and readings, there was a tendency to substitute special
psalms and readings that related in some way to the particular saint or festival,
as well as doing the same during the week following a major feast – its octave.
Since by the late Middle Ages saints' days and other festivals accounted for the
majority of the days in the year, the ancient monastic ideal of completing all
150 psalms in a specified period of time and reading sequentially through the
Scriptures was interrupted so frequently by 'proper' psalms and readings that it

effectively disappeared from view. One can only conclude that even monastic orders found that the use of selected psalms and readings better suited their devotional needs. Working out which material was to be used on any given day also made the celebration of the office an extremely complicated affair. The situation at the end of the medieval period is well summed up by the Preface to the 1549 *BCP*, which stated that 'the number and hardness of the rules called the Pie, and the manifold changings of the service, was the cause that to turn the book only was so hard and intricate a matter that many times there was more business to find out what should be read than to read it when it was found out'.

Some reform was obviously desirable, and in 1535, in response to a request from the Pope, Cardinal Francisco Quiñones produced a reformed Breviary intended to meet better the needs of those who recited the office on their own. It involved drastic simplification and a return to the ancient monastic ideal. Although all the eight hours of prayer each day were retained, they were very much shorter, each being composed of opening prayers and a hymn (except at Lauds), then three psalms (at Lauds, two psalms and an Old Testament canticle) and a collect. Lauds, Vespers and Compline had in addition a Gospel canticle, and the night office an opening canticle (Psalm 95), three substantial readings and the *Te Deum*. In this way the whole Psalter was once more completed in a week, this cycle never being interrupted even for Christmas Day or Easter, and most of the Bible read in the course of a year, with relatively few special readings for saints' days. Although warmly welcomed by the clergy, who had particularly felt the burden of the traditional offices, it was strongly opposed by conservatives, and this opposition was a major factor behind the decision made by the Council of Trent in 1568 to annul every Breviary that did not have a 200-year tradition behind it and replace it with the form of the Roman Breviary then authorized. Since this particular version did not contain quite as many secondary accretions as many other medieval forms, it was marginally better than many clergy had previously been required to use, but it was far from what they would have wished.

The Reformation in England

Since, for Luther and the other Reformers, the requirement to pray the offices was seen as 'work' intended to satisfy God, and hence stood in opposition to their central tenet of justification by faith alone, it is not surprising that a clerical obligation to recite daily hours of prayer disappeared from all the churches of the Reformation, except the Church of England. Yet, even in this last case, there was a transformation in the purpose that the office was understood to fulfil. The Preface to the 1549 *BCP*, heavily influenced by the corresponding text in Quiñones' Breviary, declared that the original purpose of the daily office, as revealed by 'the ancient fathers', had been for:

a great advancement of godliness: For they so ordered the matter that all the whole Bible (or the greatest part thereof) should be read over once in the year, intending thereby that the Clergy . . . should (by often reading, and meditation in God's word) be stirred up to godliness themselves, and be the more able to exhort others by wholesome doctrine, and to confute them that were adversaries to the truth; and further, that the people (by daily hearing of holy scripture read in the Church) might continually profit more and more in the knowledge of God, and be the more inflamed with the love of his true religion.

In other words, what was being restored here was a pure 'monastic' form and concept of the office, centred on the systematic reading of the Bible and recitation of the Psalter. Later generations of Anglicans, however, like the monastic communities before them, have often tended to interpret what they were doing in more 'cathedral' terms, as the offering of praise and prayer to God, even if the forms that they were required to use did not really correspond very well with that understanding. But what was also being restored – at least in theory, even if it did not work out widely in practice – was the idea that the daily office was something for both clergy and people to engage in together in church, not just for the clergy to recite individually, and hence the importance attached to its being in the vernacular. In this respect it went beyond Quiñones.

Also unlike Quiñones, only two hours of daily prayer were prescribed – morning and evening, the times when many clergy had recited all eight hours of the medieval round anyway. Both services had the same basic structure, incorporating elements drawn from every one of the medieval hours of prayer but producing a unique pattern centred on the reading of Scripture (see Table 1.1).

As in Quiñones' revision, hardly anything was allowed to interfere with the consecutive reading of Scripture. Very few holy days were provided with proper readings, so that the whole Old Testament was completed once each year and the New Testament three times, except for Revelation, of which only two chapters were prescribed. All 150 psalms were also recited, in their biblical order, once a month, with proper psalms being provided on only four occasions in the year. In 1552, the offices were provided with a lengthy penitential introduction, much of it from Reformed sources, and proper psalms were included as alternatives to the Gospel canticles, as the use of the latter was disliked by extreme Reformers. The *Kyries* were now also placed after the Creed with the other prayer material instead of before it. Because the laity were generally not attending the services on weekdays but continuing their traditional custom of being there only on Sundays, in the 1559 revision of the *BCP* proper first lessons were introduced for Sundays, so that they might encounter something more edifying than the next portion of the continuous reading from the weekdays. In 1662 the singing of an anthem was permitted after the

Table 1.1: The Prayer Book Pattern

Morning Prayer		*Evening Prayer*	
Lord's Prayer	⎫	Lord's Prayer	⎫
Versicles	⎪	Versicles	⎪
Gloria Patri	⎪	*Gloria Patri*	⎬ from Vespers
Venite	⎬ from Mattins		⎪
Psalms	⎪	Psalms	⎪
Old Testament reading	⎭	Old Testament reading	⎭
Te Deum		*Magnificat*	⎫
New Testament reading	⎬ from Lauds	New Testament reading	⎪
Benedictus		*Nunc dimittis*	⎬ from Compline
Kyries	⎬ from Prime	*Kyries*	⎪
Creed	⎭	Creed	⎭
Lord's Prayer	⎫	Lord's Prayer	⎫
Preces	⎬ from Lauds	*Preces*	⎬ from Vespers
Collect of the Day		Collect of the Day	⎪
Collect for Peace	⎭	Collect for Peace	⎭
Collect for Grace	from Prime	Collect for Aid	from Compline

collects, and further prayers appended at the conclusion of the services. Except for periodic attempts to revise the Lectionary and to provide proper psalms for Sundays and holy days, the Prayer Book offices have continued in this form down to the present day.

Modern Revisions

Most twentieth-century revisions have been very conservative in character, adhering to the principle that Anglican daily worship is centred on the reading of substantial portions of Scripture and the recitation of the whole Psalter in a given period of time. All they have usually tried to do is to reduce the quantities of biblical material to be read and the number of psalm verses to be recited on any occasion and to introduce some more variety into the canticles and prayers. Thus the abortive 1927/28 attempt at revision mainly allowed certain parts of the service to be omitted, and provided a range of additional prayers and some seasonal opening sentences, though it did include forms for Prime and Compline in an appendix. Most of these provisions (though not the appendix) were included in the Series 1 texts in 1966, and the Series 2 version went very little further than that. Even the ecumenical *Daily Office* produced by the Joint Liturgical Group in 1968 was really only a slimmed-down version of the traditional Anglican form, with just three readings each day (two in the morning, one in the evening) and with one canticle alone at each service, arranged on a weekly cycle. The readings were shorter, with the Old Testament being spread over a two-year period and the New Testament read only once each year, and the cycle of psalms was completed in three months instead of one. This office, with minor alterations, was adopted as one of two alternatives in Series 2 Revised Morning and Evening Prayer (the other being an amended version of the Series 2 service) authorized in 1971. In 1975 Series 3 offered modern-language versions of these two alternative forms, and these were incorporated in the *ASB*. Revisions in the rest of the Anglican Communion have mostly been of a similar kind, although the 1979 American Book of Common Prayer supplemented the offices with forms of noonday prayer, Compline, 'Daily Devotions for Individuals and Families' and an alternative 'Order of Worship for the Evening' modelled on the ancient ceremony of lighting the evening lamp. These developments were taken further in the 1985 Canadian *BAS*.

In England significant change did not emerge until a semi-official partnership of some members of the Liturgical Commission with the Society of Saint Francis produced *Celebrating Common Prayer* (*CCP*) in 1992. This appeared in two versions, one making very rich provision for the daily office, the other offering a somewhat simpler adaptation in a volume that would fit easily into a pocket. Together these moved away from the classical Anglican model by offering forms of daily prayer which embraced many of the characteristics of the 'cathedral' tradition of the fourth century and, at the same time, bore some resemblance to the Roman Catholic Church's revision of the Liturgy of the Hours (*Liturgia Horarum*) which followed the Second Vatican Council. Psalms chosen for their suitability to a particular time, day or season, such as the *Laudate* Psalms (146–150) at Morning Prayer; the provision of a collect which could be read at the end of the psalmody; the option of a blessing of light (*Lucernarium*) with the hymn *Phos hilaron* and verses from Psalm 141 at the beginning of Evening Prayer; and forms of service which encouraged public celebration rather than private recitation of the office were all conscious reflections of this 'cathedral' tradition.

In the main edition, full forms of Morning, Midday, Evening and Night Prayer were provided for each day of the week. With the exception of Midday Prayer, each of these orders was also linked to a particular season. This, together with a revision of the calendar which took forward many of the Liturgical Commission's proposals in *The Promise of His Glory* (1991), enabled a much richer celebration of the Christian year, and, in Ordinary Time, gave each day of the week its own seasonal flavour. A significant feature of the pocket edition was the provision of short passages of Scripture within simplified forms of prayer. Not only did this have the practical advantage of allowing the office to be celebrated without any further resources, but it was also a conscious imitation of the 'cathedral' pattern which placed praise and intercession, rather than the reading of Scripture, at the heart of the office.

That *CCP* enabled the Liturgical Commission to road-test some of its ideas for an official revision of the *ASB* is beyond doubt. In its 1991 report, *The Worship of the Church as it Approaches the Third Millennium*, the Commission stated that a future daily office book could provide outlines which might be suitable for use by an individual, in a family, and in a community or church setting . . . A version might be produced . . . with suggested collects, prayers, canticles, versicles and responses, etc., which varied from day to day, as on the Roman Catholic pattern. As well as forms for morning and evening, it would also include a midday form, and Night Prayer.

CCP provided just such a resource. Although, for some, its complexity compared with the *BCP* and *ASB* rendered it culpable of Thomas Cranmer's criticism that it could sometimes take longer to find out what to pray on a particular occasion than to pray it, such a disadvantage was outweighed by its ability both to meet the liturgical needs of those who looked for an enrichment of the Anglican office and to encourage individuals and groups to engage with structured patterns of prayer for the first time. Its popularity was such that, when it came to devising forms of daily prayer for *CW*, the starting point was self-evident. Integral to the process of revision was the Liturgical Commission's decision to publish a Preliminary Edition of *CW Daily Prayer* (hereafter *DP*) in 2002. This included a questionnaire inviting comment on the range of the content and the layout of the book. These comments, together with a debate in the General Synod and by the House of Bishops, guided the second stage of the revision process which led to the publication of the definitive edition in 2005.

B. COMMENTARY

Whereas Cranmer's pattern of daily prayer placed the sequential recitation of psalmody and reading of Scripture at the heart of the office, *DP* seeks to recover lost elements of the 'cathedral office' tradition of the fourth century, while remaining faithful to the Anglican principle of daily engagement with Scripture. Thus, *DP* follows *CCP* in seeking not only to enrich the *BCP/ASB* office tradition, but also to shape it in such a way as to place greater emphasis on the offering of praise and intercession, and to set the proclamation of the Word of God within this wider context.

DP provides forms of Prayer During the Day, Morning Prayer and Evening Prayer for each day of the week and season, together with a form of Night Prayer with optional daily and seasonal variations. Unlike *CCP*, the seasonal orders are printed separately from those for Ordinary Time, which are on the whole unconnected to particular seasons, except that Fridays and Sundays retain their association with the cross and resurrection respectively. Of all the forms of prayer provided, Prayer During the Day is undoubtedly the most innovative. Although an order for Prime appeared, like Compline, in the appendix to the 1927/28 Prayer Book, designed to be said 'at any convenient time before or after the saying of Morning Prayer', the Church of England has never made official provision for an order of prayer which may be used at any time of the day. The *CCP* office, which was printed in chronological sequence between Morning and Evening Prayer, was very much a Midday Office, whereas *DP*'s Prayer During the Day is deliberately designed to be flexible enough to meet the needs of a variety of groups and individuals at any point in the day.

In whatever way individuals and groups make use of these forms of prayer, undergirding each is a common structure which is clearly set out before the Notes at the beginning of each office, and contains four principal elements: Preparation, The Word of God, Prayers and Conclusion. Such a structure not only sandwiches the reading of Scripture between elements of praise and intercession but also, through the careful use of psalmody, canticles, responses and silence, allows elements of penitence, praise and prayer to be woven into the whole celebration.

Around this common structure there is a considerable degree of flexibility in the way that each order is celebrated. In addition to the introduction and the Notes which preface each office, the General Introduction provides a helpful guide to the way in which the material may be used in varying combinations to resource the daily prayer of individuals and groups, meeting a multiplicity of liturgical needs in diverse settings and contexts and encouraging the creative use of music and symbolism. It also gives guidance as to how *DP* relates to the Church of England's new weekday lectionary provision. In particular, a 'flip-flop' principle has been built into the way in which the psalms and readings for Prayer During the Day and Morning and Evening Prayer relate to each other, so that, for those who wish praise and intercession to be the focal points of their morning and/or evening worship, it is possible to use the short reading set for Prayer During the Day at Morning or Evening Prayer, and reading(s) from the *CW* Weekday Lectionary at Prayer During the Day. Likewise, for those who wish to provide a more substantial element of praise and psalmody in Prayer During the Day, either the morning or evening psalms may be used at this service, and one of the shorter Prayer During the Day cycles at Morning or Evening Prayer.

Although some may feel overwhelmed by the number of possible combinations of office and lectionary, what should guide these choices is a consideration of the bigger picture of the complete liturgical diet of any individual or community over the course of a week or a month; a diet which should take note not only of the way in which one office relates to another, but also the relationship between eucharistic and non-eucharistic worship.

Prayer During the Day
Prayer During the Day has already been referred to as one of the most innovative elements of *DP*. As its introduction makes clear, it is an order of prayer which may be used at any time of the day, either as the only act of daily worship or in combination with other orders of prayer. For example, it may be used as a liturgical framework for Quiet Time and Bible study, as a daytime

office celebrated in tandem with Night Prayer, as a simple form of Midday Prayer in addition to Morning and Evening Prayer, or as a model for the monastic offices of Terce, Sext and None. Its use is particularly commended to those approaching common daily prayer for the first time, a desire which is reflected by its simplicity and the number of 'classic texts' which are provided as prayers and canticles.

Structurally, Prayer During the Day augments the common shape which underlies all of the orders in *DP* with an element of praise following the preparation and a form of response between the Scripture reading and the prayers. Although complete orders are provided for each day of the week and season, the Notes make clear that the seasonal forms need not be used throughout a particular season, but only, possibly, at particular high points. This is, perhaps, particularly appropriate in seasons which stretch over several weeks like Epiphany, Lent and Easter.

During the seasons, many of the variable elements in each office express a number of themes related to that time of year. The weekday orders, however, while not being thematically tied, do give off the scent of particular topics and themes. Some of the daily orders, such as Sunday and Friday, have very obvious and longstanding thematic associations; on other days the scent is less strong. These themes are not exhaustive for any particular day, nor are they intended to be restrictive. For these reasons they are not printed in *DP*, but may be summarized as follows:

Sunday: creation; new creation; resurrection
Monday: economic life; business; agriculture
Tuesday: healing and wholeness
Wednesday: vocation; the needy and those who care for them
Thursday: unity; education; those in authority
Friday: the cross; penitence; reconciliation
Saturday: leisure and contemplation; saints; the dying and departed; the life of heaven.

Preparation

The form of preparation printed at the start of each order contains two versicles and responses: an adapted form of Psalm 70.1 followed by another verse from the Psalms. The use of Psalm 70.1 as an invocation at the beginning of the office goes back at least as far as St Benedict. The second psalm verse always addresses God directly, and is often in the form of an opening prayer or acclamation which celebrates a particular characteristic of the God to whom praise and prayer will be addressed. Although a pair of versicles and responses is provided at the beginning of every order, Note 1 makes it clear that this conventional opening may be replaced by a time of quiet meditation on a verse of Scripture. It also permits the use of one of the forms of penitence.

Praise

Prayer During the Day highlights praise as an important element in the preparation for worship. Although not precluding the use of the *Gloria Patri* and Alleluia as part of this, Note 2 suggests that this section might include a hymn, song, canticle or extempore praise. Each order contains a rubric which reiterates this, and also gives an example of a text which may be used. Some, like the *Te Deum* and *Gloria in excelsis*, are already well established within the Anglican liturgical tradition; others, such as the hymns of Ephrem the Syrian and Gregory Nazianzus, will be less familiar. As a resource for praise, they are intended to be as stimulating for those who are familiar to common prayer as for those who are experiencing it for the first time, but should not be interpreted as a disincentive to extemporize, sing or draw on other resources.

> *Sunday*: verses from the first section of the fourth-century canticle *Te Deum laudamus* (Canticle 79), addressed to the first person of the Trinity;
> *Monday*: a slightly adapted form of a verse from Mrs C. F. Alexander's translation of St Patrick's Breastplate, the Trinitarian hymn of praise attributed to the Patron of Ireland (372–466);
> *Tuesday*: an adaptation of verses from the *Carmina Gadelica*, a collection of Celtic prayers and other texts gathered together from the Islands and Highlands of Scotland at the turn of the twentieth century by Alexander Carmichael;
> *Wednesday*: verses from the second section of the *Te Deum*, addressed to the second person of the Trinity;
> *Thursday*: 'The Call', by the seventeenth-century Anglican priest and poet, George Herbert;
> *Friday*: The canticle 'Saviour of the World' (Canticle 87), thought to have been written by Henry Allon, a noted Congregational hymnologist of the nineteenth century;
> *Saturday*: verses adapted from one of the Syriac *Hymns on the Passion* by the fourth-century deacon Ephrem the Syrian;
> *Advent*: verses adapted from the medieval Latin Advent sequence *Salus aeterna* (Canticle 81);
> *Christmas*: the first three verses of the *Gloria in excelsis* (Canticle 78), a fourth-century composition of unknown authorship, first used in the daily morning office of the East;
> *Epiphany*: 'A Song of Christ's Appearing' (Canticle 63), which uses verses from 1 Timothy 3 and 6 to celebrate the revelation of Christ to the world;
> *Lent*: verses 1, 5–8 of what has become known as 'A Song of Anselm' (Canticle 82), written by the twelfth-century Archbishop of Canterbury;
> *Passiontide*: a compilation of three verses associated with Good Friday: 'We adore you, O Christ . . .', an acclamation of praise to the crucified Saviour traditionally used during Stations of the Cross; 'Holy God . . .', the ancient *Trisagion*, sung originally in the East during the Eucharist, and later used in

the West as part of the Good Friday Reproaches; and 'We glory in your cross, O Lord', also having its origins in the ancient Good Friday liturgy.

Easter: verses from the first *Oration* of the fourth-century doctor of the Church, Gregory of Nazianzus, which identifies the worshipper with the crucified and risen Christ;

Ascension to Pentecost: six verses from 'Bless the Lord' (Canticle 50), from The Song of the Three in the Apocrypha;

All Saints to Advent: the second section from A Litany of the Resurrection, which first appeared in *Lent, Holy Week and Easter* (1986) and was reproduced in the *CW* initiation services as a text to be used in procession to the font.

The Word of God

Notes 3 and 4 require that a psalm and at least one biblical reading are used on every occasion. For the choice of psalmody, Prayer During the Day presents four options:

- Each office suggests a psalm which may be said on any occasion when that particular order is used; for example, Psalm 133 on any Thursday, or Psalm 51.1–10 on any day in Lent. This option is likely to commend itself to those who use this office on an occasional basis, or who are new to forms of daily prayer.
- For those who are more frequent users of Prayer During the Day, a four-week psalm cycle is provided for the Sunday to Saturday orders, and a seven-day cycle for each season. Such a scheme is likely to be favoured by those who are not using this provision in addition to the morning and evening psalm cycles in the weekday lectionary.
- To celebrate Prayer During the Day as a midday office in addition to Morning and Evening Prayer, two additional psalm cycles provide schemes for saying Psalm 119 and the Psalms of Ascent (121–131 and 133) over a fortnight or a month. In addition, Note 3 allows for a portion of Psalm 119 to be used on any occasion. Psalm 119 has been associated with the lesser hours of Prime, Terce, Sext and None from as far back as the Roman monastic tradition known to Benedict.
- Finally, for those who wish to use Prayer During the Day as an office of readings, with a more substantial element of psalmody, the weekday lectionary provision for Morning or Evening Prayer may be used.

The choice of reading will, similarly, depend on how the office is being used, and whether it is being celebrated in addition to other orders of prayer.

- A four-week cycle of short biblical readings is provided for each day of the week, together with an additional reading which may be used whenever a particular order is being followed. As with the psalmody, this option will be particularly appropriate for new and occasional users of the office. The choice of readings covers a wide variety of Old and New Testament texts and some are scented with the themes loosely associated with each weekday.

- Each season has its own seven-day cycle of short readings (with the exception of the period from Ascension Day to Pentecost, when a different passage of Scripture is provided for each of the eleven days) together with an additional reading which may be used on any day in a particular season. Once again, these cover a wide range of biblical texts, but have strong seasonal associations.

- For those who are using Prayer During the Day as an office of readings, or who require more substantial engagement with Scripture than is possible with the printed texts, Note 4 permits the use of one or more readings from the Weekday Lectionary (including the eucharistic provision), and on Sundays and Principal Holy Days, one or both of the readings appointed for the Third Service.

Response

An integral feature of Prayer During the Day is the way in which groups and individuals respond to their engagement with Scripture. This may take several forms, depending on the context. Note 5 refers to silence, group discussion, responsive prayer and singing; a form of penitence may also be used at this point in the service. Alternatively, each of the orders prints a versicle and response, which should probably conclude a period of silence after the reading. Carefully chosen to reflect some of the themes associated with each order, in Ordinary Time they are based on the 'I am' sayings of John's Gospel, whereas the seasonal orders make creative use of the Beatitudes.

Prayers

The prayers offered at this point in the service are also part of the response to Scripture, and it is likely that many of the concerns expressed here will have arisen as a result of engagement with the Word of God. Each order suggests five topics which may also be used as a focus for prayer. These are drawn from the Ordinary Time and seasonal cycles of intercession, and are intended to ensure that a broad range of topics is covered rather than to restrict the freedom of groups or individuals to offer their own intentions. Note 6 refers to a litany, extempore prayer, the General Thanksgiving and a pattern of intercessions, such as those included within the section of prayers, as also being appropriate. Whatever form the intercessions take, they may, of course, include a period of silence, and are followed either by the Collect of the day or another prayer. One possibility of another prayer is that printed within each order, which may be described as a 'classic prayer'. These do not appear anywhere else within *DP*, but are examples of well-known texts from a variety of different Christian spiritual traditions. As in Morning and Evening Prayer, the Lord's Prayer concludes the intercessions.

Conclusion

Note 7 suggests several ways of ending the office. Printed within each order is a simple prayer of blessing, which is thematically related to the rest of the service. The weekday forms all come from the Midday Office in *CCP*, whereas in seasons these are new compositions. Alternatively, the service may close with a concluding prayer, a dismissal or another ending. If a priest is present, another ending could be a blessing, and one example of a concluding prayer would be the Grace. *DP* also allows the Peace to be exchanged at the end of any order (General Note 9). Although many may be surprised to experience this corporate act of fellowship outside the context of the Eucharist, the invitation, 'Let us offer one another a sign of peace, God's seal on our prayers', alludes to Tertullian's description of the Peace as 'the seal of prayer', and therefore an appropriate conclusion to any office.

Forms of Penitence

For the most part, penitential material is not printed within the individual orders of *DP* but has been grouped together into a resource section which may be used within Prayer During the Day, Morning Prayer or Evening Prayer. Night Prayer and the Thanksgiving for the Word contain their own forms of penitence, and Note 4 permits the use of this material, together with appropriate parts of the Litany and the *CW* main volume confessions and absolutions.

Forms of penitence have played a significant part within the daily worship of the Church of England since the 1552 *BCP*. *CW*, however, in its attempt to recover some of the characteristic features of the 'cathedral' office, has moved away from the *BCP* model in a number of significant respects. By not printing the penitential material at the beginning of Morning and Evening Prayer, it has more clearly signalled its optional nature and the primary importance of praise. Moreover, each of the four forms provided in *DP* clearly expresses penitence and forgiveness as a liturgical dialogue between different members of a worshipping community rather than a hierarchical confession and absolution.

Whether or not a form of penitence is incorporated into an office will depend on a number of factors. Among these, Note 1 refers to it being less appropriate when the Eucharist, the Thanksgiving for the Word or Night Prayer are being celebrated on the same day. Equally important will be a consideration of the number of other opportunities for acts of penitence during the course of a week, as well as whether the sacrament of reconciliation plays a significant role within the life of the community.

Form 1, which also appeared in *CCP* in a slightly different form, begins with three versicles and responses which make use of Isaiah 55.6–7. After a time of silence there is a corporate confession based on verses from Psalm 51 followed by a prayer for forgiveness which picks up the imagery of cleansing and restoration. Both of these texts are contained in the *CW* main volume, and are based on prayers from the 1989 *Patterns for Worship* report (GS 898). The use of an italicized 'us' and 'our' rather than 'you' and 'your' in the prayer for forgiveness is not simply for occasions when a priest is not present to pronounce an absolution; rather, to pray for forgiveness rather than to declare it is to express something of the theology of a mutual act of penitence referred to above. The rite concludes with two further versicles and responses based on Psalm 28.7, 9.

Form 2 encourages the lighting of a candle as a focus for silent reflection before a versicle and response invoking the Holy Spirit to 'search our hearts with the light of Christ'. This is followed by the Summary of the Law and a further period of reflection which leads into a corporate confession based on Hosea 6. This, again, is a text from GS 898 and, together with the prayer for forgiveness, is included in the *CW* main volume.

Form 3 does not contain texts for confession and absolution which have been authorized by the Church of England, and so these may not be used at the Principal Service on a Sunday, Principal Feast or other Principal Holy Day. It contains seven versicles and responses based on verses from Psalm 103. The first three celebrate the unbounded mercy of God, and these lead into a period of silence which concludes with the *Trisagion*. The final four versicles give thanks for God's mercy expressed in the forgiveness of sins before concluding the rite with an ascription of praise and thanksgiving.

Form 4 is framed by a pair of versicles and responses based on Psalm 107. The first pair encourages trust and confidence in the God who delivers his people from trouble, and this leads into a form of penitence in which short sentences are inserted within the petitions of the *Kyrie eleison*. GS 898 is, again, the source for the prayer for forgiveness, and the final versicles and responses conclude the act with a note of praise and thanksgiving.

The three confessions that follow the four forms of penitence (which include a modern-language version of the *BCP* confession for Morning and Evening Prayer) are all taken from the *CW* main volume, as are the absolutions.

Morning and Evening Prayer

DP provides fifteen fully worked-out forms of Morning and Evening Prayer, one for each day of the week and for each of the seasons, together with a skeletal form for Ascension Day. In terms of shape, they are identical to *CCP*, and provide sufficient flexibility to cater for those who wish to follow a pattern of prayer which, descended from the office tradition of the *BCP* and *ASB*, focuses on the reading of Scripture, as well as those who wish to imitate the 'cathedral' shape, and thereby place greater emphasis on praise and intercession. As distinct from other orders in *DP*, a vertical red line is printed in the margin of services to highlight mandatory material. These minimal requirements, summarized in Note 1, are intended to provide an order of prayer with a simple structure and appropriate balance of praise and intercession together with an engagement with Scripture.

The Acclamation of Christ at the Dawning of the Day and the Blessing of Light

The Acclamation of Christ at the Dawning of the Day, which may replace the Preparation at Morning Prayer, is a development of the more extended introduction to Morning Prayer in *CCP*. An opening response (Psalm 51.16) is followed by five verses from the *Venite* or another hymn or canticle. If the *Venite* is used, it may be sandwiched between one of three optional refrains, each inspired by the hymnody of Charles Wesley (1707–88). The first two are drawn from the first verse of 'Christ, whose glory fills the sky', itself based on 2 Peter 1.19; and the third combines the penultimate line of the first verse of 'Love divine, all loves excelling' with Psalm 51.13b. This opening act of praise is followed by a choice of one of two ferial thanksgiving prayers, or a seasonal prayer from the seasonal orders. These are examples of what have been called *berakah* prayers, being based on ancient Jewish blessing prayers (*barak* being the Hebrew verb 'to bless') which follow a common pattern of acclamation, remembrance, petition and doxology.

The Blessing of Light, which may replace the Preparation at Evening Prayer, also appeared in *CCP*, and is based on the ancient *Lucernarium*, a thanksgiving for light which was one of the characteristic features of the 'cathedral' office. Although the lighting of a lamp or candle is optional, the Blessing of Light makes little liturgical sense without this simple symbolic action. In Advent, it may be the candles of the Advent wreath which are used; in Eastertide, it will more likely be the Easter candle. The theme of light is developed throughout the first part of this liturgy. The opening sentence makes use of Psalm 27.1 and, after the greeting, the *berakah* Prayer, if used, picks up the themes of creation and incarnation from the Acclamation of Christ in the morning. The optional hymn *Phos hilaron* has already been identified as an established feature of Evening Prayer in the East in the fourth century, and is printed here in John Keble's translation so that it may easily be sung as other candles are lit. Psalm 141 has similar liturgical roots, and its responsorial use is particularly suitable when accompanied by the burning of incense in a pot or thurible. If incense is used here, it may also be burned during the Gospel canticle, when it is appropriate to cense the altar.

The Preparation

The basic structure of the Preparation is identical in every order. In Ordinary Time, Psalm 51.16 and Psalm 70.1 are used invariably as the versicles and responses at the beginning of Morning and Evening Prayer respectively. In seasons, these are followed by a further versicle and response which have seasonal associations, most of which make use of verses from the Psalms:

Advent: Psalm 63.3b
Christmas: Psalm 102.26
Epiphany: Psalm 97.11, 6 (morning); Psalm 113.3 (evening)
Lent: Psalm 119.149

Passiontide: Psalm 67.2
Easter: non-biblical, but traditional
Ascension Day: Psalm 93.3
Ascension to Pentecost: Luke 24.29
All Saints to Advent: Psalm 145.10b, 12b

The use of Psalms 51.16 and 70.1 was known to Benedict and, in the Sarum and Roman Breviaries, Psalm 51.16 began the first office of the day, whereas all others used Psalm 70.1, the *Gloria Patri* and, except from Septuagesima to Easter Day, Alleluia. While *DP* continues this tradition by beginning the office with a psalm versicle, and concluding the second response during Eastertide with an Alleluia, the new provision has replaced the doxological *Gloria*, which Cranmer also included in 1549 and 1552, with the choice of more extended forms of praise: one or more of an opening canticle, a prayer of thanksgiving or a hymn. Despite the fact that no order contains an example of all three, this should not be interpreted as a disincentive to using a form of praise which is not printed. In particular, where individuals and communities feel confident enough to sing, a suitable hymn or song (historically, the 'office hymn') is particularly appropriate during the Preparation. The *berakah* prayer and opening canticle may also be sung, and Note 5 allows for the prayer to be varied or improvised by the officiant. However, it should also be borne in mind that it is possible to overload the Preparation and thereby create an office which is too heavily balanced in favour of praise. As to which elements should be chosen, communities will develop their own preferred patterns, which may well vary according to the time of day and season as well as the number of worshippers. In *DP* a suggested opening canticle is printed in every Ordinary Time order, whereas the seasons contain, in the morning, a prayer of thanksgiving and an opening canticle, and, in the evening, a prayer of thanksgiving and a hymn. These seasonal hymns are provided to meet the need of those who wish to sing on an occasional basis without needing a hymn book in front of them. Individuals and communities who wish to sing more frequently will need to make use of other resources.

The majority of opening canticles are made up of portions of psalmody, with the exception of Morning Prayer on Sunday and in Christmas, Epiphany, Passiontide and Easter, and Evening Prayer on Thursday and in Passiontide, Easter and from All Saints to Advent, where appropriate texts from the Old Testament or Apocrypha are suggested. Where the opening canticle is not printed in the order itself, a rubric directs the worshipper to the bank of canticles. Whether the canticle is said antiphonally or in full, it is important that the doxology is said by everyone, thus articulating a strong corporate expression of praise at the end of the canticle.

The *berakah* prayers make use of a wealth of scriptural and other imagery associated with particular seasons. To distinguish the prayers used in the morning and evening, the opening acclamations give God 'praise and glory' and 'glory and praise' respectively. With the exception of Evening Prayer in Advent, most were written for *CCP* by David Stancliffe or the late Michael Vasey.

The Preparation, Acclamation of Christ and Blessing of Light conclude with an optional opening prayer which, like the Collect at the Eucharist, helps effect a smooth transition between Preparation/Gathering and the Word of God. Both morning and evening texts (with the exception of the evening bidding) are taken from *CCP* and, again like the Collect, consist of four parts: bidding, silence, prayer and congregational Amen. The evening invocation of God's mercy to cleanse the heart of the worshipper introduces a penitential element into the Preparation.

If a penitential rite is to be incorporated into Morning or Evening Prayer, Note 3 to the Forms of Penitence indicates that it may either replace the Preparation or be inserted after the Prayer of Thanksgiving, hymn or opening canticle.

The Word of God

Within The Word of God, it is possible to follow one of three tracks: the first, based on the office tradition of the *BCP* and *ASB*, sandwiches an Old Testament reading, canticle and New Testament reading between psalmody and a Gospel canticle; the second, drawing on the 'cathedral tradition' as expressed in *CCP*, places the psalmody and canticle together, followed by one or two readings and the Gospel canticle; the third, being a minor variation of the second at Morning Prayer, follows the Roman *Liturgia Horarum* by placing one of the *Laudate* Psalms (117, 146–150) after the canticle and before the reading(s). If desired, when following track one or two, the *Laudate* Psalm may be said at the end of the psalmody before the first reading or canticle. The structure of The Word of God within Morning Prayer is therefore as shown in Table 1.2.

Table 1.2: The Word of God within Morning Prayer

1	2	3
Psalmody	Psalmody	Psalmody
(*Laudate* Psalm)	(*Laudate* Psalm)	
First reading		
(Canticle)	(Canticle)	(Canticle)
		Laudate Psalm
Second reading	Reading(s)	Reading(s)
(Responsory)	(Responsory)	(Responsory)
Gospel canticle	Gospel canticle	Gospel canticle

As to lectionary provision, mention has already been made to the flip-flop principle which allows one of the psalm cycles and/or a short reading from Prayer During the Day to be used at Morning or Evening Prayer in place of the provision in the Weekday Lectionary. Once again, the decision as to which track should be followed, as well as the number of elements to be included within The Word of God, will be influenced by a number of factors, not least the number and content of the other offices being celebrated on any particular day. For example, in some communities, it may seem appropriate to place greater emphasis on praise at Morning Prayer by following track 3 with the optional canticle but only one biblical reading, and to use Evening Prayer, following tracks 1 or 2, as an opportunity for more extended engagement with Scripture, using both biblical readings with a period of silence rather than a canticle between them.

Although the optional canticles are apportioned in such a way that those from the Old Testament and Apocrypha are printed in the morning, and those from the New Testament in the evening, there is nothing to stop a wider range of canticles being used at any office. This may be particularly appropriate if only Morning or Evening Prayer is being celebrated each day. In addition to the canticle printed in each order, the rubric also refers to one or two others which are appropriate to particular days and seasons.

Whichever track is followed, it is important that silence is included as a response to the proclamation of God's word. In some communities, if two readings are used, an extended period of silence after the second may be more effective than two shorter periods, one after each reading. *DP* also encourages further response in the form of a song, hymn or responsory. Historically, the responsory consists of a series of versicles and responses, originally taken from a psalm but later from other parts of Scripture. Although we have no definite information as to their form until the Roman Office of the ninth century, Benedict's Rule makes reference to their use, if not their content.

The climax of The Word of God is the proclamation of the Gospel canticle. Following the Western medieval tradition, adopted by the *BCP* and *CCP*, *DP* commends the use of the *Benedictus* and *Magnificat* at Morning and Evening Prayer respectively. They thus function as a bridge between the proclamation of God's word and the offering of prayer. An optional refrain or antiphon is printed in each order. In Ordinary Time these are taken from the Gospel canticles themselves, whereas in seasonal time they make use of a wider range of sources, many of them with longstanding associations to particular seasons, and which already have an established place within the Western tradition. Nearly all of them were also used in *CCP*, and can be traced back through earlier editions of the Franciscan office. The following list looks beyond *CCP* to the original source of each refrain:

Advent to 16 Dec. MP: Baruch 4.36
17 Dec. to Christmas Eve MP: adapted from *Liturgia Horarum*
Advent to 16 Dec. EP: adapted from *Liturgia Horarum*
17 Dec. to 23 Dec. EP: the Advent Antiphons; although author and date of
composition are unknown, they were already part of the Roman use by the
eighth century
Christmas MP: Luke 2.11, 13–14
Christmas EP: Wisdom 18.14–15
Epiphany MP: Luke 9.35; Revelation 22.2
Epiphany EP: Isaiah 42.1
Lent MP: Matthew 5.6
Lent EP: Isaiah 55.7
Passiontide MP: 1 Corinthians 1.18
Passiontide EP: Romans 5.8
Easter MP: adapted from *Liturgia Horarum* responsory
Easter EP: Psalm 118.22
Ascension Day MP: 1 Timothy 3.16
Ascension Day EP: John 20.17
Ascension to Pentecost MP: Psalm 68.17
Ascension to Pentecost EP: Psalms 8.1 and 113.4
All Saints to Advent MP: Psalm 73.24
All Saints to Advent EP: Matthew 13.43

If a sermon is to be preached as part of the community's response to the
reading of Scripture, Note 8 suggests that it may be delivered between the
responsory and the Gospel canticle, or before or after the Prayers. Equally, if
the office is to include a Creed or Affirmation of Faith, Note 9 places it after
the Gospel canticle or sermon, if there is one. Normally, this would only
be appropriate if the office is being celebrated as the Principal Service on a
Principal Feast or Holy Day.

Prayers

For many users of the *BCP* and *ASB*, the provision of Lesser Litany, Lord's
Prayer, Versicles and Collects provided sufficient intercessory material to
enable them to conclude their daily office after the Third Collect without recognizing the need to supplement these with additional intercessory material.
In *DP* this is not an option. Since praise and the proclamation of God's word
are both springboards for intercession, it is important that this part of the
service contains sufficient flexibility to enable the worshipper to respond
appropriately to these elements, but in such a way that requires more than the
repetition of set formulae. As the Introduction makes clear, 'the offering of
intercession is as integral as praise to the nature of the service, and should not
be minimized unless another service containing a substantial element of intercession is to follow immediately'. To assist in this, the rubrics suggest that

morning intercessions should include prayer for the day and its tasks, the world and its needs and the Church and its life; whereas, in the evening, thanksgiving may be made for the past day, and prayer should be offered for peace, and for individuals and their needs. Within these broad parameters it is left to each individual worshipper and community to decide how this should best be expressed. Two cycles of intercession, referred to above, encourage the coverage of a broad range of intentions.

DP also provides a large resource of forms of intercession for different times of the day and year, together with litanies and other prayers. Where one simple refrain is repeated throughout the intercessions, it will usually be unnecessary for anyone other than the intercessor to follow the text being used. Moreover, despite the richness and variety of the forms provided, on many occasions, extempore prayer, inspired by the psalmody and readings, may well be more appropriate than set forms. Whatever material is chosen, a period of silence will often provide an opportunity for the offering of individual intentions or personal reflection before the intercessions are summed up by the Collect of the day or the prayer printed in each order. The latter will be particularly appropriate if the office is celebrated in close proximity to a Eucharist, in which the Collect of the day is used. The collects and prayers contained in the main orders are from the following sources:

Sunday MP: *CW* Additional Collect of Easter Day

Sunday EP: adapted from the *BCP* Third Collect at Evening Prayer

Monday MP: from Prayer in the Morning, *The Methodist Worship Book* (1999)

Monday EP: from the *CCP* Vigil Office, attributed to Columba of Iona

Tuesday MP: adapted from the *ASB* alternative Third Collect at Morning Prayer

Tuesday EP: adapted from a Lutheran prayer book

Wednesday MP: adapted from the *BCP* Third Collect at Morning Prayer

Wednesday EP: *CW* Additional Collect of Epiphany 2

Thursday MP: adapted from the *BCP* Second Collect at Morning Prayer

Thursday EP: adapted from the *BCP* Second Collect at Evening Prayer

Friday MP: *CW* Additional Collect of Lent 5

Friday EP: from *CCP* Midday Prayer on Thursday

Saturday MP: *CW* Collect of Easter Eve

Saturday EP: adapted from *The Book of Common Worship of the Church of South India* (1963)

Advent: *CW* Collect of Advent Sunday

Christmas: *CW* Collect of Christmas 1

Epiphany: *CW* Collect of Epiphany 2

Lent: *CW* Collect of Ash Wednesday

Passiontide: *CW* Collects of Lent 5 and Palm Sunday

Easter: *CW* Post Communion of Easter Day

Ascension: *CW* Collect of Ascension Day
Ascension to Pentecost: *CW* Collect of Easter 7
All Saints to Advent: *CW* Collect of All Saints' Day

In every *DP* office the Lord's Prayer concludes the intercessions. This follows the pattern in *CCP* and is a reversal of the order in the Roman *Liturgia Horarum*, where the Lord's Prayer precedes the Collect. The rationale behind the *DP* position is that it allows the Collect to function as a prayer which both gathers together the intercessions which have been offered and acts as a bridge between those intercessions and the Lord's Prayer. In Ordinary Time, the optional words of introduction reflect those which may be used at the Eucharist. In the rest of the year, this is prefaced by a line which introduces a seasonal emphasis. Words of introduction may also be improvised, or other forms used, as indicated by Note 12.

Note 13 allows for the Prayers and the Conclusion to be replaced by one of the Thanksgivings which follow the forms of Morning and Evening Prayer, or the Prayers for the Unity of the Church or Prayers at the Foot of the Cross. The Thanksgivings all appear in the *CW* main volume. The other two forms are adapted from those that appeared in *CCP*. The first includes the prayer from the *BCP* Accession Service which draws on Ephesians 4 together with a series of versicles and responses from John 15. The second makes use of material traditionally associated with the veneration of the cross on Good Friday, some of which is used in Prayer During the Day.

By way of preparation for the Sunday Eucharist, Note 14 allows for the Sunday Gospel to be read between the Prayers and Conclusion at Evening Prayer on Saturday, making use of responses from the Thanksgiving for the Mission of the Church or the Vigil Office, which also include a proclamation of the Gospel of the morrow.

Following the Roman Breviary and *CCP*, Note 15 permits the use of the *Te Deum* immediately before the Conclusion on Sundays (outside Advent and Lent), Principal Feasts and Festivals. Developing this tradition, the same note also allows the *Gloria in excelsis* to be used at the end of Morning Prayer and the *Nunc dimittis* at Evening Prayer.

Conclusion

Morning Prayer in Ordinary Time contains the simple 'us' form blessing from *CCP*, which was adapted from one of the concluding formulas of the Roman office. At Evening Prayer in Ordinary Time the Grace is used as the concluding prayer. In seasons, the morning and evening endings are identical and reflect particular themes associated with each season. The final response, also derived from *CCP* and the *Liturgia Horarum*, is optional and appears at the end of every order, concluding the office on a note of praise. As with Prayer During the Day, Note 16 allows for the Peace to be used in place of or in addition to whichever form is printed.

Additional Material for use at Morning or Evening Prayer

Reference has already been made to the thanksgivings and prayers for unity and at the cross which may be inserted into Morning and Evening Prayer. *DP* also provides two forms which may replace the office as a whole, A Commemoration of the Resurrection and a Vigil Office.

The former is designed to be used as an early Sunday morning celebration, especially during Eastertide. It is derived from the ancient weekly Sunday vigil of the resurrection, but its fundamental structure is the same as the other offices. Notable features include two versicles and responses from Night Prayer which begin the Preparation, the second of which looks forward to a celebration of the Eucharist later the same day. The Word of God contains an optional Scripture reading and Old Testament canticle before the proclamation of a Gospel of the resurrection or of one of the resurrection appearances. This is followed by the Easter Anthems, rather than a Gospel canticle.

The Vigil Office is taken from *CCP* and may appropriately be used on the eve of a Sunday or Principal Feast. Beginning with the Blessing of Light, what distinguishes it from Evening Prayer is the way in which The Word of God is structured. It begins with an Old Testament reading which is followed by a psalm, silence and a collect. A New Testament reading leads into a canticle, silence and a second collect, before the proclamation of the Gospel of the morrow and the *Magnificat.*

Night Prayer (Compline)

The basic form of Night Prayer is identical to that in the *CW* main volume (with the exception of printing the *Gloria Patri* in bold). In addition, there is a section of daily, seasonal and other variations. In Ordinary Time this consists of psalmody, a short reading, and a Collect. In seasonal time and on feasts of the Blessed Virgin Mary and other saints, a refrain for the Gospel canticle and concluding blessing are also provided. All of these variations are optional and follow the Sarum rather than Latin use. Those who want to preserve Night Prayer as a simple office may wish to use an unchanging form on every occasion. The psalm provision in Ordinary Time is basically the same as that outlined in the *CW* main volume, except that the ancient Compline Psalms (4, 91 and 134) have been included so that they are not omitted by those who follow this cycle on a daily basis. Much of the material in this section is taken from *CCP* and many of the refrains and collects go back to the Sarum Breviary.

Prayers

With its emphasis on intercession arising out of the offering of praise to God and an encounter with him in Scripture, it is unsurprising that *DP* provides such a substantial resource of intercessory material. Divided into six main sections, it is designed to encourage individuals and communities to use a variety of material as they explore different ways of fulfilling the Church's priestly task to 'pray without ceasing'. Those who make use of the two cycles of intercession should not be constrained by the themes suggested there. Although a deliberate attempt has been made to extend some of the more common categories of intercession, particularly with respect to the workplace, many parishes will want to supplement these with their own cycles of prayer as well as those devised by their diocese, the Anglican Communion or mission organizations that are supported locally.

Within the Forms of Intercession, the first section consists of twenty-one responsive intercessions for particular times of the day and year. Following a common pattern, each is addressed to the first person of the Trinity, and concludes with an invitation to the worshipping community to commend themselves to God, together with those for whom they have prayed, using extempore and/or silent prayer. This open prayer is then drawn together by the Collect and Lord's Prayer. Many of the forms are new compositions, but a number have been adapted from *CCP* (nos. 4, 7, 12, 14, 16–18) or from *New Patterns for Worship* (3, 5, 9, 13), and no. 20 is adapted from *ECY*.

With the exception of the forms for Lent and Ordinary Time, the Seasonal Acclamations are adapted from those which appeared in *CCP* (without responses) as Ambrosian Acclamations. These were translated by George Guiver from the revision of the Ambrosian Office undertaken in the 1980s, when they replaced a twelvefold *Kyrie*, the remnant of a previously existing litany. Each acclamation is addressed to Christ and is more of a litany of praise than a form of intercession, and hence the rubric which suggests that, if one is used, it should be preceded by short biddings or open prayer, thus setting it within the context of intercession. The repeated responses give an added seasonal flavour to each acclamation.

Six short litanies from *CCP*, largely based on the Psalms and compiled by George Guiver, are also provided. They may be used as a series of versicles and responses, or with a congregational response after each petition. The Litany itself is also printed in full, as in the *CW* main volume. Note 10 suggests that it is especially suitable at Morning or Evening Prayer on Ash Wednesday, Fridays in Lent and All Souls' Day.

The final section contains a selection of 'Other Prayers', many of them classic texts from different periods of the Church's history. Each prayer has its own attribution, and although they may not be used on a regular basis, some of them will be appropriate on particular occasions, and the collection as a whole offers a valuable resource for public and private prayer.

Collects and Suggested Canticles and Refrains

One of the distinctive features of *DP*, as compared with the *BCP* and *ASB*, is the possibility of celebrating the *temporale* (cycle of seasons) and *sanctorale* (festivals and saints' days) with a degree of richness hitherto unknown in the Church of England. Thus, in addition to Collects for Sundays, Principal Feasts and Holy Days, Festivals and Lesser Festivals, a number of Gospel canticle refrains are provided and alternative canticles suggested to enrich the Seasonal and Ordinary Time orders. Faced with the possibility of such elaboration, it is important that this material is used appropriately, so that the office does not become overly complex or the use of proper material detract from the continuous celebration of a particular season. To this end, Note 5 makes clear that, on Lesser Festivals, the use of a common refrain with the Gospel canticle is optional. As with alternative canticles, it is likely that they will only be appropriate if, for some reason, a Lesser Festival is being observed as a Festival or Principal Feast, as, for example, on a Patronal Festival. The provision of a refrain for the *Magnificat* on the eve of a Festival is also optional, and is only likely to be needed on a Saturday evening, or if the Festival is being kept as a Principal Feast, when a 'First Evensong' is celebrated.

At Morning and Evening Prayer, the celebration of Festivals may be further enriched by the optional use of different seasonal orders to accompany particular observances. Note 10 in the General Notes at the beginning of the book lists these, and there is a further note to this effect beneath the title of each Festival to which it applies. Thus, for example, the Christmas orders may be used on Festivals of the Blessed Virgin Mary, and the Passiontide orders on Holy Cross Day. Appropriate alternative canticles are also suggested to replace those within the main orders, including the use of the *Te Deum* at Morning Prayer on feasts of Apostles and Evangelists. To simplify the use of refrains on such occasions, they are printed above the collect of each Festival, so that all the 'proper' material is located on one page. Festivals falling in Eastertide, such as George and Mark, have an Alleluia added to the end of the refrain. Where Alleluia appears in brackets, this indicates that it should only be used if the Festival, such as Matthias, falls within the fifty days of Easter. Further directions on the celebration of the Christian year are provided in the Seasonal Notes at the beginning of the book. These include a model for the celebration of a very simple form of Morning, Evening or Night Prayer during the Easter Triduum.

As well as the collects which were first authorized in *Calendar, Lectionary and Collects* (1997), *DP* also includes five of the Additional Collects, authorized in 2004, one for each of the seasons (for Advent, that of Advent 4; for Christmas, that of Christmas Day; for Epiphany, that of Epiphany 2; for Lent, that of Lent 2; and for Easter, that of Easter 3). In addition to these, which may be used on any day in their respective seasons, it is of course possible for the appropriate Additional Collect to replace the standard *CW* collect on any occasion.

Under the heading 'Special Occasions', collects, refrains and alternative canticles are suggested for a number of different occasions on which it may be appropriate to celebrate an office with a particular theme or intention; for example, 'The Guidance of the Holy Spirit' before a church meeting, or 'Mission and Evangelism' during a Parish mission.

Canticles

The eighty-seven canticles that appear within the 'canticle bank' are a telling indicator of the extent to which *DP* offers choice and variety in the celebration of the office. Almost three-quarters of the biblical canticles are printed within the main orders for Morning and Evening Prayer. The rest are referred to as alternative canticles in Ordinary and Seasonal Time, and may be used to enrich the celebration of Festivals and Holy Days. This variety is further increased by the permission given in General Note 7 at the beginning of the book for any canticle to be replaced by an appropriate hymn or a metrical paraphrase. Such liberty is granted in order to encourage individuals and groups to celebrate the Church's daily prayer with the sung as well as the spoken word. To this end, metrical versions of the *Benedictus* and *Magnificat* are also provided.

The 'bank' is divided into four sections. The first consists of eighteen Psalm canticles, the majority of which are printed as optional opening canticles in the Ordinary Time and seasonal orders for Morning and Evening Prayer. Of the thirty-four canticles from the Old Testament and Apocrypha, all but four appeared in *CCP*. Of these four, A Song of the Rock, A Song of Trust and The Prayer of Habakkuk are contained within the provision for Morning Prayer in the modern Roman Catholic office. All of the twenty-four New Testament canticles were used in *CCP*, with the exception of the metrical versions of the *Benedictus* and *Magnificat*, referred to above.

Except for the Psalm canticles, Bless the Lord, the *Benedicite*, the Gospel canticles and the Easter Anthems, each of the biblical canticles is printed with an optional refrain, or antiphon, which may be used at the beginning of the canticle and after the *Gloria*, thus providing an interpretative framework. The majority of these make use of or are inspired by verses from the canticle itself; the following are derived from other sources:

20	Deuteronomy 30.14
21	Luke 1.45
29	Isaiah 40.9
40	new composition
53	Matthew 5.12, 14
58	Romans 8.11
64	Revelation 7.15; Colossians 1.12
67	*CCP*
68	*CCP*, adapted
71	Psalm 86.9
75	Revelation 22.20

Of the eleven post-biblical canticles, four did not appear in *CCP*. The Song of Ephrem the Syrian contains verses from his tenth *Hymn on the Faith* and is particularly suited to the feast of the Baptism of Christ and the season of Epiphany. *Salus Aeterna* is derived from an Advent sequence, whose original

Latin text dates back to before the eleventh century, and which skilfully juxtaposes Christ's first and second comings. *Victimae Paschali* and *Veni Sancte Spiritus* are also based on medieval sequences. In the Roman Rite, they remain the only sequences appointed to be sung before the Gospel at mass on Easter Day and Pentecost respectively. *Victimae Paschali* includes a dialogue in which Mary Magdalene testifies to her encounter with the risen Christ at the garden tomb. *Veni Sancte Spiritus* is an invocation of the Holy Spirit, based on the Golden Sequence.

Of the other post-biblical canticles, the *Gloria in excelsis*, *Te Deum* and *Saviour of the World* are all referred to in Volume 1 of this *Companion*. *Phos hilaron* is printed here in a version which is likely to be favoured by those who would prefer to say rather than sing this fourth-century hymn during the Blessing of Light. Though separated by three hundred years, the Song of Anselm and the Song of Julian of Norwich are linked by their description of Jesus as mother. The Anselm text first appeared as a canticle in *ECY*, in a version written by Michael Vasey. The Song of Julian of Norwich is taken from chapter 60 of her *Revelations of Divine Love*.

The Psalter

DP prints the *CW* Psalter in full together with optional refrains and psalm collects. As with the canticles, the former may be used at the beginning and end of each psalm or section of psalmody, as in the Latin monastic tradition, to provide an interpretative framework within which the psalm may be read and prayed. Alternatively, in line with the principles of the 'cathedral' office and the earliest evidence for the Christian use of psalms during meals, the psalms may be performed responsorially, with the refrain repeated at the beginning of the psalm and at the points indicated by the refrain markers [R], the rest of the text being read or sung by one voice.

The use of psalm collects goes back to the early centuries of Christianity, where their purpose was to provide a christological interpretation to the Psalter. The optional use of psalm prayers in *DP* continues this tradition, encouraging the worshipper to use the psalms as texts for prayer, praise or reflection. Since the prayers are, to some extent, doxological as well as christological, the *Gloria* should be omitted when they are used. As with the collect at the Eucharist, it is important that a period of silence is kept before the prayer is read. This allows the biddings which arise as a result of the worshipper's engagement with the psalm to be articulated in the silence before they are summed up in the psalm collect, to which the whole community adds its assent with the Amen. The introduction to the Psalter gives further guidance on how psalmody may be said or sung. The notes also provide the text of a non-gender-specific *Gloria* which first appeared in *CCP* and which may be used as an alternative to the *Gloria Patri*.

Although over half of the psalm prayers are new compositions, a number have been taken or adapted from *CCP* (those to Psalms 24–26, 28, 33–37, 47,

51–54, 56–78a, 80–84, 86, 89a, 89b, 91, 94, 95, 119b, 119g–121, 123–125, 127, 128, 131, 132, 138, 141, 142, 145, 148, 150), or are the work of John Eaton (those to Psalms 23, 38, 55, 110, 126, 130, 133, 140), and were published in 2003 as part of his commentary on the Psalms. Those for Psalms 27 and 88 are the Additional Collects of Trinity 20 and Easter Eve respectively. Table 1.3 indicates the sources of the refrains. All are taken from the Psalter, the majority of them have verses taken from the psalm in which they are used. For those psalms which have their own internal refrain, no additional refrain has been provided.

Further Reading

Paul F. Bradshaw, *Daily Prayer in the Early Church*, SPCK, London, 1981.

Paul F. Bradshaw, *Two Ways of Praying*, SPCK, London, 1995.

John Eaton, *The Psalms: A Historical and Spiritual Commentary*, T & T Clark, London, 2003.

George Guiver, *Company of Voices*, 2nd edn, Canterbury Press, Norwich, 2001.

Joseph A. Jungmann, *Christian Prayer Through the Centuries*, Paulist Press, New York, 1978 (now out of print, but a new edition, with notes, is forthcoming from the Alcuin Club).

Pierre Salmon, *The Breviary Through the Centuries*, The Liturgical Press, Collegeville, MN, 1962.

Robert F. Taft, *The Liturgy of the Hours in East and West*, The Liturgical Press, Collegeville, MN, 1986.

Gregory W. Woolfenden, *Daily Liturgical Prayer: Origins and Theology*, Ashgate Publishing, Aldershot, 2004.

Table 1.3: Sources of psalm refrains

Psalm	Refrain	Psalm	Refrain	Psalm	Refrain	Psalm	Refrain
1	1.6a	40	40.5a	79	79.9a	117	117.2c
2	28.10	41	41.10a	80	–	118	118.21
3	3.3a	42	–	81	95.1a	119a	119.33a
4	4.8a	43	–	82	82.8a	119b	119.47a
5	5.14a	44	44.27a	83	1.5a	119c	119.75a
6	6.4a	45	84.8	84	84.3a	119d	119.107b
7	7.8a	46	–	85	85.7a	119e	119.124a
8	–	47	47.6a	86	86.9a	119f	119.130a
9	9.10b	48	48.9a	87	132.14a	119g	119.174a
10	9.10b	49	40.4a	88	142.5b	120	120.2a
11	11.4b	50	50.15a	89a	89.18a	121	121.7a
12	12.7a	51	51.18a	89b	132.11	122	84.1a
13	116.1a	52	52.8b	89c	132.10	123	123.3a
14	111.10a	53	111.10	90	7.1a	124	124.7a
15	5.7a	54	54.4a	91	17.8a	125	87.2
16	16.7b	55	55.24a	92	92.8b	126	126.4a
17	17.14a	56	56.4a	93	10.17	127	121.8a
18	18.29b	57	–	94	119.137	128	31.19a
19	19.8b	58	9.16a	95	95.6a	129	34.22a
20	20.7b	59	59.10b	96	96.9a	130	130.5a
21	21.7a	60	85.4a	97	97.9a	131	131.4a
22	22.19a	61	61.3	98	98.3a	132	132.8a
23	23.6b	62	62.5a	99	–	133	85.10
24	24.10b	63	42.2a	100	100.4a	134	103.1a
25	25.5a	64	64.10a	101	112.1a	135	135.3a
26	26.8,	65	66.1a	102	121.2a	136	–
	adapted	66	66.3a	103	103.8a	137	122.6a
27	27.1a	67	–	104	104.35	138	138.8b
28	28.8a	68	68.4a	105	105.5a	139	139.23a
29	29.10b	69	69.19a	106	106.46a	140	140.4a
30	30.3a	70	70.5b	107	–	141	141.3a
31	31.5a	71	71.12a	108	108.5a	142	142.7a
32	32.12a	72	97.1a	109	109.25b	143	143.8b
33	33.5b	73	73.28b	110	93.1a	144	144.16b
34	34.8a	74	74.21a	111	111.4b	145	145.3a
35	35.25a	75	75.7a	112	112.6b	146	146.10a
36	36.9a	76	9.7b	113	113.3	147	147.5a
37	37.40a	77	2a	114	114.7a	148	113.1b
38	38.22	78a	92.5a	115	115.12a	149	98.5a
39	39.5a	78b	114.7a	116	116.4a	150	150.6

Chapter 2

The Weekday Lectionary

A. HISTORY

Early and Medieval Practice

Within Western Christendom there are two traditions for reading Scripture in worship, both of ancient origin. The first is known as *lectio continua*, where Scripture is read in course, and the other is *lectio electa*, where readings are chosen according to a theme or according to the day. The first is probably the more ancient practice and seems to have been inherited from the continuous reading of the Torah in the Jewish synagogue on the Sabbath and at the Monday and Thursday services. This tradition continued in Christian Services of the Word, which happened on Sundays alongside the Eucharist and were eventually combined with it, and also on Wednesdays and Fridays. *Lectio electa* seems to have featured at first only on great Festivals, and to have been extended very gradually to other occasions as the liturgical year developed. Although educated and wealthy individuals may have had their own copies of the Bible and read them on a daily basis, Scripture reading was originally not part of the daily prayer pattern of most individuals. The earliest forms of the people's office were instead times rather of praise and intercession.

The earliest monastic movements of the fourth century, however, do seem to have adopted the communal reading of Scripture passages as part of their daily pattern, especially during the hours of darkness when other work could not be done. We find this practice continued in the later Rule of St Benedict in the West, where in the long winter nights there were three substantial readings in the night office: one from the Old Testament, one from the New, and a third drawn from the writings of the Fathers, or on a saint's day from the life of the saint. On summer nights and at the times of prayer during the day, there was only one very brief passage of Scripture, recited from memory. This pattern became the basis for all medieval monastic rules in the West, and through the eventual imposition of the monastic daily office on the clergy, for the Western Church as a whole. Sundays and Festivals were assigned special readings, outside the *lectio continua* of the daily sequence, but with the enormous proliferation of saints' days and other festivals in the later Middle Ages, often with octaves attached to them, the sense of *lectio continua* was gradually lost from the daily office and it became little more than a series of unrelated readings, many of which were frequently repeated while other parts of the Bible were hardly ever read at all.

An attempt was made in the sixteenth century to remedy this defect. In the reformed Breviary produced by Cardinal Francisco Quiñones and authorized by the Pope in 1535, a more continuous reading of the Old and New Testaments was restored to the night office, with very few feast days being permitted to break up this provision. While this reformed office was swept away at the Council of Trent, some of its features were incorporated into Roman Catholic revisions of the twentieth century, and it served as a major influence on the composition of the daily offices in the first English Prayer Book of 1549.

The Church of England

The forms of Morning and Evening Prayer in the 1549 *BCP* provided for two readings at each service every day, one from the Old Testament and one from the New. The lectionary tables arranged for each book of the Bible to be read continuously, with a whole chapter being assigned for each reading. This meant that the Old Testament would be read through, with few omissions, once a year, while the Gospels were read three times a year at Morning Prayer, and the Acts of the Apostles and the Epistles three times a year at Evening Prayer. A feature of this lectionary was that it was based almost entirely on the civil calendar and, apart from a few major feast days, paid scant attention to the liturgical year except in Advent, to which portions of the book of Isaiah were assigned. For the rest of the year books of the Bible were read in their biblical order. Thus, on 1 January the reading of the Old Testament at Morning Prayer began with Genesis and the reading of the New Testament with Matthew. As part of the same reforms, the Psalter was divided into sixty equal portions to be used in numerical sequence, morning and evening, throughout each month. In those months with thirty-one days the provision for the thirtieth day was simply repeated. This arrangement was only interrupted four times a year, when selected psalms were designated for the feasts of Christmas, Easter, Ascension and Pentecost. To this scheme, proper Old Testament lessons for all Sundays and proper Old and New Testament lessons for the rest of the major feast days were added in 1559, and selected psalms for Ash Wednesday and Good Friday in 1662.

The lectionary was thereafter little altered until 1871, when a more substantial revision was planned and executed. Like its predecessor, the 1871 lectionary, which still forms part of the *BCP*, retained the civil rather than the liturgical calendar as its basis for weekday provision. However, on the whole, this new lectionary had a very different look. Many lessons were shortened and substantial portions of Ezekiel and 1 and 2 Chronicles, hitherto omitted, now found a place in the revised order. Perhaps the most substantial change, however, was in the fact that the New Testament was now only read twice a year, once in the morning and once in the evening, rather than three times a year as in the earlier scheme. In comparison to the earlier lectionary the number of passages used from the Apocrypha was substantially reduced.

A further change came about with the 1922 lectionary, which remains available for use as an alternative to the 1871 lectionary in the *BCP* and which is still printed in some copies of the Prayer Book. This lectionary, the surviving portion of a much wider proposed reform of the *BCP* that had failed to get through Parliament, was the first to pay attention to the liturgical rather than to the civil year. Another feature of the 1922 lectionary is that on weekdays after the Trinity, material from the Gospels is arranged to form a composite life of Christ. In this, its compilers were greatly influenced by the 'quest for the historical Jesus' movement and especially by W. Hershal's *The Gospel Monogram* of 1911. More readings from the Apocrypha were included in this lectionary and lessons were also provided for the first Evening Prayer of holy days. From 1939 to 1961 the Convocations of Canterbury and York worked on a further revision of the 1922 lectionary with the aim of shortening many lessons and spreading the Sunday readings over a two-year cycle. This work was authorized from 1962 and was generally used by those adhering to the Prayer Book offices until 2000.

From the Joint Liturgical Group's Daily Office to the ASB

The lectionary in the Joint Liturgical Group's *Daily Office* (1968) provided a distribution of the psalms over thirteen weeks as an alternative to the thirty-day psalter, and the biblical readings were arranged according to a two-year rather than a one-year cycle. This lectionary proved to be very popular. It was appended to Morning and Evening Prayer Series 2 Revised as an alternative to the existing provision and was authorized for use from November 1971. In 1975 a table of lessons for holy days was appended to Morning and Evening Prayer Series 3 and was authorized from November of that year. The next step was the drawing together of this and other new material in a document entitled *Calendar, Lectionary and Rules to Order Services* (GS 292) in 1976. After amendment, this was finally authorized for use in 1979 and incorporated subsequently into the *ASB* in 1980.

What had emerged by this time was a weekday lectionary the purpose of which was to ensure that the whole Bible was read in the course of one year (if both offices were said) or in the course of two years if only one office was said. The *ASB* lectionary, like several of its predecessors, had a seasonal feel about what was read at certain times of the year (e.g. Isaiah and Thessalonians during Advent, Genesis and Exodus in the weeks before and after Easter, and 2 Peter during Eastertide itself). Where this lectionary differed from its predecessors, however, was that all four tracks of readings (Old and New Testament for both Morning and Evening Prayer) were now separate and distinct. Thus books from the Old Testament were no longer read through continuously at both Morning and Evening Prayer. Some Old Testament books were inevitably not read through in their entirety, namely Leviticus,

Chronicles and Ezekiel, while duplicate material and long genealogies were omitted. As far as possible when the historical books were read at one service, the prophets and other Old Testament books were read at the other service, with the exception of Isaiah, where, in order to retain the traditional disposition of the book, Isaiah 1—39 was read in the morning and Isaiah 40—66 was read in the evening during Advent. The New Testament was planned so that the Gospels were always read at one service while the rest of the New Testament was read at the other. The four Gospels were read in their entirety in the course of the year. In Holy Week, Easter Week and in the days before and after Christmas this pattern of continuous reading was abandoned in favour of selected passages that were felt to be particularly appropriate to the season. Apocryphal readings also had their place in the *ASB* lectionary, although in every case alternative provision was also made from the canonical books.

In terms of psalmody, the *ASB* weekday pattern was based not on the more traditional thirty-day or on the thirteen-week cycles but upon a ten-week cycle read in course, except on Festivals and in Holy Week. No differential was made between psalms on the basis of whether they were read in the morning or the evening.

Daily Eucharistic Lectionary

One element that was missing from GS 292 was a eucharistic lectionary intended for use on weekdays. The House of Bishops opposed proposals made by the Liturgical Commission regarding a new weekday eucharistic lectionary in 1976. A little later, however, it was proposed in General Synod that the Roman Catholic daily eucharistic lectionary should be adopted on the grounds of both expedience and ecumenical co-operation. On the other hand, it was recognized that such a lectionary was designed to follow a different Calendar. A compromise was reached whereby the Liturgical Commission was asked to prepare a lectionary *based on* the Roman lectionary for those weekdays for which no separate provision had been made. This lectionary was finally approved in November 1979 and incorporated into the *ASB*.

Celebrating Common Prayer

Although the *ASB* Lectionary and daily office were to continue in use for more than twenty years, many of those who prayed the office regularly began to wish for something more. Into this vacuum came *Celebrating Common Prayer* (*CCP*), a pattern of daily offices drawn up for use by the Society of St Francis but offered to a wider praying public in 1992. In terms of lectionary provision, it provided a number of alternatives. Short one-reading lectionaries were provided in the Simple Celebration of Morning and Evening Prayer, with the readings suggested over a four-week cycle. There were also short thematic lectionaries, based on a seven-week cycle, as at Midday Prayer. And there was a longer set of lections, beginning at All Saints' tide with a Kingdom Season and intended for use at Morning and Evening Prayer, which was based on a continuous reading of Scripture with seasonal flavour where appropriate. Although this was a two-office, two-reading pattern throughout the year, it did not always include a reading from the Gospels. In terms of psalmody, there was a seven-week cycle during Ordinary Time with certain psalms being allocated to certain days of the week on the basis of their content, while in the liturgical seasons there was a more selective cycle, with the chosen psalms tending to be repeated on the same day each week.

The CW Temporary Weekday Lectionary (GS 1341/1341A)

The launch of *CW* necessitated that the whole question of weekday lectionary provision be revisited. This work was gathered together in two reports, GS 1341 and GS 1341A, the latter being sent to General Synod for approval in October 1999. The provision thus made was authorized for a period of five years beginning on Advent Sunday 1999. The overriding principle of the temporary weekday lectionary (henceforward GS 1341A) was to provide adequate readings and psalms for a variety of different contexts. For a parish which had both a daily Eucharist and Morning and Evening Prayer said each day, no fewer than six readings and three sets of psalms would be needed. For a parish or community where the same group of people were to share in every service throughout the week, a degree of *lectio continua* was also desirable. At the same time the report recognized that there were very different needs in places (such as cathedrals at Evensong) where the congregation was different on almost every occasion. To meet these needs, three different tracks were provided.

The first provision, marked 'Eucharistic Lectionary', was an Anglican adaptation of the Roman Catholic eucharistic readings as previously used in the *ASB*. It was intended principally for use in parishes with a daily, or near-daily, weekday Eucharist. It made use of readings from the Apocrypha, although on each such occasion a canonical alternative was also given.

The second provision, marked 'Office Lectionary', was adapted from an original used in the Episcopal Church in the USA and in the Anglican Church of Canada via the Church in Wales and the Scottish Episcopal Church. The original had provided three readings a day over a two-year cycle. This was adapted to two readings a day, but in the process the provision of a daily Gospel was lost for considerable portions of the year. The rationale behind this office lectionary was that of *lectio continua*. Passages were selected as far as possible according to the seasons of the Christian year but so as to honour the Anglican tradition by almost continuous reading of the Bible over two years. It was intended primarily for use in those places where there was a regular congregation for the office. In the rubrics it was envisaged that this lectionary would probably be mostly used for Morning Prayer.

A third provision was entitled 'Second Office/Alternative Eucharistic Lectionary', but was also known colloquially as the 'Pillar Lectionary'. This was compiled especially for GS 1341A. Its intention was to meet the needs of those who attended services on an occasional basis, as at cathedral Evensong. It was also envisaged as being of use in those parishes where there were only one or two Eucharists during the week and where the more continuous approach to Scripture of the Daily Eucharistic Lectionary might not be considered appropriate. For part of the year this lectionary consisted of independent series of readings from both the Old and New Testaments, read continuously or semi-continuously. For other parts of the year one reading, usually the second, functioned as the 'controlling reading', the other reading being chosen to provide complementary, reflective, contrasting or contextual material to it. Each reading was intended to stand alone, although some books were read consecutively but with many 'linking' verses omitted between successive days' readings.

The intention of GS 1341A was also to provide a more seasonal flavour to the pattern of psalmody. Thus the psalms were only said in sequence from the day after the Presentation in the Temple until Shrove Tuesday and from the Day after Pentecost until All Saints' Eve. During the seasons the psalms were chosen for their appropriateness to the liturgical time of year. Here a weekly pattern, derived from that in *CCP*, was visible, with certain psalms being said on certain days of the week throughout a season. Again following the conventions of *CCP*, a seasonal flavour was also given to the period between All Saints Day and the Saturday before Advent, although the use of 'seasonal' psalms at this point was optional. Since the main psalm tables in Ordinary Time were designed to be used continuously, with the psalm at Evening Prayer following numerically that used at Morning Prayer, a separate table of psalms was also provided for the use of those who only said either Morning or Evening Prayer each day. A further psalm table, designated 'Alternative Eucharistic Lectionary' was also given, presumably to be used in conjunction with the Second Office/Alternative Eucharistic Lectionary. Although the notes claim that this is 'largely the cycle in the Book of Common Prayer', the similarities between these two psalm tables are not immediately obvious.

Long before its experimental period was over, use had revealed a number of shortcomings in the temporary weekday lectionary set out in GS 1341A. The main concern was the close repetitions, which had become apparent, between some of the readings in the Office and the Second Office Lectionaries where these were being used side by side as lectionaries for Morning and Evening Prayer. Perhaps the most frequent complaint among those who wrote in to the Liturgical Commission on this matter concerned the Book of Ruth, which was read in the Office Lectionary in Year 1 in the week beginning 17 February and which was then repeated in the Second Office Lectionary a fortnight later. Another area of complaint was the desire to have two tracks of *lectio continua*, which could be used at Morning and Evening Prayer for those who said two offices daily. Having weighed all these issues, and having commissioned detailed research on the number of overlaps and close parallels between the various lectionaries, the Liturgical Commission decided not to revise the provision of GS 1341A when it came up for re-authorization but instead to replace it with an entirely new weekday lectionary. Meanwhile the authorization of GS 1341A, due to expire on 27 November 2004, was extended until 31 December 2007 in order that the proposed new weekday lectionary provision might be properly cross-checked with both the Daily Eucharistic Lectionary and with the Lectionary for Sundays, Principal Feasts and Holy Days, and Festivals, and might also be used experimentally for a period of several months. In the end, 566 parishes in England, nominated by their respective diocesan bishops, used the lectionary experimentally between Advent Sunday 2003 and Easter 2004. General Synod took its first look at the proposed new weekday lectionary material set out in GS 1520 on 12 February 2004, from where it was sent to the Revision Committee. The Revision Committee did its work quickly, and an amended text was represented to Synod as GS 1520A in July 2004. No further amendments being proposed, the new Weekday Lectionary was given final approval in February 2005. From that point it became authorized for use, although the temporary weekday lectionary provision provided in GS 1341A also remained authorized until December 2007.

Since the Daily Eucharistic Lectionary of the *ASB*, re-authorized as part of the temporary weekday lectionary provision in GS 1341A, would have ceased to be authorized in December 2007, it was once more re-authorized in GS 1520A. As it had served the Church of England well since 1980, and enquiries did not disclose any intention of an early review of it in the Roman Catholic Church, no changes were proposed or made to it then, although some errors in GS 1341A, which had become apparent during the compilation of the annual lectionary booklet, were corrected. The opportunity was also taken to insert some necessary rubrics so that this lectionary is used in the Church of England in the same weeks as it is in the Roman Catholic Church.

In the General Synod debate on the Weekday Lectionary in February 2004 a plea was made for the provision of another 'pillar lectionary', along the lines of that in 1341A, which might be used in places, such as cathedrals, where the congregation was occasional rather than regular. The Revision Committee, however, did not believe that it was part of its brief to compile such a lectionary, nor did it wish to hold up the authorization of the weekday lectionary until such time as the Liturgical Commission might produce one. The report, which went back from the Revision Committee to Synod, therefore recommended that the weekday lectionary provision in GS 1520A be allowed to proceed without such an additional track being appended, but it recommended that the Liturgical Commission be asked to look at this matter as a separate piece of liturgical business. A questionnaire sent to all cathedrals and Oxbridge colleges about the need for and shape of such a lectionary, however, did not bring in an enthusiastic response for its composition. Various options considered by the Liturgical Commission for adaptation of existing lectionaries as a 'pillar lectionary' have also proved to be problematic, since none of them provides a suitable 'off-the-peg' alternative but would need to be substantially reworked. The only remaining alternative would be to commission a new lectionary altogether. Both these options would require careful and extensive checking of the material to be carried out in order to ensure that it did not produce too many overlaps with the current Weekday Lectionary, with the Daily Eucharistic Lectionary or with the Lectionary for Sundays, Principal Feasts and Holy Days, and Festivals. The decision was therefore taken by the Liturgical Commission not to proceed with the provision of such a lectionary until the need for it in more than a few places was established beyond doubt.

B. COMMENTARY

The new Weekday Lectionary (GS 1520A) replaces the temporary provision made in GS 1341A with a two-reading, two-office pattern. The New Testament provision is presented in two columns, New Testament 1 (NT1) and New Testament 2 (NT2), which are simply reversed from year to year for Morning and Evening Prayer. NT1 is used for Morning Prayer in years when Advent Sunday falls in an odd-numbered year (e.g. 2005–6) and NT2 for Morning Prayer in years when Advent Sunday falls in an even-numbered year (e.g. 2006–7). The Old Testament provision is also presented in two columns during Seasonal Time, as Old Testament 1 (OT1) and Old Testament 2a (OT2a). OT1, like NT1, is used for Morning Prayer in years where Advent Sunday falls in an odd-numbered year (2005–6). In Ordinary Time, however, the Old Testament material is divided between three columns: OT1, OT2a and OT2b. While OT1 continues to be used in the same years as in Seasonal Time for Morning and Evening Prayer, OT2a and OT2b are used alternately in Ordinary Time in years where Advent Sunday falls in an even-numbered year according to the four-year cycle (see Table 2.1).

Table 2.1: Distribution of Scripture

Year	Morning Prayer Seasonal Time	Evening Prayer Seasonal Time	Morning Prayer Ordinary Time	Evening Prayer Ordinary Time
2005–6	OT1–NT1	OT2a–NT2	OT1–NT1	OT2a–NT2
2006–7	OT2a–NT2	OT1–NT1	OT2a–NT2	OT1–NT1
2007–8	OT1–NT1	OT2a–NT2	OT1–NT1	OT2b–NT2
2008–9	OT2a–NT2	OT1–NT1	OT2b–NT2	OT1–NT1

Rationale

The weeks are designated by the preceding Sunday. As far as possible, readings have been arranged in such a way that each book occupies a multiple of complete weeks. In order to decide on the best beginning and ending points for readings, the compilers looked at the demarcation of readings in GS 1341A and the *ASB* and in the 1922 and 1961 lectionaries. The length of readings varies, the determining factor being sense rather than an attempt to attain any uniformity in the length of the passage. Occasional overlaps between consecutive readings have been made to assist the sense of each passage. Chapter and verse references are to the NRSV, but when a reading ends at the end of a chapter, 'end' rather than the verse number is given. When a reading consists of a whole chapter, no verse references at all are given. A full stop divides chapter and verse numbers; a comma divides verse numbers within a chapter.

The basic principle on which this lectionary is constructed is that of a continuous or semi-continuous reading of individual books of the Bible, with four lessons offered for each day, two for the morning and two for the evening. Used in this way, most of the Old and New Testaments are read each year. Where only one office is said each day, a complete coverage of Scripture will still be achieved, but over a longer period. Each day's New Testament readings include both a Gospel and a non-Gospel reading. As far as the Old Testament and Apocrypha are concerned, the pattern of the *ASB* lectionary has been followed by putting the historical books in one column and the prophetic and wisdom books in the other.

The Weekday Lectionary begins on the Monday after the Fourth Sunday before Advent, the pre-Advent and Advent seasons being treated as a continuous whole. The Gospel of Matthew is read sequentially at either Morning or Evening Prayer, thus straddling two liturgical years. For practical purposes, however, the lectionary, as printed, continues to run from Advent Sunday in any given year and will continue to be printed in that way also in the annual lectionary booklets.

Because of its commitment to the continuous reading of each book of the Bible, there will be occasions when a passage which occurs in its natural sequence in GS 1520A will be in close proximity to its occurrence in another lectionary such as the Daily Eucharistic Lectionary or the Lectionary for Sundays, Principal Feasts and Holy Days, and Festivals. Where this happens, the sequence of the readings in the Weekday Lectionary has been kept in order to maintain the principle of reading Scripture continuously. Such proximity between readings as do occur will, in any event, not happen every year in view of the different cycles over which the different lectionaries operate. Every effort has been made to avoid the same passage occurring on the same day in this lectionary and in the Daily Eucharistic Lectionary. However, a few such overlaps do occur, mainly in the reading of John at Christmas and Easter.

Coverage of the Bible

The Gospels
In the compilation of GS 1520A, the practice of the consecutive reading of Luke–Acts, first used in the *ASB* lectionary, has been followed, beginning in NT1 on the Monday after Easter 3 (called Easter 2 in the *ASB*). Mark is used

as the Gospel in NT2 from the Monday after Trinity 9 during the reading of Acts. Matthew is read from the Monday after the Fourth Sunday before Advent and is then read consecutively through Advent and Epiphany, excluding the Christmas period, which has its own special readings. The Gospel of John is not read consecutively as a whole but split between the different seasons of the liturgical year. Thus John 1 and 2 are read in the period between 29 December and 5 January; John 13—20 in the period between the Feast of the Presentation in the Temple and the Saturday before the First Sunday before Lent; John 3—12 is read during Lent itself; and John 20—21 in the week following Easter 2.

Other New Testament Books

Revelation is read, according to convention, in the period before and during Advent in parallel to Matthew's Gospel. Ephesians and 1 Peter, as one might expect, come in Eastertide. The remaining portions of the New Testament are distributed rather more mathematically according to which suitable book will fit into a certain period of time – 1 and 2 Thessalonians, Jude and 2 Peter occur during Advent after the reading of Revelation has been completed; 1 John, 2 John and 3 John appear between 7 and 12 January; and 1 Corinthians is read during the Epiphany season. Philippians, 1 and 2 Timothy, Titus and Philemon are read before Lent and completed if that season is short in the last few weeks of the Trinity season. Galatians and Hebrews are assigned to Lent. That leaves Romans, 2 Corinthians and the Letter of James, which are all read during the weeks after Trinity.

The Old Testament

In the reading of the Old Testament, too, there are some well-established conventions, which have been followed by the compilers of GS 1520A. For example, Isaiah is read in the run-up to Christmas, as it has been in every Church of England lectionary ever devised. The Pentateuch is begun in the Sundays before Lent and is read through in such a way that the Exodus and the crossing of the Red Sea occur about Easter time. Other portions of the Old Testament do not necessarily belong in particular seasons but are read together in sequence. So in the period before Lent we begin to read the narrative sequence contained in 1 and 2 Chronicles, Jeremiah 39—44 and Ezra–Nehemiah, while during Trinity we read all the former prophets together (Joshua, Judges, 1 and 2 Samuel and 1 and 2 Kings). How necessary it is to read Genesis sequentially was an issue of debate. In the initial draft of the Weekday Lectionary (GS 1520) the primeval myths in Genesis 1—11 were detached from the other two parts, the Abraham and Jacob saga (Genesis 12—35) and the Joseph story (Genesis 37—50). This was done in order to keep the Joseph cycle in Lent every year, no matter how long or short the period was between Epiphany and Lent. However, those who used the lectionary experimentally and those who wrote in to the Revision Committee did not like this arrangement, and so in the final draft (GS 1520A) Genesis was rearranged in OT1 in order, beginning on the Monday after Epiphany 1 and continuing to the end of Epiphany 4. The cycle is then taken up again in the third week before Lent. Exodus and Numbers follow Genesis and are so arranged as to be completed in time for Pentecost. The only other portion of the Pentateuch to be detached is the reading of Deuteronomy, which occurs in OT2a in parallel with Exodus and Numbers, beginning on the Monday after Easter 2. The wisdom books and the minor prophets are divided between the OT2a and OT2b columns during the weeks before Lent and in the season of Trinity. Jeremiah is begun in Lent but is completed during Trinity in OT2a. Ezekiel is also read during Trinity in OT2b. For the arrangement of the remainder of the books of the Old Testament see Table 2.2 on pp. 48–9.

The Apocrypha

Like most other Church of England lectionaries, including that in the 1549 *BCP*, the Weekday Lectionary in GS 1520A includes in both the OT2a and OT2b columns readings from the Apocrypha, in conformity with Article 6 of the Thirty-Nine Articles. However, since there are people within the Church of England who cannot in conscience accept the Apocrypha as part of Scripture, and as there are many churches and individuals who do not have the Apocrypha in their Bibles, the convention of the *ASB* has been followed, namely that in each place where an apocryphal reading occurs, a canonical alternative is also provided. The compilers took great care, however, to ensure that the alternatives never occur near to the place where they would be read in course, so that it is unlikely that anyone will feel a sense of repetitiveness even if they use the alternatives. On the other hand, those who do use the readings from the Apocrypha will not lose any canonical ones, since they all appear somewhere else in the Lectionary as well.

Psalmody

In compiling the Weekday Lectionary in GS 1520A, the Liturgical Commission tried to keep to the principles of both appropriate psalmody in seasons and a continuous reading of the psalms in Ordinary Time. The seasonal provision is less constrained than that provided in GS 1341A. It was considered important to keep a distinctive feel to each of the main seasons of the liturgical year, which had become familiar to many people in *CCP*, but within that pattern of psalmody to offer more than a single weekly cycle repeated throughout the season, since that tends to be over-repetitive and limits too much the coverage of psalms. Care was therefore taken not to repeat the same psalms on the same day of the week throughout a season. The compilers also tried to maintain a sense of proximity between the psalms chosen for any one office, so that the amount of turning backwards and forwards through the Psalter could be reduced. For those who only wish to say one psalm a day, the psalm which is to be preferred is indicated in the text.

Psalms for Ordinary Time are used from the day after the Presentation in the Temple until Shrove Tuesday. A proposal to make 'seasonal' provision for the weeks before Lent was rejected by the Revision Committee and thus did not make it into GS 1520A. The cycle resumes on the day after Pentecost and is used until the eve of the Fourth Sunday before Advent. Alternatively, the psalm table for weekdays in Ordinary Time can be used throughout the year, except for the period between 19 December and the Epiphany and from the Monday of Holy Week to the Saturday of Easter Week. Rubrics are provided to ensure that this provision follows the same sequence in Ordinary Time as would be followed by those who also use the seasonal tables. For those who wish to use wholly continuous psalmody throughout the year, the table of psalms from the *BCP* remains authorized.

During Ordinary Time the psalms follow a seven-week cycle. The pattern provided is semi- rather than wholly continuous. Attention was paid in particular to psalms which refer to specific hours of the day. Thus Psalm 5 is not said on the Evening of the Monday of Week 1 because of verse 2, 'In the morning when I pray to you'. Psalm 119 is also not read in course, but portions of it are used alternately at Morning and Evening Prayer on Wednesdays and the whole psalm completed over the seven-week cycle. Some attempt has also been made to use appropriate psalms on Fridays and on Saturday evenings, even though this breaks the sequence to some extent. Despite some pleas from a few of the experimental parishes for a return to saying the psalms strictly in course during Ordinary Time, the care taken in differentiating between morning and evening psalms and the breaking-up of Psalm 119 into digestible portions has been generally welcomed. Less happy was the proposal in GS 1520 to omit certain psalms (8, 63, 67, 95, 103, 134) used as invitatory psalms in *Daily Prayer*. The Revision Committee took the view that, since in many parishes the invitatory psalm is replaced by a hymn, there was a danger that these psalms would never be used. So they were reinstated and in GS 1520A appear in brackets with a note that they are to be omitted if used as an invitatory psalm. Certain psalms are also asterisked. These may be shortened as pastoral needs dictate.

C. RELATED CALENDRICAL ISSUES

The process of compiling annual lectionary booklets has in the last few years revealed a number of lacunae in the rules and rubrics contained in *Calendar, Lectionary and Collects* and in Rules for Regulating Authorised Forms of Service. Other mistakes or lacunae were at the same time drawn to the attention of the Liturgical Commission. The opportunity afforded by the passage of the Weekday Lectionary through General Synod was taken as an opportunity to address these issues.

Lesser Festivals: Rules for Regulating Authorised Forms of Service

Two amendments were made here. The first gave force to the convention that Lesser Festivals should not be observed on Sundays and (as when they fall on Principal Feasts, Holy Days and Festivals) should normally lapse, though they may be transferred 'where there is sufficient reason'. It also provided that Lesser Festivals should not be celebrated between Palm Sunday and the Second Sunday of Easter. The second amendment makes explicit one such example of transferring a Lesser Festival, namely the case of All Souls' Day, and permission is given to transfer this to a Monday when it would fall on a Sunday.

The Second Sunday of Christmas: Collects and Lectionary

Amendments here make it clear that when Christmas Day falls on a Sunday and, by local decision, the Naming and Circumcision of Jesus is transferred to Monday 2 January, Sunday 1 January becomes the Second Sunday of Christmas. However, in these circumstances the liturgical provision for the First Sunday of Christmas should be used on 1 January.

The Epiphany: Rules for Regulating Authorised Forms of Service

The rubrics in *CW* state that if there is a Second Sunday of Christmas, the Epiphany may be celebrated on that day. This, however, needed to be changed to prevent a conflict with the rubric relating to the Second Sunday of Christmas above. The combined effect of these rubrics is that the Epiphany is celebrated on a Sunday if 6 January is a Sunday and may be celebrated on the preceding Sunday if 6 January is a Monday, Tuesday, Wednesday or Thursday. Only in the two years out of every seven when the Epiphany falls on a Friday or a Saturday may it not be transferred to a Sunday. However, if parishes become accustomed to celebrating the Epiphany on a Sunday in five years out of seven, it is likely that many will be tempted to transfer the Epiphany forward to 7 or 8 January, whatever the rubrics say.

The question was further complicated by the fact that the Roman Catholic Church's General Norms for the Liturgical Year and Calendar allow Bishops' Conferences to assign the Epiphany to a Sunday occurring between 2 January and 8 January inclusive. In England and Wales, the Bishops' Conference has decided that the Epiphany should be celebrated on 6 January unless 6 January is a Saturday (in which case it is celebrated on Sunday 7 January) or a Monday (in which case it is celebrated on Sunday 5 January). Thus the one year in which the *CW* rules forbid celebration of the Epiphany on a Sunday, and one of the two in which this would still be forbidden by the amendments relating to the Second Sunday of Christmas, is a year in which all Roman Catholic churches in England and Wales *do* celebrate the Epiphany on the nearest Sunday. This may increase the likelihood of churches transferring the Epiphany forward in that year despite the *CW* rules. In view of all of this, the Liturgical Commission recommended that the *CW* rubrics should be changed to allow the Epiphany to be celebrated *for pastoral reasons* on the Sunday falling between 2 and 8 January inclusive, and this amendment was approved.

The Date of the Baptism of Christ: Calendar, Collects and Rules

The Festival of the Baptism of Christ is normally celebrated on the First Sunday of Epiphany. In the Roman Catholic Church, when the Epiphany falls on a Sunday, the Baptism is celebrated on the following Sunday (13 January). However, no such provision was made in the *CW* rubrics, and as a result, if the Epiphany falls on a Sunday, the Baptism of Christ must, according to the *CW* rules, be transferred to the Monday. If the Epiphany is a Sunday, the following Sunday must be the Second Sunday of Epiphany.

Amendments were made, therefore, to provide that the Baptism of Christ should normally be observed on the Sunday following the Feast of the Epiphany in every year, but that this Sunday should be counted as the Second Sunday of Epiphany when 6 January is a Sunday. However, if the Epiphany is itself transferred forward for pastoral reasons to what would otherwise be the Festival of the Baptism of Christ, then the Baptism of Christ must be transferred to the Monday. (This is also what happens in the Roman Catholic Church if the Epiphany is transferred forward.) Provision also needed to be made for the readings to be used on the Sundays of Epiphany in years in which 6 January is a Sunday. It is clear that as in those years everyone will keep the Baptism of Christ on 13 January (the Second Sunday of Epiphany), the readings for the Baptism of Christ should be used on that day.

The Sundays of Epiphany: Lectionary

Amendments ensure that insofar as the Church of England's Lectionary uses the same readings and psalms as those in the Revised Common Lectionary during Epiphany, they are used on the same Sunday. The Church of Ireland and the Church in Wales are making similar provisions on this issue.

Holy Week: Lectionary

The Second and Third Service lectionaries for the weekdays of Holy Week were designed with a view to the Second Service lectionary being used in the morning and the Third Service lectionary in the evening on the Monday, Tuesday and Wednesday, on Maundy Thursday and on Easter Eve. On Good Friday, however, the readings in the Second and Third Services are designed to be used the other way round, the Third Service lectionary being intended for morning use, and the Second Service lectionary for evening use. The amendments therefore provide for the readings concerned to be used in the morning and the evening as intended.

Sundays of Easter: Lectionary

For the Principal Services on Ascension Day and the Feast of Pentecost, a reading from Acts is provided as the first reading in *CW*. An optional Old

Testament reading is also provided, but a rubric requires that the reading from Acts must be used as either the first or the second reading. Old Testament readings are also provided, in a table, for the Principal Service on Easter Day, Second, Third, Fourth, Fifth, Sixth and Seventh Sundays after Easter. A rubric requires that if the Old Testament reading is used on these Sundays, then the reading from Acts must be used as the second reading. However, if the Old Testament reading is not used, there is no requirement to use the reading from Acts at all. Amendments remove this anomaly by requiring the use of the Acts reading as either the first or the second reading on these Sundays also.

The Martyrs of Uganda: Calendar

In the *CW* Calendar, 3 June is the Commemoration of 'The Martyrs of Uganda, 1886 and 1978'. However, it has been pointed out that these dates are incorrect, because three of the martyrs died in 1885 and one in 1887 and because it is not clear which martyr died in 1978 (Archbishop Luwum is commemorated separately on 17 February and in any case he died in 1977). Therefore the dates have been corrected to '1885–1887'.

Further Reading

G. J. Cuming, *A History of Anglican Liturgy*, Macmillan, London, 1969.

Mark Earey and Gilly Myers (eds), *Common Worship Today*, HarperCollins, London, 2001, pp. 230–42.

Gordon Giles, 'The Sunday Lectionary' in Paul F. Bradshaw (ed.), *Companion to Common Worship*, vol. 1, SPCK, London, 2001.

George Guiver, *Company of Voices*, 2nd edn, Canterbury Press, Norwich, 2001.

Table 2.2: Biblical material covered in the Weekday Lectionary by seasons

Season	OT1	OT2a	OT2b	NT1	NT2
Before Advent	Daniel Isaiah 40—42.17	Isaiah 1—24		Revelation 1—18	Matthew 1—11
Advent	Isaiah 25—39 Zephaniah; Malachi; Nahum; Obadiah	Isaiah 42—56; 58; 63		Matthew 12—19; Matthew 23	Revelation 19—end; 1 Thessalonians; 2 Thessalonians; Jude; 2 Peter
Dec 29–31	Jonah	Isaiah 57.15–end; 59		Colossians 1.1—2.7	John 1.1–34
Jan 2–5	Ruth	Isaiah 60—62		Colossians 2.8—end	John 1.35—2.end
Jan 7–12	Baruch or messianic oracles	Isaiah 63—66		Matthew 20 and 23	1 John 3—5; 2 John; 3 John
Epiphany	Genesis 1—24.28	Amos; Hosea		Matthew 21; 24—28	1 Corinthians 1—14
Before Lent	Legal material from Torah; Genesis 24.29—41.24	From 1 Chronicles 10—29 From 2 Chronicles 1—16 Jeremiah 1.1—4.18	Song of Three; Susannah; Bel and the Dragon; Prayer of Manasseh or Malachi; Nahum and Obadiah; Joel; Ecclesiastes 1—12	Philippians; 1 Timothy; 2 Timothy; Titus; Philemon	John 13—20; John 3—4
Lent	Genesis 41.25–end; Exodus 1—11	Jeremiah 1—25		Galatians; Hebrews	John 5—12
Easter	Exodus 12—end Numbers 9—32	Song of Solomon; Deuteronomy		1 Corinthians 15; Colossians; Luke 1.1—9.17	John 20—21; Ephesians; 1 Peter; 1 John

Table 2.2 (continued)

Season	OT1	OT2a	OT2b	NT1	NT2
Pentecost and Trinity	Joshua; Judges; 1 Samuel; 2 Samuel; 1 Kings; 2 Kings; Judith or legal material from Torah	2 Chronicles 17.1—36.11; Ezra; Nehemiah; Esther; Jeremiah 26—end; Micah; Habakkuk; Haggai; Zechariah; Ecclesiasticus or Ezekiel + Ecclesiastes	Job; Ezekiel; Proverbs; Wisdom 1—2; Maccabees or 1 & 2 Chronicles; Tobit or Micah + Habakkuk	Luke 9.18–end Acts; Philippians; 1 Timothy; 2 Timothy; Titus; Philemon *If not used before Lent*	Romans; 2 Corinthians; James; Mark; John 13—20

Chapter 3

Times and Seasons

The Times and Seasons volumes (hereafter = TS) are intended to replace and extend *Lent, Holy Week and Easter* (1986 = *LHWE*) and *The Promise of His Glory* (1991 = *PHG*), and include material drawn from those books, from *New Patterns for Worship* (2004 = *NPFW*), itself based on the earlier *Patterns for Worship* (= *PFW*), and from privately produced but widely used resources such as *Enriching the Christian Year* (1993 = *ECY*), as well as wholly new provisions and compositions. By its nature, TS builds on the principles of the *CW* Calendar (see Chapter 3 in Volume 1 of this *Companion*), expands on the seasonal provision of the *CW* main volume, of the President's Edition of that book (= *CWPE*) and of *CW Daily Prayer* (=*DP*), and also supplies resources for special services on single occasions in the liturgical year. As such, it is a vital addition to the *CW* library and offers many opportunities for a rich observance and exploration of liturgical time. The material is set out season by season, and within each section material is usually grouped by genre, for example 'Introductions to the Peace' or 'Prefaces'. There are also detailed schemes, including full orders of service, for the major feasts, and practical directions where these are essential. Each season has its own historical and pastoral introduction.

The commentary given here will follow the order of the material through the liturgical year, giving information on the history of each of the seasons and of days within them, the sources of the liturgical texts provided (if known or identifiable: many were written by members of the Liturgical Commission without individual attribution), indications of their theological significance and, where appropriate, advice as to the practical usage of each item. The latter may often be inherently suggested by the provenance of the material, for example how it was used in *PHG* or is identified in *NPFW*. For reasons of space, it has not been possible to be exhaustive or as detailed as, for example, the *Companion to the ASB* was on the relatively slender seasonal resources in that book. However, it is hoped that an impression at least is given of the breadth of sources and the scope of the Christian liturgical tradition covered by what is by any standards a very great deal of material.

In addition to the seasons, a digest of material is added for occasions in the agricultural year, which will be welcomed by rural communities and others as an acknowledgement of the often-forgotten symbolic connection between the cycle of the natural seasons and those of the Church, and as an encouragement of and resource for good practice in this regard. Unfortunately space does not permit detailed comment on this material and for the purposes of this *Companion* it is felt that the seasons and major feasts of the Christian year, being universal, have the prior claim. The same principle applied to the resources for Festivals of the Liturgical Year, for each of which is provided material for the Eucharist in the same categories as for the seasons and major feasts, and drawn from the same range of sources. It is hoped that the pastoral principles of selection and use which emerge from the main commentary will lend themselves to these occasions also.

A. ADVENT

Although in historical terms the most recent of the seasons to emerge, if the *CW* treatment of 'Epiphanytide' is discounted, the origins of Advent are not clear. It had a penitential character in the middle centuries of the first millennium which may have been linked to Epiphany baptism, but neither this nor the alternative view that it represented a Christianizing of the pagan winter fast can be certain. Contrary to its modern acceptance as the beginning of the liturgical year, Advent may in earlier times have struggled against a persistence in Rome to see Christmas in this role; certainly the emphasis on penitence in Gaul and Spain was contrasted in Rome by a focus on the joyful expectation of the coming of Christ.

As a distinct season Advent is overshadowed in secular society by preemptive celebration of Christmas. The positive realities of this are discussed in Chapter 3 of Volume 1 of this *Companion*. However, it is possible and desirable that even if occasions are observed for sound pastoral reasons in advance of Christmas for particular communities such as schools and colleges, Advent is not to be obscured by these as the principal focus of the community at prayer before 25 December. Advent has a rich potential for reflection on powerful themes in the economy of salvation, for example the first and second comings of Christ and, traditionally, the 'four last things': death, judgement, heaven and hell. An earlier emphasis on penitence, although not universal, tends to be downplayed, and as the introduction to the material in Times and Seasons states, Advent is now seen as 'a season of expectation and preparation', although of course preparation properly includes a measure of penitence. The texts provided reflect this balance.

Seasonal Material

Invitations to Confession
Three alternatives are given, all scriptural texts: 1 Corinthians 4.5 (an altered version, also given in the *CW* main volume, of a provision in *PHG*) recalls the Advent images of darkness and light; John 1.23 the exhortation of John the Baptist to 'make straight the way of the Lord'; and Matthew 3.10 the promise of divine judgement.

Kyrie Confessions

Three options are suggested, the first and third of which appeared in *PHG*. The first, originally from Portsmouth Cathedral, uses verses from Psalm 85 to express the balance between the consequences of sin, the compassion of God and the promise of salvation to those who hear and repent. The second is new to TS and is composed from Romans 2.16, Matthew 7.21 and a recurring phrase in Revelation 2 and 3. The emphasis is on judgement linked to the prospect of heaven and the consequent need to listen to the prompting of the Spirit. The third text (originally in the Roman Missal) is ecclesial in composition, directly addressed to the coming Christ and framing present encounter with him in word and sacrament with statements of the expected gathering of the nations in peace and the hope of salvation which will accompany the parousia.

Gospel Acclamation

The text of Isaiah 40.3 is reproduced from the main volume, and anticipates the Baptist's use of this prophecy. As such, it suggests the proclamation in the Gospel and the present reality of that which was long ago foretold.

Intercessions

Two forms are provided. The invitation, petitions (altered) and response of the first are a *PHG* text with a strong emphasis on expectation, and a suggestion of the sense in which Advent is a profitably unsettling season ('Break into our lives . . .'), and yet one which looks to the communion of saints as co-inheritors of the kingdom. The concluding collect is also from *PHG*, the authorship unattributed. It communicates an urgency that heightens the desire for the Lord's coming. The invitations and petitions of the second form are in *CCP* and repeated in *DP*. They pick up the themes of watching and waiting for, and experiencing, the healing presence of the Lord. The collect is an adapted form of one found in the *Scottish Prayer Book 1929* of the Scottish Episcopal Church, included in *PHG*. It complements the watching and waiting of the petitions with a reminder of the Christ who seeks and finds us.

Introductions to the Peace

Four alternatives are supplied. The first comprises verses taken from the *Benedictus* (Luke 1.78, 79) and is included in the *CW* main volume, with the theme of the light of Christ dispelling the world's darkness. The next, underlining the promise of peace which results from a turning towards God, is based on Psalm 85.8 and 1 Samuel 12.20 and appears in *NPFW*. The third is also included in *NPFW*, and echoes the call to holiness in 1 Thessalonians 5.23. The final alternative is from the Canadian *BAS*, where it appears in responsorial form as part of material for the beginning of the Daily Office in Advent, and is also to be found in *NPFW* as an introduction to the Peace. It alludes to the kingship of him who 'comes in the name of the Lord', thus looking back to the Sunday before Advent (Christ the King) and forward to the acclamation of his entry into Jerusalem heard on Palm Sunday.

Prayers at the Preparation of the Table

The first of the three forms is in two parts, with a response based on *Didache* 9.4 and as previously included in *PHG*, although there among the material for Epiphanytide: perhaps more appropriately for Advent, it brings together the symbol of bread with the image of scattering and reuniting to aspire to the unity of the Church, and that of wine with the notion of Christ the personification of Wisdom as the builder of the house and the host at the table. The second form is in the *CW* main volume, contrasting mercy with judgement and love with hatred as our need and our means respectively in the transformation of frail praise into a worthy response to God's glory. The third option has also been transposed from the Epiphanytide material in *PHG*, where it was part of a longer unattributed text and had instead the response 'Maranatha! Come, Lord Jesus!' It appears in its revised form in the *CW* main volume without seasonal identification. Again the image of scattering and reuniting is used to good effect.

Prefaces

1 From the *CW* main volume, was in *PHG* borrowed in modified form from the ECUSA 1979 *BCP*, clearly associated in terms of its themes of redemption and judgement with the first Collect of Christmas Day in that book, a prayer which was based on the Sarum Collect for the *Missa in Gallicantu* (see Vol. 1, p. 185), and in turn included in the *ASB* for use on Christmas Eve. This may suggest its use in the fourth week of Advent as an allusion to what is to come.

2 Originating in the Roman Missal, modified in *PHG* and further altered ('as a man' becomes 'in human flesh') in *NPFW*. The reference to Christ's humbling of himself recalls Philippians 1.5–11, and connects it with the plan of salvation 'formed long ago' and to be fulfilled at his coming again.

3 In *NPFW* and *CWPE*, from the *ASB* unaltered, recalling the role of John the Baptist and therefore especially appropriate on the Third Sunday of Advent since it ties in with the Collect of that day.

4 From *PHG* and *NPFW*, explicitly inclusive in compactly recounting the foretelling, announcing, conceiving and proclaiming of the birth of the Messiah to 'men and women of every race'.

5 Modified from the *ASB* in *NPFW*, recalling the vision of John in Revelation 21.5 ('Behold, I make all things new'). The immediacy of the language suggests use in the final days before Christmas, perhaps from *O Sapientia* (17 December) onwards.

Extended Prefaces

The first is for use from the First Sunday of Advent until 16 December. It appears in the *CW* main volume, and is an extended form of the second short preface. The second extended preface is for use from 17 December (*O Sapientia*) until Christmas Eve and is a modified version of a preface in *PHG* and also in the *CW* main volume. Appropriately for the final days of Advent and conscious of the imagery and scriptural provision of the foregoing weeks, the roles of the prophets, the Blessed Virgin Mary and John the Baptist are drawn into the same narrative, which bursts with joyful anticipation of the great feast about to be celebrated but without pre-empting it.

Blessings and Endings

Two simple and two solemn blessings are supplied, with an additional 'ending' that is neither a blessing nor a dismissal in the strict sense, and is therefore more suited for use at the daily office. The first of the two short blessings was in the *ASB* and *PHG* and is also in the *CW* main volume, employing the title 'Sun of Righteousness' for Christ, again emphasizing the contrasted light and darkness of Christ in relation to the world and looking forward to his coming as judge. The second short blessing was in *PHG*, is included in *NPFW* and focuses on the call to holiness and wholeness in spiritual and physical terms.

The first solemn blessing was composed by Michael Perham and included in *PHG* and *CWPE*. Properly Trinitarian in shape, it alludes to the role of the persons of the Trinity in the first and second comings of Christ in relation to the hope of renewal in our lives. The second solemn form was unattributed in *PHG* (although incorporating the title of that volume) and is also in *CWPE*. In Trinitarian shape, it contains the themes of judgement, 'the promise of his glory' and the strengthening of the Pauline attributes of faith, hope and love.

The 'ending' is simple in form, with a responsorial form of the final verse of the Book of Revelation and an aspiration to readiness for the coming of Christ.

An Alternative Dismissal for Advent Sunday

A combination of existing and new material, this provision comprises an Acclamation, a Dismissal Gospel, a Blessing and a Dismissal formula. The Acclamation with repeated response is followed by Mark 1.14–15, framed by the usual *CW* announcement and conclusion. The model is clearly the pre-conciliar Roman Catholic 'Last Gospel', the reading of John 1.1–14 with which the president concluded the Latin Mass, and which was also included in some unofficial Anglican liturgies. This imaginative reworking of a hitherto presumed obsolete element of the liturgy recurs at other points in the TS material, although it might be argued that the Gospel passages chosen, while presumably as brief so as not to detract from the liturgical Gospel earlier in the rite, are also too short to have any real impact at this point. Nevertheless the desire to underscore the beginning of the season is in general a good one. The Blessing may consist either of the solemn form suggested (the second in the previous section), or another suitable form, presumably from those specifically provided. The Dismissal is a slightly lengthened version of either the familiar 'Go in peace to love and serve the Lord' or '. . . go in the peace of Christ' texts.

Short Passages of Scripture

The introduction by the Liturgical Commission to the Report containing the first draft of TS is very clear in intending these seasonally suggested passages, which are in fact single verses called in the *ASB* 'sentences of scripture', to be used flexibly and optionally within a rite as circumstances suggest. In this they differ from the *ASB* provision, in which such sentences were anchored to particular points in the liturgy. They do not preclude the selection of others which may be thought suitable.

Carol Services in the Advent Season

PHG recognized the increasing popularity of so-called 'Advent Carol Services', and sought to provide appropriate structures and resources. Much of the material in TS is taken from this earlier compilation.

Bidding Prayers and Introduction

All three suggested forms (presumably alternatives could be composed locally or those provided adapted) of bidding and introduction are accordingly of *PHG* provenance. They appeared there having been first composed for Christ Church, Oxford by E. W. Heaton, for Portsmouth Cathedral by David Stancliffe, and by Michael Perham for St George's, Oakdale respectively. The adapted version of a text from Westminster Abbey which appears in *PHG* is not reproduced in TS, although as implied above it could presumably still be used if desired. Of the three given, the Portsmouth text follows the pattern classically set by the bidding prayer for the Nine Lessons and Carols at King's College, Cambridge (for which see below) in including as its climax the Lord's Prayer recited in common, here in either traditional or contemporary form (or indeed in the 'ecumenical' text included in the supplementary material in the *CW* main volume). All three are good examples of attempts to encapsulate the great themes of Advent so as to 'set the scene' for the sequence of readings and music to follow. Accordingly they contain elements of liturgical greeting, theological exposition, call to repentance and invitation to prayer.

It is not entirely clear whether the rubric which follows the three texts and which directs a period of silent prayer followed by the Collect of Advent Sunday is meant to apply to all three or only the last. It would certainly be appropriate in all three cases, and perhaps in its *BCP* form if the traditional form of the Lord's Prayer has been used.

Patterns of Readings

The four options in TS are all from *PHG*, each focusing on a different scriptural 'route' through the Advent mysteries. In the case of sequence 3, an appropriate element of social responsibility is incorporated in the form of 'A vigil for prisoners and those who sit in darkness'. It may be that such themes could be woven into other patterns of readings, given the Advent characteristic of disturbance and challenge to comfort and security otherwise all too easily taken for granted.

Conclusions

Although reflecting the fondness of the compilers of *PHG* for sequences of versicles and responses, the responsorial forms suggested as conclusions to Advent Carol Services are entirely appropriate theologically and would be most effective if sung. The first from the Canadian *BAS* employs psalmody (Psalms 80.8; 85.6, 7), the second a combination of an echo of the *Benedictus* (Luke 1.68), the entry into Jerusalem and the Davidic ancestry and destiny of Jesus (Matthew 21.9; Mark 11.10) and ending with a blessing of God's name (Psalm 113.2). The third is shorter and employs the opening words of the Liturgy of St John Chrysostom and Luke 19.38. The fourth and fifth are similar, in that they each comprise three versicles and responses beginning with Psalm 48.9, and continuing with either Isaiah 40.5 and Psalm 85.7 or Psalm 121.2 and the formula 'Let us bless the Lord/Thanks be to God'. The final option in this section is a shortened version of a *PHG* text, beginning with Romans 13.12, which may well be familiar from the traditional form of Compline, and part of the Collect for Advent Sunday. Three versicles and responses follow: Psalm 86.4a (altered) with Revelation 22.20b as the response, a possible allusion to the invitatory for Christmas Eve in the Roman Catholic *Divine Office* ('know today that the Lord will come: in the morning you will see his glory') and Luke 1.79 from the *Benedictus*. The closing text is an adaptation of Revelation 22.16, 20.

The Advent Wreath

The use of the Advent wreath in the context of the liturgy began in Germany in the seventeenth century. As an aspect of Christian devotion its precise origins are uncertain, but it seems likely it draws on a pagan tradition whereby the return of the sun was expressed in ritual. Consequently the birth of Christ is heralded by the increasing number of candles lit on the wreath as Advent progresses.

TS gives extensive resources for use with the wreath, allowing for a number of different foci and teaching opportunities. The introductory text allows for red or blue candles around a white or gold one. The possibility of three purple and one pink (or rose-colour) candles surrounding the central 'Christ' candle is not mentioned, presumably because thought obsolete. However, the *CW* Calendar specifically mentions the custom in some places of rose-colour as the colour of the day on the Third Sunday of Advent, the *Gaudete* Sunday of lightened mood with its 'splash of colour' mentioned in the introduction to the TS Advent material. Therefore it seems a shame to omit this option in respect of the candles for use where such an emphasis is recalled. Nevertheless, such observance may serve to distract from the principal liturgical emphases of the four Sundays, which the use of the wreath and its candles can effectively underscore. Thus the introduction (almost identical to *PHG*) restates the 'Patriarchs, Prophets, John the Baptist, Virgin Mary, Christ' sequence followed by the Principal Service Lectionary. Suitable prayers are then provided to accompany the lighting of each candle on its Sunday, each addressed to God and inviting the response 'Blessed be God for ever'. It is suggested that for each Sunday the second and third have children in mind. The third is designed for common recitation by the congregation. All are adapted from *PHG*, the second and third prayers for each Sunday having originally been used at St George's, Oakdale.

In terms of their position, TS adds to the *PHG* provision in suggesting that the wreath may be used in connection with the Prayers of Penitence, with additional, dedicated material as an alternative to using the first set either after the Gospel, before the Peace or as the post-communion prayer (presumably replacing the existing *CW* provision). The penitential material takes the form of a *Kyrie* confession for each Sunday of the season, with an absolution from the *CW* main volume preceded by a 'may' rubric that implicitly permits any authorized alternative. The petitions reflect the main focus of the Principal Service Lectionary. It is not suggested when exactly the candle may be lit: perhaps immediately before the absolution would be best, to associate the light with the forgiveness for which the assembly prays.

The Advent Antiphons

Although practically obsolete after the Reformation, the inclusion of *O Sapientia* on 16 December in the *BCP* Calendar suggests at least a residual awareness of the traditional *Magnificat* antiphons, the 'Great Os', which in the Roman use from at least as early as the eighth century occurred on the seven days leading up to Christmas, beginning on 17 December. Sarum began the sequence on 16 December, however, adding *O Virgo Virginum* ('O Virgin of Virgins') on 23 December in honour of the Virgin Mary. The antiphons, originally sung to relatively elaborate chant, ask God to come in the form of what TS calls 'a tapestry of scriptural titles and pictures which describe his saving work in Christ'. Some cathedrals and other churches have revived the practice of using these antiphons in their original context before and after the *Magnificat* at Evensong. They will also be familiar to many in the form of the hymn 'O come, O come, Emmanuel'. TS provides a translation of each antiphon with an indication of its scriptural allusions and a suggested lectionary from Norwich Cathedral for Evening Prayer on the relevant days, as an encouragement to continue the revival of these wonderfully rich and evocative texts. Not included, but still possible, is the *PHG* suggestion and provision that they be used as the framework for 'A Service of Hope and Expectation'. In any event the antiphons are most effective when sung, however simply.

Resources

Advent Prose

This is a translation in contemporary language of a traditional text, *Rorate coeli desuper*, probably by the prolific hymn-writer Aurelius Clemens Prudentius (348–413), later found in both the Latin office and Mass; the opening words (the Vulgate text of Isaiah 45.8) are used by the late medieval Scottish poet William Dunbar to begin his *On the Nativity of Christ*. The Advent Prose (an alternative term for the liturgical 'sequence') is rendered in the *New English Hymnal* (no. 501) 'Drop down, ye heavens, from above'. The Latin verb *rorare* has the sense of falling like moisture, perhaps light rain or dew, so perhaps 'Pour down, O heavens, from above', as here, is nearer the image intended by the writer. Another, older version has 'Mystic dew from heaven / Unto earth is given', more of a paraphrase but confirming the sense of the original. In *PHG* the text is given as an appendix to the penitential material for Advent, and is indeed markedly penitential in character, although culminating in a powerful note of hope. For this reason, and in order to maintain the finely balanced character of the season, the *Rorate coeli* should be used with care. Whenever it is used it should be sung, perhaps most effectively to the plainsong melody, a cantor singing the verses and the whole assembly the refrain, although other settings are available.

Further Reading

J. Neil Alexander, *Waiting for the Coming: The Liturgical Meaning of Advent, Christmas and Epiphany*, Pastoral Press, Washington, DC, 1993.

Patrick Cowley, *Advent: Its Liturgical Significance*, Faith Press, London, 1960.

Thomas Merton, 'The Sacrament of Advent in the Spirituality of St Bernard' (1952) and 'Advent: Hope or Delusion?' (1963) in his *Seasons of Celebration: Meditations on the Cycle of Liturgical Feasts*, Farrar, Straus & Giroux, New York, 1965, pp. 61–87, 88–100.

T. J. O'Gorman (ed.), *An Advent Sourcebook*, Liturgy Training Publications, Chicago, 1988.

Michael Perham and Kenneth Stevenson, 'Advent' in *Welcoming the Light of Christ: A Commentary on 'The Promise of His Glory'*, SPCK, London 1991, pp. 38–53.

Thomas J. Talley, *The Origins of the Liturgical Year*, 2nd edition, The Liturgical Press, Collegeville, MN, 1991, pp. 147–53.

B. CHRISTMAS

December 25 probably became fixed as the date of the celebration of the birth of Jesus in Rome in the fourth century. This was taken up elsewhere remarkably rapidly, such that it was near-universal by the mid-fifth century. Constantinople, Antioch and Palestine followed later, having previously established 6 January as the more significant 'epiphany'. Two main strands of scholarly opinion have accounted for the adoption of 25 December. The 'history of religions' thesis associated it with the pagan festival of the sun, *natalis solis invicti*, in opposition to pre-Christian religion. A more recent argument is based on calendrical calculation: early Christians may have associated the presumed date of the conception of Jesus on 25 March with a presumed birth nine months later on 25 December. From relatively early on in Rome three Masses were celebrated: midnight, dawn and during the day.

TS acknowledges the modern issues of commercial anticipation of Christmas. Perhaps the fact that it is far more than a birthday party, but nothing less than the celebration of the 'mystery of God's dwelling among us in the fullness of humanity' lessens the absolute necessity of focus on the date itself (see Chapter 3 of Volume 1 of this *Companion*) and to some extent justifies the frequent pastoral need to anticipate the feast and enables the major feasts of saints on the days immediately following 25 December to be properly observed.

Medieval and modern forms of celebration that are now firmly associated with the season are given full recognition and provision: the crib and the carol service, and the New Year, which while strictly a secular occasion is nevertheless an opportunity for Christian reflection and commitment, as in the Methodist custom of the 'Covenant' service. In addition, an 'alternative tradition' is encouraged whereby the Christmas 'season' is extended through Epiphany to the Feast of the Presentation (Candlemas) on 2 February, a full forty days underscored by lectionary provision and consistency of liturgical colour.

Seasonal Material

Invitations to Confession
Three forms are provided. The first quotes directly Matthew 1.21, and is also to be found in the *CW* main volume. The second first appeared in *PHG* for use on Christmas Night or Day as the introduction to an extended form of penitential prayer to be used at the crib, but in TS independent use at the Midnight Eucharist is suggested, since it speaks of the dispelling of darkness by Christ the Light of the world. The third form is based on Malachi 4.2, and is from *NPFW*, where it is associated with relationships, healing and incarnation.

Kyrie Confession
A single provision draws on John 1 ('full of grace and truth'), the poverty of Jesus' birth and the obedience of Mary to the work of the Spirit.

Confession
An alternative form of confession with a response to five petitions, from *PHG* and reproduced in the *CW* main volume. The petitions have as their themes our unworthiness, the obedience of Mary, the poverty of Christ's birth, the shepherds and the wise men.

Absolutions
Both forms are drawn from the alternatives given in the *CW* main volume. The first alludes to John 1 ('behold the glory' and 'the Word made flesh'), the second to John 3 ('God who loved the world so much').

Gospel Acclamation
John 1.14, from the seasonal provisions in the *CW* main volume.

Intercessions
1 Adapted from *NPFW*, addressed to Christ.
2 Addressed to either Christ or to God the Father, and inviting specific locally chosen topics for intercession before each response.
3 Intended for Christmas Night but adaptable to other occasions in the season, addressed to God the Father and using the Gospel birth and infancy narratives (the inn, angels, shepherds) and traditional phraseology (e.g. 'this holy night'; 'heaven is come down to earth, and earth is raised to heaven'). Adapted from *NPFW*.
4 A 'Litany for the World' from *PHG*, where it is part of suggested material for 'A Service for Christmas Morning', implicitly non-eucharistic.
5 Specifically intended to encourage and offer the prayers of small children. Very simple petitions mention both scriptural and traditional aspects of the birth narratives (Mary, the manger, animals, shepherds, kings), each associated with themes for suggested specific items and people: families, the homeless and refugees, creation, nations, races and peoples, those in especial need.

Introductions to the Peace
Two forms are given. The first is from the *CW* main volume, and also *PHG*, based on Isaiah 9.6; the second quotes Luke 2.14.

Prayer at the Preparation of the Table
Jesus the Word made flesh (John 1) is addressed, and contrasts the human poverty he shares by the incarnation with the riches which, in the Eucharist, we are enabled to share by the power of the Spirit.

Prefaces
All six short prefaces are drawn from existing resources:

1 From *CW*, originally in the *ASB*.
2 From *CWPE*, originally in the *ASB*.
3 From *NPFW*, originally in the *ASB*.
4 Adapted in *PHG* from a prayer for use in Christmastide by Eric Milner-White, in his *After the Third Collect* (1952), based on words in Lancelot Andrewes' fourth sermon on the nativity.
5 In *CWPE*, from the *ASB*. For the Holy Family, and thus suitable for use on

the Sunday within the Octave of Christmas as observed by the Roman Catholic Calendar. Although the title is not used in the *CW* Calendar, the Gospel readings for the Principal Service on this day in years A and C are virtually the same as in the Roman Catholic Lectionary, and the post-communion prayer has this theme.

6 In *CWPE*, from the *ASB* and also in *ECY*, with a focus on the role of the Blessed Virgin Mary, alluding to the *Magnificat.*

Extended Preface

Included in the *CW* main volume in the seasonal material for Christmas Day until the Eve of the Epiphany. Its rich language evokes Philippians 2 ('humbled himself') and John 1 ('in this mystery of the Word made flesh'). The phrase 'in him we see our God made visible and so are caught up in the love of the God we cannot see' appeared in a short preface in *PHG*. 'This mystery' and 'the God we cannot see' in respect of the incarnation perhaps echo Ignatius of Antioch's *Letter to the Ephesians*, 19.

Blessings and Endings

1 An adaptation of a blessing from the *ASB*, given for the season in the *CW* main volume. The revised version places more emphasis on the consequences of the incarnation by adding 'make you partakers of the divine nature'.

2 In *CWPE*, from *PHG*, adapted from a prayer for use at the Dedication of the Crib (also in *PHG*) and originating in a form for the blessing of the crib published by the Church Literature Association which was later included in Silk, *PUAS*. In TS it is given as a blessing for general use in the Christmas season, whereas in *PHG* it was in the 'Service for Christmas Morning' only.

3 In *CWPE*, from the *ASB*, later in *ECY* among the resources for the Blessed Virgin Mary.

4 A solemn blessing in *CWPE*, from the *PHG* 'Eucharist of Christmas Night or Morning', correctly Trinitarian in structure. Its use on Christmas Day especially would serve to balance any *over*emphasis on the second person of the Trinity to which the season of Christmas may lead.

Despite the title of this section, the four options given are in fact all blessings, although of course their use need not be confined to the Eucharist.

Acclamations

1 Based on Isaiah 9.2, 6; Luke 2.14. Used as an introduction to a carol service in *PHG*, alternative or possibly in addition to a bidding prayer.

2 Based on Luke 1.68; Psalm 97.11; Luke 2.14. From the Canadian *BAS* and in *PHG* as a conclusion to a carol service.

3 Based on 1 John 1.1–3. In *PHG* (carol service conclusions), *CCP* (Morning Prayer in Christmastide) and the *CW* main volume.

4 Based on 1 John 3.1; Hebrews 1.5; John 1.12, from *PHG* (carol service conclusions).
5 From *CCP* ('After the Office'), and in *PHG* as a carol service conclusion and as an introduction to the blessing for a crib service or Christmas Eve vigil.
6 Based on John 1.14. From *DP*.

Short Passages of Scripture

These have been selected with flexible use in mind.

Eucharist of Christmas Night or Morning

In addition to resources for the season generally, a choice of material for a Eucharist for Christmas Day itself is given, based on that offered in *PHG*. Night *or* morning is suggested, but many if not most communities will celebrate the Eucharist at both midnight and in the morning, and so the opportunity could be taken to vary the material using resources from the preceding general section. This is entirely in keeping with the historical tradition of three masses with different propers.

The order begins with a rubric offering the possibility of beginning at the crib, and includes the option of dedicating it. The next rubric, 'a hymn or carol may be sung', does not necessarily indicate that either the congregation *or* the choir will so do: as an alternative to a Christmas hymn, a simple carol arrangement may be sung by all, and there are in any case strong grounds for encouraging corporate singing at the beginning of the Gathering, and on this occasion something well known.

The optional opening words from *In the Holy Nativity of Our Lord* by Richard Crashaw (?1613–49) may not be suitable as the very first words spoken when many people are present who are not regular worshippers (or even if they are), since they may at first wonder if they themselves are being welcomed as 'all wonders in one sight'! A liturgical greeting with some additional words of introduction leading into this quotation would be preferable, if it is to be used. The alternative responsive form, from Silk, *PUAS*, might be better from the point of view of establishing the relationship between president and assembly.

Unlike in *PHG*, a liturgical greeting is now given, one of the possibilities in the *CW* main volume, although presumably it does not preclude any of the others. The option of the Trinitarian invocation is not suggested: if used, this and the greeting formula could easily, and preferably, come *before* the Crashaw quotation or the responses.

The dedication of the crib is to be omitted here if it is to be dedicated on another occasion, in which case the liturgy moves to the Prayers of Penitence. The introductory words and the prayer are as in *PHG* and Silk, *PUAS*. Nothing is said in the rubric about the possibility of the image of the child being carried in the procession to the crib and placed in it, which is a feature of the Christmas liturgy in many churches of more catholic tradition; indeed in some it is placed on the altar.

PHG directed that the Prayers of Penitence 'are used at the Crib', since there the dedication of the crib was not optional at this point. In TS they 'may' be so used, to reflect its flexibility on the point. The words of invitation to confession are the same in TS as in *PHG*, and silence is also directed, but thereafter TS has the first *Kyrie* confession from the general seasonal resources. That set in *PHG* is, however, also in the general resources and this may well be a point at which a midnight and a morning Eucharist use different forms. Given that the *Kyrie* form includes the words 'full of grace and truth' it would be appropriate to use that form if John 1.1–14 is to be read as the Gospel. Apart from these provisions, a rubric allows another authorized form of confession to be used if desired. The absolution is from the *CW* main volume (authorized alternatives), and is very appropriate in its allusion to John 1.

After the prayers of penitence, if they are not already there the ministers move to the place where the Liturgy of the Word is to be celebrated, and the *Gloria in excelsis* may follow: on this of all days perhaps its omission should not be an option since it so directly reflects the song of the angels.

A collect for both night and daytime is given: commentary on these and all the *CW* collects may be found in Volume 1 of this *Companion*. The *CW* Additional Collect is also given, for either occasion; it is addressed to Christ, celebrates his birth at Bethlehem, drawing the worshipper to kneel in wonder, and asks for the acceptance of this praise.

A canticle, which may be replaced with a psalm, a hymn or a carol, should follow the first reading. It is from *DP* and was previously (with a longer response) in *CCP*. The scriptural basis is Isaiah 11.1–4a, 6, 9, and the response is used in *A New Zealand Prayer Book*. Two optional acclamations are given that may immediately precede the Gospel, from *PHG* and the *CW* main volume respectively, the second quoting John 1.14 which may inform when it is used.

A possible form of intercession is given for use either in the night or during the day (with the substitution of 'holy night' for 'on this holy day'), with the injunction that any local additions in the indicated places be brief. This form is an adaptation of one in *NPFW*, originally written by Michael Perham for *PHG*.

Introductions to the Peace are given for use at night and during the day, the first recalling the message of the angels to the shepherds (Luke 2.14) and the second the prophecy of the birth of the Messiah fulfilled on this day (Isaiah 9.6). The latter is also in the *CW* main volume, and was in *PHG*.

The suggested prayer at the preparation of the table is that included in the general resources section, as are the three prefaces, two short (nos. 3 and 4 above) and the extended preface.

A special invitation to communion is provided as a versicle and response, from *PHG,* where it appeared in conjunction with 'Draw near with faith . . .' rather than as an alternative to it, reflecting the *ASB* direction for the Eucharist on Sundays, which made the longer text mandatory even if other forms were also used, a rubric *CW* does not preserve.

The post-communion prayers are those of the *CW* main volume, for night and day use respectively. The first, however, is modified in TS by making the final sentence a congregational response. The two alternative or additional congregational prayers in the main text of Order One are also given here. In the second of these, the first half – 'Father of all . . .' to '. . . gate of glory' – might be said by the president alone, the rest by the congregation to avoid the difficulties of lengthy corporate recitation.

As noted in the Advent resources, the concept of an optional Dismissal Gospel is introduced in TS. For Christmas Day it is in the form of what was once the unvarying 'Last Gospel' of the Latin Mass, John 1.1–14, to be proclaimed either before or after the Blessing. Self-evidently, if this Gospel has been read earlier in the service it should not be repeated here.

The suggested Blessing is the solemn form from the general resources, although another may be substituted. The dismissal formula once again reflects the 'Word made flesh' imagery of John 1.

Carol Services in the Christmas Season

Bidding Prayers and Introductions

The first two of the three texts are reproduced almost exactly from *PHG*. The first is that used at King's College, Cambridge on Christmas Eve, written by Eric Milner-White for the first service of Nine Lessons and Carols in 1918, broadcast live since the 1920s on BBC Radio. On the one hand, it is of its time in terms of content and syntax, but on the other is still powerful and moving in its familiarity and resonances. The Lord's Prayer follows in traditional form.

The second form is modified. The rather stiff opening words of the *PHG* version are replaced with more natural and therefore more accessible and genuine-sounding words of welcome. Later, the abrupt 'But first we pray' is changed to the more theologically communicative 'As we gather together in the name of Christ, we pray for the world he came to save'. This bidding also concludes with the Lord's Prayer in either contemporary or 'modified traditional' form.

The third form is new to TS, is much shorter and succinct, and implicitly intended for use on Christmas Eve, since it is followed by the Collect of that day. The text of the bidding encapsulates and associates in very few words the liturgical journey of the Church through Advent to Christmas, the scriptural journey of Mary and Joseph, and the spiritual journey from revelation to faith.

Patterns of Readings

Three sequences are given, all from the series of patterns of readings in *PHG* for a 'Service of Light' after All Saints and in Advent and Christmastide, but without the concluding collects there suggested. Five of the *PHG* patterns were deemed suitable for Christmas carol services. TS reduces these to three: Good News for the Poor (Lukan), the Gospel of Luke, and the Christmas Eve

Pattern from King's College, Cambridge. The reduction in options has the effect of omitting Matthew and John as dominant scriptural bases for a carol service, which will be a disappointment to some. However, the patterns are only suggested as a guide, and local modification or wholesale substitution is entirely possible, as indeed, presumably, is the addition of non-scriptural but appropriate readings, for example of a patristic or a poetic variety, although the place of Scripture must not thereby be obscured or minimized.

Christingle Services and Crib Services

Given the fact that these tend to be all-age services, the material in TS is gathered in one section, preceded by separate outlines which encourage those preparing these services to adopt a clear liturgical structure comprising theologically appropriate yet accessible texts and vivid visual symbols. The resource material is set out by genre, for selection as appropriate. Much of it is to be found also in *PHG* or *NPFW*. In *PHG* there is much more detail about the origin and meaning of the Christingle Service, and greater practical direction, to which many may find it useful to refer.

The Christingle Service has its origin in the Moravian Church but has been widely adopted by the Church of England, especially in connection with the Children's Society, to which collections at these services are often donated. It is entirely right therefore that they should be particularly attractive to children and young people, and that the visual, musical and verbal expression of the Christmas message be in accord with that aim. The visual element is largely supplied by the distribution (and sometimes making) of the 'Christingle' ('Christ light'), an orange decorated with cloves and with a candle fixed on top, symbolic of Christ the Light of the World.

The crib appears only in the Gospel of Luke, as the feeding-trough or manger (*phatne*) in which the infant Jesus is laid, but its veneration is not recorded before the time of Jerome in the year 385. It is not mentioned in the fourth-century diary of Egeria, which otherwise contains much detail about ceremonies and devotions in Bethlehem. The beginnings of devotion surrounding the crib really lie in nativity plays of the twelfth and thirteenth centuries, and in the writings of Francis of Assisi, which assured the crib a firm and enduringly popular place in the devotional lives of Christians at Christmas.

Greeting/Introduction/Acclamation

1 A much-abbreviated and simplified form of a text found as a 'Preparation' for use at a Christingle Service in *PHG*, beginning with 1 Peter 2.9 as a versicle and response. The TS revision is less specific and could also be used at a Crib Service.

2 A simple responsory including the lighting of a candle and incorporating the titles of Jesus as way, truth and life, from *NPFW*, in which the lighting of the candle is optional.

3 A brief Johannine form using John 1.14 as a versicle and response, from *PHG* and *NPFW.*

4 A slightly modified version from *NPFW* of an Introduction for a Service for Christmas Morning in *PHG*, which is a composite of responses and narrative scripture. The opening pair of versicles and responses comprise Luke 2.10b–11a and Isaiah 9.6a. The continuous text of Luke 2.15–16 follows, and the conclusion is a non-scriptural but suitable acclamation and response with Alleluias.

5 An extended and modified form of an Introduction with a 'resurrection' theme in *NPFW.* The TS version begins with a versicle and response (Isaiah 40.5a), and a candle is lit. A responsory follows (John 1.5; Luke 2.8b, 9b; Psalm 139.12; Luke 24.29).

6 A prayer to the infant Jesus, modified from one in *PHG* from Silk, *PUAS,* which itself was an altered version of a prayer by Frank Colquhoun in his *Parish Prayers* (1967).

Invitation to Confession

The first text is by Kenneth Stevenson, in *PHG* and *PFW* as an introduction to a responsive form of confession (given in the general seasonal material in TS), and standing alone in *NPFW.* It is based on the light and darkness contrast also typical of the Advent season, and is therefore very suitable for a Christingle Service. The second form is from *PHG* and in *NPFW,* associating the worshippers with the kneeling shepherds.

Prayers of Penitence

A *Kyrie* form linked to Invitation 2 above in *PHG,* and a prayer of confession for use with small children, simple and direct, presumably to be said by the president or another minister on their behalf.

Absolutions

The first is Johannine in flavour and written by Kenneth Stevenson as part of a complete penitential rite in *PHG,* for a Crib Service or Christmas Eve vigil. One of the authorized forms of absolution in the *CW* main volume, it is also in *NPFW,* where it is associated with 'Relationships and healing' as well as 'Incarnation'. The second text is from the *CW* main volume, and in *NPFW,* where it is given the theme 'Living in the world'.

Thanksgivings

A rubric encouraging the use of a 'prominently placed Christingle', a candle or the Advent wreath (implicitly according to when in the Advent and Christmas seasons the service takes place) precedes the alternatives offered. All are responsive in form.

1 From *PHG*, using the 'Son' titles of Jesus (Mary, David, Man) to invite the response 'Glory to God in the highest'. The concluding prayer is for a response of love, service and discipleship to the light of Christ symbolized by the Christingles. Also in *NPFW* as an acclamation for 'Incarnation'. The source of this text is the Lutheran Church in the USA, from the *Manual on the Liturgy: Lutheran Book of Worship*.

2 From *PHG*, also in *NPFW* for 'Incarnation', and slightly adapted from *PFW*. Based on John 1.

3 Adapted from *NPFW*, where it includes a final section enabling its use as an extended preface. A text originally used at Holy Trinity, Wealdstone, it has resonances of Matthew 1.21, 23 and Philippians 2.9–11. *NPFW* encourages the insertion, before the closing section of the unaltered version, of the appropriate text from the three final alternatives given (a separate text in *NPFW*). TS does not repeat this note since it is not here intended as an extended preface: the additional versicle and response are added according to the time of celebration.

4 From *NPFW*, for 'Incarnation'.

Before a Bible Reading

The versicle and response (Psalm 119.105) given here for use *before* a reading are given in *PHG* for either the beginning *or* end of *each* reading at a Christingle Service. This form is among several possible alternatives to 'This is the Word of the Lord/Thanks be to God' which may see wider use on a seasonal basis at the Eucharist. Examples of such texts were in *PFW* among the 'Short acclamations and responses', and are included as 'acclamations' in *NPFW*.

Intercession

It is envisaged that resources from elsewhere in the Christmas material will be used, but this need not and should not preclude local composition. A special prayer for the Children's Society by David Rhodes is provided here, particularly appropriate for a Christingle Service.

Affirmation of Faith

One of the briefer authorized texts from the *CW* main volume, with Ephesians 3 as its basis.

Blessings and Endings

The first is from the conclusions in *NPFW*, an altered version of a *PFW* prayer after communion or ending for a Service of the Word, originally in the Canadian *BAS* as the prayer after communion for the Eucharist of Christmas Day. The second text is altered from a conclusion in *NPFW*. The third is the Aaronic blessing (Numbers 6.24, 25), in *NPFW* and in *CWPE* as an additional blessing. The final text is from *NPFW* ('Father, Son and Spirit; Relationships and healing'). Other blessings and endings appropriate to the season may be preferred, as indicated by a rubric to this effect.

Additional Prayers for Use at Christmastide
A collection of material mainly from *PHG* which may be used on the occasions indicated.

Blessings of the Crib
The *PHG* form for 'The Dedication of the Crib' for use on 'other occasions' is given, which includes a short reading from the Book of Wisdom (18.14–15a). There follow the same two prayers of blessing as found in *PHG*: the first was in Silk, *PUAS*, from material originally produced by the Church Literature Association. The second is longer and is an adaptation of an original written in 1941 by Eric Milner-White for use at York Minster, later included in his *After the Third Collect*.

Prayers at the Crib
1 Adapted in *PHG* from a prayer for use in Christmastide by Eric Milner-White, in his *After the Third Collect*, based on words in Lancelot Andrewes' fourth sermon on the Nativity.
2 From a Milner-White original written for York Minster in 1941, later in *After the Third Collect*, adapted for *PHG*.
3 A prayer by Archbishop William Temple (1881–1944), also in *PHG*.
4 Extracted for *PHG* from a Meditation before the Crib in Silk, *PUAS*, and originating with the Church Literature Association.
5 As number 4.

Resource Material for the Beginning of a New Year
Although not a liturgical feast, the turn of the secular year has become an occasion for prayer and rededication in many traditions, not least the Methodist Church. TS provides a selection of resources, partly drawn from the section 'Prayers at the New Year' in *PHG*, the rubrics of which direct the reader to 'The Service of Light' in that publication for further guidance for a vigil service.

Invitation to Confession
A new composition based on Psalm 90.12.

Kyrie Confession
From the Epiphanytide material in *PHG*, originally from the Roman Missal.

Collects
1 *PHG*, adapted from Silk, *PUAS*. A translation of a prayer in the Mozarabic Sacramentary. The original begins 'Lord Christ, Alpha and Omega, the beginning and the end'.

2 *PHG,* from Silk, *PUAS,* where it appears under 'Advent Sunday'. A translation of words of Gregory of Nazianzus.
3 From *PHG.*

Gospel Acclamation
This reflects the self-description of Christ as the Alpha and Omega in Revelation 22.13.

Intercession
From *NPFW,* where it has the theme 'Living in the world'. It was also in *PFW,* 'origin uncertain', and *PHG.*

The Renewal of the Covenant
The material is drawn from *The Methodist Worship Book* (1999). It introduces the theme of the covenant made by God with Israel, renewed in Jesus Christ for all people. A responsive penitential rite follows, which concludes with the congregational recitation of Psalm 51.1–2, 11, 13, using a modified translation in the TS version. The absolution is an adaptation of the Methodist form. The words of renewal, said by all, are the climax of Wesley's original composition.

Introduction to the Peace
The text of Matthew 5.9, a form also among the Introductions to the Peace in the *CW* main volume.

Prayer at the Preparation of the Table
The third option in the *CW* main volume.

Preface
A new composition in which the phrase 'you have redeemed our time' recalls Ephesians 5.16, a text upon which Wesley preached in January 1782 (Sermon 93). The phrase recurs in verse 2 of the hymn 'Let bells peal forth the universal fame' by Peter Baelz, a hymn which could well form part of a service to mark the New Year.

Blessings and Endings
1 In *NPFW* with the themes 'General (time)' and 'Lament'. It appeared in at least one service for the turn of the millennium, 1999–2000 but its origin is uncertain.
2 The Aaronic blessing (Numbers 6.24, 25), in *NPFW* and in *CWPE* as an additional blessing.
3 In *NPFW* for 'Father, Son and Spirit; Relationships and Healing'.
4 In *NPFW* with the theme 'Living in the world', and a rubric encouraging all to face the open doors of the church building.

Acclamation

In *NPFW* with the themes 'Living in the world' and 'General (morning)'. A cento of Psalm 90.4, Revelation 22.13; 3.20, and a non-scriptural but scripturally resonant final couplet.

Short Passages of Scripture

A selection of single verses suggested on the same basis as earlier equivalent sections, and one longer passage (Luke 4.18–19).

Further Reading

J. A. T. Gunstone, *Christmas and Epiphany*, Faith Press, London, 1967.

Michael Perham and Kenneth Stevenson, 'Christmas' in their *Welcoming the Light of Christ: A Commentary on 'The Promise of His Glory'*, SPCK, London, 1991, pp. 54–69.

Susan K. Roll, *Towards the Origins of Christmas*, Liturgia Condenda 5, Kok Pharos, Kampen, The Netherlands, 1995.

C. EPIPHANY

Epiphany is of Eastern Christian origin, only later becoming part of the Western Calendar, celebrated on 6 January. An 'epiphany' is an appearance or manifestation, of God in a religious context, but also in ancient times the birth or visit of a monarch. Clement of Alexandria is the earliest witness to the feast in about 215, but the fourth century brings the full flowering of the scriptural associations and their liturgical celebration, having in view the baptism of Jesus, his nativity, the visit of the Magi and the wedding at Cana. The Church in Rome, however, came to place an almost exclusive emphasis on the visit of the Magi, consequently inherited by the Western Church in general. The significance of the date is uncertain: various arguments have been advanced, including the Christian opposition to a pagan festival at this time, a complex calendrical calculation arising from the date of the birth of Jesus, and even a Christian adaptation of the Jewish Feast of Tabernacles. Of these, the calendrical solution suggested by Thomas Talley seems the most likely.

The increasing emphasis on Christmas has led to a decline in the perceived importance of the Epiphany, an imbalance that the Church of England provisions beginning with *PHG* and now further enriched in TS have sought to correct. The intention has been not to imply a relative devaluing of Christmas but rather to integrate the Christmas and Epiphany seasons and make the important scriptural connections more explicit, thus recovering some of the richness of the early centuries in respect of this time of the liturgical year. As the Introduction to the season makes clear, this has been done to the extent of regarding the Feast of the Presentation of Christ (Candlemas) on 2 February as the end of the season which begins at Christmas. This is reflected in lectionary provision and in suggested liturgical colours. TS supplies an extensive directory of material which also includes forms for use in connection with the Week of Prayer for Christian Unity, and the theme of Mission, as well as worked-out examples of Eucharists for the Epiphany, the Baptism of Christ and the Presentation.

Seasonal Material

Invitations to Confession
1 For use from the Epiphany to the eve of the Presentation; in the *CW* main volume, and based on Titus 2.11–14.
2 For the Baptism of Christ; by Michael Perham, based on Titus 3.5, in *ECY*, among the resources for 'Baptism'.
3 For the Baptism of Christ; based on Romans 12.1.

Kyrie Confessions
For use from the Epiphany to the eve of the Presentation.

1 From Portsmouth Cathedral and based on Psalm 67.1, 2 and 98.3; also in *NPFW* ('Living in the world').
2 From English translations of the Roman Missal, and in *PHG* for Epiphanytide.
3 From English translations of the Roman Missal, in *PHG* for Epiphanytide, in the *CW* main volume ('Spirit'), and in *NPFW* ('Holy Spirit; Relationships and healing').
4 Based on Luke 2.

Gospel Acclamations
1 The *CW* main volume provision for Epiphany, based on 1 Timothy 3.16.
2 For the Epiphany; the response of the Magi in Matthew 2.2.
3 For the Baptism; the voice from heaven in Matthew 3.17.
4 For the Presentation; the *CW* main volume provision, based on the Song of Simeon, Luke 2.32.
5 For the Presentation; from the Song of Simeon, Luke 2.30, 32.

Intercessions
1 For Epiphany; adapted here from a form in *NPFW* ('Incarnation'), but clearly originating in a set of intercessions by Michael Perham for the Feast of the Epiphany in *PHG*.
2 For Epiphany; adapted here from *NPFW* ('Church and mission'), originally a Liturgical Commission composition in *PHG*, where it is wrongly attributed to the Church Pastoral Aid Society's *Church Family Worship* (1986).
3 For Epiphany; based on Isaiah 61.1–3, a Liturgical Commission composition, in *PHG* with the title 'For the Ministry and Mission of the Church' and adapted in *NPFW* ('Living in the world; Christ's coming'), the version used here.

4 For the Baptism. This is unattributed and so is presumably a new composition for TS, although the final collect is a modified version of that for Epiphany 2.
5 For the Presentation; a modified form of the intercession for the Eucharist of Candlemas in *PHG*, where it is unattributed.

Introductions to the Peace
1 For Epiphany to eve of Presentation; the *CW* provision based on Isaiah 9.6, 7.
2 For Epiphany to eve of Presentation; from *PHG*, based on 2 Corinthians 5.17.
3 For the Baptism; one of the *CW* main volume's options for general use.
4 For the Baptism, for which it is appropriate, although given in the *CW* main volume for Ascension to Pentecost; based on 2 Corinthians 1.22.
5 For the Presentation; the provision for this day given in the *CW* main volume, and based on Luke 1.78, 79 (the Song of Zechariah or *Benedictus*).
6 For the Presentation; based on 1 Peter 2.9.

Prayers at the Preparation of the Table
For Epiphany to the eve of the Presentation from the Canadian *BAS*, for Epiphany to the eve of the Presentation (unattributed), for the Baptism from *A New Zealand Prayer Book*, and for the Presentation (unattributed). It is interesting to note that these prayers have no reticence in the matter of the language of offering: 'accept the offering of your Church' appears in two of them.

Short Prefaces for Epiphany
1 The *CW* main volume short preface, originally in the *ASB* as a preface for 'Incarnation', there being no explicitly separate provision for Christmas and Epiphany.
2 Unattributed, but containing familiar Epiphanytide turns of phrase such as 'by the leading of a star' which recalls the *BCP* Collect of the Epiphany.
3 From the Roman Missal and in *NPFW*.
4 From *PHG*, adapted there from the Canadian *BAS*; Johannine in feel, as in 'the mystery of the Word made flesh'. Without this phrase it bears distinct similarities to another preface for 'Incarnation (Epiphany)' in *NPFW* originating with the Liturgical Commission and previously included in *PFW*.
5 From *PHG*, adapted there from the Canadian *BAS*.

Short Prefaces for the Baptism of Christ
1 Unattributed, and so presumably a fresh composition.
2 Adapted in *PHG* from the Canadian *BAS*, and explicitly making the connection between Baptism and Eucharist.

Short Prefaces for the Presentation

1 The *CW* main volume preface, itself an adaptation of one of the prefaces for the Eucharist of Candlemas in *PHG*. The phrase 'he brings judgement on the world' is replaced by 'he comes near to us in judgement' in the newer version, a needless softening, it may be thought.

2 A new composition, unattributed, although the phrase 'shares your eternal splendour' and other indications identify the Roman Missal Preface of the Presentation as the basis. The preface recalls the Song of Simeon in such phrases as 'the glory of Israel' and the aspiration that 'all peoples might find him the light of the world.'

3 The second *PHG* preface, which recalls the role of Mary at the Presentation and the prophecy of her witnessing the crucifixion.

Extended Prefaces

1 Epiphany to eve of Presentation; the *CW* main volume text, written by S. A. J. Mitchell, including references to most of the scriptural themes of the season.

2 Baptism of Christ; adapted from the *PHG* version which was intended for use as an inserted preface with the *ASB* eucharistic prayers, both based closely on the Roman Catholic preface for this day.

3 Presentation; the *CW* main volume text, containing once again the phrase 'comes near to us in judgement' (see short preface 1 above). The Collect is also in view in the phrase 'in substance of our flesh', as is the scriptural account of the event in the words 'destined for the falling and rising of many'. It effectively combines and enhances short prefaces 1 and 3 above.

Blessings

Epiphany to eve of Presentation:

1 A simple blessing, the *CW* main volume text; an expansion of the *ASB* preface for Epiphany, which original version was in *PHG*.

2 A simple blessing, in *CWPE* and *PHG*.

3 A solemn blessing, in *CWPE* and *PHG*, recalling the visit of the Magi, the wedding at Cana and the baptism of Jesus.

4 A solemn blessing, in *CWPE* and *PHG*, with light as the connecting theme.

A single simple blessing is then offered for the Baptism of Christ, from *CW Initiation Services* and by David Stancliffe; also in *NPFW*. Two simple blessings are given for the Presentation: the first originates with the Church Mission Society and is also found in rites of the Church in Wales. The second was a Christmas blessing in the *ASB*, was set in the Candlemas Eucharist in *PHG*, and is the *CW* main volume text for the day.

Short Passages of Scripture
A selection of single verses suggested on the same basis as earlier equivalent sections.

Seasonal Material Connected with the Theme of Unity
Since the Week of Prayer for Christian Unity falls within the Epiphany season, TS draws mainly on the *PHG* material to suggest suitable resources. The three Invitations to Confession are those in *PHG*, the last modified to improve the phrasing, omitting the clumsy 'we meet together with one accord from our various churches', and inserting the more directly penitential 'let us acknowledge our sin'. The suggested congregational confession is the starkly honest *PHG* text from Silk, *PUAS*. Two *Kyrie* confessions follow, the first of which is in *PHG* and also found elsewhere for general use in Roman Catholic and other sources. The second is based on Ephesians 4.4–6, and is also a familiar confession of this type, wholly appropriate here. Further 'Acts of Penitence' are provided, the first is a contemporary-language version of the noble prayer for unity found in the *BCP* Accession Service, added to that service at the accession of the House of Hanover in the person of George I. The second Act of Penitence is a prayer to be said over a vessel of water with which the people are then sprinkled, in *PHG* but adapted from David Silk's *In Penitence and Faith* (1988).

The Collects for Unity are both in *CWPE*, the first from the *ASB*, the second based on the introduction to the Peace in the Roman Missal. The three Gospel acclamations are based on Colossians 3.15, Ephesians 4.5 and John 17.21 respectively. The single set of intercessions is one of the forms in *PHG*, and was written for the Lima Liturgy of the World Council of Churches assembly in Vancouver in 1983, and published in *One Lord, One Faith, One Baptism* (British Council of Churches). It includes the option of free prayer by the congregation.

Of the four introductions to the Peace, the first is based on Philippians 2 and, like the second, is from *PHG*. The third is among the alternatives in the *CW* main volume, and the fourth based on that in the Roman Missal, itself echoing John 14.27. The Prayers at the Preparation of the Table are from very diverse sources:

1 Based on the *Didache*, chapter 9, and among the options in the *CW* main volume.
2 Adapted from the Roman Missal.
3 From *PHG*, again recalling the *Didache* and also Proverbs 9.2.
4 From the *Book of Common Order* of the Church of Scotland, where it forms part of the order for Remembrance Day.

Prefaces

The two short prefaces are from *CWPE* and adapted from the Roman Missal respectively. The extended preface originates with the Roman Catholic International Commission on English in the Liturgy, although not in any current Roman Catholic liturgy. It is here modified but still very rich in language and imagery.

Post Communions

The first is in *CWPE*, from *PHG*, the original prayer written by William Temple (1881–1944) here modified and drawing on the Johannine prayer of Jesus for unity of the disciples. The second is from *PHG*, adapted from the Roman Missal, Preface of the Holy Eucharist II.

Dismissal Rites

The single simple blessing appeared in *PHG* as a prayer for use 'at the end of any service' on the theme of unity. TS modifies the final clause to enable a blessing to be added. New to TS is the Alternative Dismissal, a scriptural acclamation (Ephesians 4), a Dismissal Gospel as provided for other occasions in TS, here either John 17.21b–23 or John 10.14–16, a simple blessing recalling the unity of the Trinity as the basis for Christian living and witness, and a special form of dismissal to prefix either 'Go in peace to love and serve the Lord' or 'Go in the peace of Christ' and their respective responses.

Acclamations and Short Passages of Scripture

The three forms are all based on Scripture: the first combines 1 John 3.11 with a versicle and response from the 'Unity in Christ' form of 'After the Office' in *CCP*; the second is based on Ephesians 4; the third is text of an introduction to the peace in the *CW* main volume. The short Scripture passages, mostly Pauline, gather up several appropriate texts not already used in another form.

Seasonal Material Connected with the Theme of Mission

PHG also provided such material in connection with the Epiphany theme of reaching out to the world and, as with the unity texts, TS selects from that earlier provision and makes some additions to reflect the *CW* approach to structure and options. The invitations to confession are precisely those in *PHG*, and may also be found in other contexts. All begin with Scripture: 1 John 2.1–2; Acts 20.24; Matthew 6.31, 33. The *Kyrie* confessions also repeat the *PHG* provision, the first drawing on Matthew 25 and the second an adaptation of a confession in *NPFW*. The collects are that for Trinity 13 in the *CW* main volume, associated with mission in *CWPE*, and an adaptation of the Collect of Pentecost in the *ASB*, a prayer not retained for that day in *CW*. Gospel acclamations, not in *PHG*, are scriptural: Matthew 28.19–20; Mark 16.15; John 3.16. The Intercession is an adapted form of that in *PHG*. TS adds a concluding collect referring to our union with the saints and asking that 'we may ever be supported by this fellowship of love and prayer', which would seem to confirm that it is now acceptable, at least in a 'commended' resource if not an 'authorized' one, to assume the reality of the prayers of the saints if not directly to ask for them.

The introductions to the Peace are all from *PHG*. The first prayer at the Preparation of the Table is based on Malachi 1.11, and perhaps recalling in the first line, 'Father, look upon the face of Jesus Christ', the hymn 'And now, O Father, mindful of the love' by William Bright (1824–1901), of which verse 2 begins 'Look, Father, look on his anointed face'. The second prayer is adapted from the Canadian *BAS* where, with the addition of the phrase 'like the apostles' in the second sentence, it is the Prayer over the Gifts for the Feast of St Bartholomew.

The first of two extended prefaces is adapted and condensed from a form in *NPFW* for 'Church and mission', which has in view Acts 17.25, 26 and Ephesians 1.9–13; 2.13–17. Particularly pleasing and theologically weighty is the phrase 'in him you show us the mystery of your purpose', which relates directly to the mystery theology in the letter to the Ephesians. The second preface is an extension of the single *PHG* provision, and also in *NPFW*.

The material in this section concludes with another Alternative Dismissal, with an acclamation based on Romans 5.6, 8 and in *NPFW*, adapted from the Canadian *BAS*. The Dismissal Gospel is either Matthew 28.19–20 or John 20.21–22. The blessing is solemn and Trinitarian in form, also in *NPFW*, and has distinct echoes of the Ascension ('The Father, whose glory fills the heavens'; 'The Son, who has ascended to the heights'). The dismissal prefix is based on Matthew 28.19. There are then the usual short passages of Scripture, all but two of them single verses.

Complete Orders of Service

As with Christmastide, and like *PHG*, complete orders of service using the seasonal material are provided. There are eucharistic texts for the Epiphany, the Baptism and the Presentation, and, as in *PHG*, an additional non-eucharistic 'Service for the Festival of the Baptism of Christ'. As with Christmas, these orders should be taken as examples rather than as prescriptive. Given the amount and variety of resources provided by TS, their exploration and pastoral use is to be encouraged, but with care not to embrace variety at the expense of liturgical stability, particularly where a liturgy is being introduced for the first time.

The Epiphany Eucharist

The most distinctive feature of this liturgy, and thus requiring comment, is the possibility of including the presentation of the traditional gifts of gold, frankincense and myrrh at the crib. The forms of prayer used for each are of the 'Blessed are you' variety with the response 'Blessed be God for ever', as in *PHG* and as originally used at Portsmouth Cathedral. It is suggested that this occur after the Gospel but before the sermon. This has the advantage of allowing the preacher to explore the symbolic significance of what has just taken place, although this must not detract from the centrality of the Gospel reading and its implications. If the gifts are presented, however, the later use of the second prayer at the Preparation of the Table which says that the people's gifts are 'not gold, frankincense or myrrh, but hearts and voices raised in praise', although of course true on one level, might nevertheless seem strange put in those terms. The matter might well be addressed by the preacher so that the contradiction is seen in its proper and creative light.

The Eucharist of the Baptism of Christ

The distinctive feature of this liturgy is the Thanksgiving for Holy Baptism, after the sermon. This comprises elements drawn from *PHG* (which provides the basis for the modified form), the *CW* main volume and *CW Initiation Services*. The words which accompany the pouring of water into the font are from *CCP* (first form, also *PHG*) and *PHG* (also part of the Thanksgiving for Holy Baptism in the *CW* main volume). The prayer over the water is from *CW Initiation Services*. There is a hint of Genesis 1 in the phrase 'May your holy and life-giving Spirit move upon these waters', and indeed the overall tenor of the prayer is 'new creation'. The suggested chant which follows begins with the words of the *Vidi aquam* ('I saw water': Ezekiel 47.1), a chant used in the Roman Rite from Easter until Pentecost instead of the *Asperges* at the beginning of Mass. In the present version, a responsory is based on Ezekiel 47.1, 9, 12 and Revelation 22.1–3. It appears in *NPFW* as a thanksgiving with the theme 'Relationships and healing'. The act of penitence and dedication is optional, and is the *PHG* form, now with only one possible collect. The sprinkling (optional: individuals signing themselves with the cross is an alternative) is accompanied by the *PHG* words (Revelation 22.17), with an added absolution in 'us' or 'you' form. This is followed by the Peace. Since the Thanksgiving for Baptism incorporates the penitential rite, the latter is not, of course, part of the Gathering. The prayer at the Preparation of the Table is worthy of note since it implies a very definite catholic eucharistic theology in asking 'send your *transforming* spirit on us and on these gifts' (present writer's emphasis). There is an extended dismissal rite incorporating a Dismissal Gospel (John 1.32–34).

A Service for the Festival of the Baptism of Christ

This is to all intents and purposes a revised version of the service in *PHG*, which, as the rubric in both states, 'with suitable hymns and carols . . . forms an Epiphany Procession or Epiphany Carol Service, at the climax of which is the Renewal of the Covenant or of baptismal vows'. As such it mirrors the processions and carol services of Advent and Christmas, and therefore can serve to underscore the encouraged sense of a single season ending at the Presentation. Consequently the liturgical material includes provision for the presentation of the traditional Epiphany gifts and for baptismal recommitment. As in *PHG*, it may be combined with the Eucharist, but this is perhaps not necessary in view of the other provisions, and should probably be avoided in order to preserve a service of appropriate length. The sources are diverse and include Scripture, *CCP*, Portsmouth Cathedral, the *ASB*, the Byzantine Rite (part of the prayer over the water), the *Methodist Worship Book* (the renewal of the covenant) and seasonal material already discussed here.

The Eucharist on the Feast of the Presentation of Christ in the Temple

The distinctive feature of this liturgy, as the rubric states, is the procession with lighted candles, which may occur at the end of the service (in the default order) at the beginning or before the Gospel (as alternatives). Historically as a liturgical observance deriving from the Gospel account of the Presentation, this feast has had various emphases in East and West. In the East, where it is of fourth-century origin, it is known as the 'meeting' (*hypapante*): the five persons in the story symbolize a new community in Christ. Western observance has been ambiguous in that it has variously been principally either a Marian feast or a feast of the Lord, but is now very clearly the latter. In England it came to be popularly called 'Candlemas', and still is, on account of the procession.

Traditionally, and in the modern Roman Rite, the procession is at the beginning, and can form in this way an extended Gathering rite if the people assemble in a separate place such as a church hall and process to the church (as 'temple') from there, as they may well do on Palm Sunday in commemoration of that solemn entry on the part of Jesus. There is merit in an explicit association (in a rubric and/or by the preacher) of these two processions, since Candlemas is the 'hinge' which looks back with joy to the birth and forward (prophetically in the Gospel for the day) to the Passion. The option to place the procession before the Gospel, while not inconceivable and with some symbolic merit, has the danger of overshadowing the proclamation of the Gospel itself.

PHG is again the immediate principal source, with *CW* main volume additions and adaptations, most of which have already received comment above as 'seasonal material', to which the reader is referred. The procession includes the singing (preferably) of the *Nunc dimittis*. Either the contemporary English Language Liturgical Commission (ELLC) version or the *BCP* 1662 text may be used. The final responsory is by Michael Perham, and makes effective use of the double-edged nature of the celebration in looking back and forward, as mentioned above, in particular 'Here we turn from Christ's birth to his Passion'. While intended to conclude the procession when placed at the end of the service, it could perhaps be used as part of an extended dismissal rite. With the regard to the latter, there is no Dismissal Gospel provided in the case of the procession having occurred at the beginning of the service, which might be seen as inconsistent with the pattern established for other days in the season.

Further Reading

J. A. T. Gunstone, *Christmas and Epiphany*, Faith Press, London, 1967.

Michael Perham and Kenneth Stevenson, 'Epiphany' and 'Candlemas' in *Welcoming the Light of Christ: A Commentary on 'The Promise of His Glory'*, SPCK, London, 1991, pp. 70–85, 86–101.

Kenneth Stevenson, 'The Origins and Development of Candlemas: A Struggle for Identity and Coherence' in *Time and Community*, ed. J. Neil Alexander, Pastoral Press, Washington, DC, 1990, pp. 43–80.

Thomas J. Talley, *The Origins of the Liturgical Year*, 2nd edition, The Liturgical Press, Collegeville, MN, 1991, pp. 103–47.

Gabriele Winkler, 'The Appearance of the Light at the Baptism of Jesus and the Origins of the Feast of the Epiphany: An Investigation of Greek, Syriac, Armenian and Latin Sources' in *Between Memory and Hope: Readings in the Liturgical Year*, ed. Maxwell E. Johnson, The Liturgical Press, Collegeville, MN, 2000, pp. 291–347.

D. LENT

It is difficult to be certain of the process whereby Lent emerged as a distinct season. In the past scholars have argued that it is an expansion backwards of an originally much shorter period of fasting before Easter, to mirror liturgically the temptation of Jesus in the wilderness in length and ascetical practice. Preparation for Easter baptism and public penance became part of this scheme. More recently, however, it has been suggested that the expansion occurred the other way, and that we should see a post-Epiphany, pre-baptismal period of fasting in the church at Alexandria as the true beginnings of Lent. These two theories are not necessarily mutually exclusive – that the result of the development was a period leading up to Easter in which penitents were reconciled and catechumens prepared for their baptism is not in doubt, although these practices fell into relative disuse until recent revival in Western Churches. The precise length has varied depending on how its significance has been viewed and how the days have been calculated. For example, Ash Wednesday as the beginning of Lent owes its origin to a medieval concern in the West for Lent to last exactly forty days when Sundays are excluded, which intention meant the addition of the four days before the first Sunday. The introduction to the season in TS enlarges on some of these themes and places them in their theological and devotional context.

Ash Wednesday

The fortieth day before Easter, if Sundays are excluded, Ash Wednesday has become the distinctive Western beginning of the season, although the Roman Catholic Church regards the first Sunday as the true beginning, with the days immediately after Ash Wednesday as a 'pre-Lent' period. The Church of England does not make this distinction. The distinctive feature of the Liturgy of the day is the (optional) marking of a cross of ash on the foreheads of each person as a reminder of mortality and a sign of repentance, following the biblical tradition of ashes covering the head in mourning. The ash is traditionally obtained by burning the blessed palm leaves of the previous year's Palm Sunday liturgy.

TS gives a full order of service, first setting out the structure. It follows the basic pattern established in *LHWE*, with further enrichment and conformity to *CW* norms. The Liturgy of Penitence, which includes the imposition of the ashes, is placed after the Liturgy of the Word.

The Gathering

The president's introduction is a condensed and improved version of the rather stilted *LHWE* text, which at certain points sounded rather like a lecture on liturgical history. The tone is now entirely devotional and exhortatory. It would presumably not be inappropriate for the president to introduce the liturgy in his or her own words if desired. The *Trisagion* (in English) is inserted at this point, although another chant or song of a penitential nature may be used. This need not automatically be assumed to be the *Kyrie eleison*. The Collect of Ash Wednesday may be replaced by the *CW* additional Collect of the day, although this would be at the cost of the fine language and imagery of the longer prayer. There is nevertheless a challenging directness about the shorter prayer ('our lives are laid open before you').

The Liturgy of the Word

The acclamation is from the *CW* main volume, and of course does not use the word 'Alleluia', which is traditionally not used anywhere in the liturgy (including hymns) from Ash Wednesday until it 'returns' at the Easter Vigil in celebration of the resurrection.

The Liturgy of Penitence

Two forms of self-examination and confession are given, but may be replaced by 'another suitable form', perhaps the shorter forms in the Roman Missal or of the *Methodist Worship Book*, the latter itself largely derived from Anglican sources. Form A combines a short litany of penitence with the first sentence of one of the *CW* authorized confessions. It continues with a litany from the 1979 *BCP* of ECUSA, but originating in an Ash Wednesday liturgy used at Epworth Chapel on the Green, Boise, Idaho, and also appearing in the Canadian *BAS*. Form A concludes with the rest of the corporate confession of which the first sentence is used earlier. Form B repeats the *LHWE* provision, and with slight alteration begins with parts I, II, III and VII of the *CW* Litany, which is based on that of the *ASB*. The versicle and response and the corporate prayer are those of *LHWE*: the confession is the *ASB* alternative confession C, now one of the *CW* authorized confessions, originally written by Professor David Frost and with echoes of Julian of Norwich.

The Imposition of Ashes is optional and if used follows Form A or Form B, the service otherwise continuing with an authorized absolution and the Peace.

The opening invitation is the *LHWE* form sensibly abbreviated. The prayer over the ashes is the same as in *LHWE*, and is from the 1979 *BCP* of ECUSA. The president is to receive the ashes first, from another minister, an appropriate visible example to be followed, like the president's receiving communion first at the Eucharist. The words of imposition are slightly modified from those in *LHWE*. The first sentence is used in the 1979 *BCP* of ECUSA, and similar forms are to be found in the Roman Missal. It is preferable that the whole undivided formula be used for each person. Alternatively, the ashes may be imposed in silence. The first concluding prayer is the first *LHWE* provision, and is the *CW* Collect of the First Sunday after Trinity, based on the 1662 *BCP* Collect, and ultimately the Gelasian Sacramentary. The alternative prayer is a *CW* authorized absolution, which might well be used to conclude the self-examination and confession if there is to be no imposition of ashes.

The Liturgy of the Sacrament
Most of the material in this section is drawn from the directory of seasonal material which follows in TS, and includes that in the *CW* main volume for use from Ash Wednesday until the Saturday after the Fourth Sunday of Lent and some items from *CWPE*. Unique to Ash Wednesday, however, are the first prayer at the Preparation of the Table, adapted from the Canadian *BAS*, and the second, unattributed and so presumably having originated in the Liturgical Commission. Both reflect the particular penitential character of the day. There is also an optional Dismissal Gospel: the parable of the lost sheep (Luke 15.4–7).

Seasonal Material

Invitations to Confession
The first form is from the *CW* main volume and is based on Psalm 51. The second is based on Daniel 9.9 and from David Silk's *In Penitence and Faith*. The third focuses on the temptation of Jesus in Luke 4.

Kyrie Confessions
The first is from Portsmouth Cathedral, based on Psalm 51 and in *CW* main volume for general use. The second is also based on Psalm 51 and in *NPFW* (B63). The third form is *NPFW* (B60).

Gospel Acclamations
Four alternatives, based on Psalm 95.7–8 (and in *CW* main volume for the season), James 1.2, John 8.12 and Psalm 119.105 respectively. All use the unvarying response 'Praise to you, O Christ, king of eternal glory', but there are other possibilities such as 'Praise and honour to Christ Jesus' (in Jonathan Priestland Young, *Enriching the Liturgy*, 1998, where the acclamations are not directly addressed to Christ), and 'Glory and praise to you O Christ' (Roman Missal).

Intercessions

Both forms are from *ECY*. The first uses a litany from the Canadian *BAS* and a collect from Silk, *PUAS*. The second was written by Trevor Lloyd, and includes points where local, specific petitions may be inserted.

Introduction to the Peace

The *CW* main volume Lent provision (Romans 5.1).

Prayers at the Preparation of the Table

Two forms, the first adapted from the Canadian *BAS*, and both taking the Word as their focus, and a third unattributed prayer with journey as its theme.

Prefaces

The first short preface repeats the *CW* main volume provision, an enriched version of the *ASB* (and before that Series 3) form, which adds a reference to the 'paschal mystery'. The other two forms were in *ECY*, from the Canadian *BAS* and adapted from the Roman Missal respectively. The extended preface is the provision in the *CW* main volume for the season, which successfully picks up many of the scriptural and devotional themes of the season, among them the 'desert of repentance', 'prayer and discipline', fasting, and service of neighbour, but with the joy of Easter always in view. The phrase 'you bring us back to your generous heart' is especially memorable.

Blessings and Endings

Forms from the *CW* main volume and the *ASB*, and a solemn blessing from *CWPE*.

Acclamations

A text based on 1 John 4.12, also *NPFW* (G50), and a form from *DP*.

Short Passages of Scripture

Fewer are provided than for the preceding seasons, perhaps because others are easily found. All are single verses.

The Way of the Cross

The inclusion of resources for devotions in connection with the Way of the Cross is a recognition that this has for long been part of the diet of many Anglican parishes (many of which have pictorial or numerical Stations of the Cross in their church building) and not an exclusively Roman Catholic practice. It is not necessary to give a history of the 'Stations of the Cross' here, since this is given in TS and easily found in other works of reference, nor to give exhaustive comment on each section of the devotions, since they are in effect their own commentary on the stages of the Passion and many forms exist, often locally composed. Comment may be made, however, on the fact that TS chooses to provide 'scriptural stations' and not material for the 'traditional stations', although it does list what the latter are. The justification for this decision is reasonable: 'those churches which have non-scriptural tableaux in place will probably have the resources already'. It is also acknowledged that the stations may not be liturgical as such, but may equally be used for personal devotion. It is suggested, however, that 'a few of the stations' might form part of a definitely liturgical celebration. This would require care and imagination, and a close reading of the notes TS provides: a Eucharist, for example, could be seriously overbalanced by an excessive concentration on 'stations' material.

E. PASSIONTIDE AND HOLY WEEK

The title of this section is misleading in that 'Passiontide', an English name, is by custom taken to begin on the Fifth Sunday of Lent, called 'Passion Sunday', whereas TS clearly views it as coterminous with Holy Week and by implication assumes the Lenten material to cover the period right up to the Saturday before Palm Sunday. Confusingly the Roman Catholic Church now calls Palm Sunday, 'Passion Sunday'. A note would have been helpful to clarify this matter: the Introduction to the Season focuses entirely on Holy Week.

In the East called the 'Great Week', Holy Week originates in the Syrian and Egyptian churches of the third century as an expansion of a shorter fast of one or two days before Easter. The emergence of Jerusalem in the fourth century as a popular destination for pilgrims encouraged the devising of liturgical celebrations to mirror the events of the last days of the Lord's life. Because of the pilgrim traffic, these became part of Western observances too, grew in length and variety, and became more 'representational' rather than 'rememorative', to use Kenneth Stevenson's distinction. This is a danger to be borne in mind today by the teacher and preacher, if the risk of mere 'acting out' is to be avoided in favour of true participation in the liturgical mystery of the Lord's Passion and death. Holy Week has been revived liturgically in full or in part by the Church of England, and what began as borrowing from the Roman Catholic Church has now become, via private publication and local initiative, indigenous 'commended' provision in the form of *LHWE* and now the abundant material of TS. The Introduction to the Season in TS explains scriptural, theological and devotional aspects of the week in relation to their liturgical expression, and adds an important note of caution in reminding us of the former anti-Jewish emphasis of some of the week's liturgies, such that 'those who lead the keeping of Holy Week today have a heavy responsibility, both to be faithful to the act of collective memory, and to be sensitive to the damage to which a careless use of inherited readings and prayers can lead'.

Seasonal Material
It is to be assumed that this material is intended for use on those days which do not have a unique liturgy, that is the Monday, Tuesday and Wednesday of Holy

Week. However, where 'Passiontide' is taken to begin on the Fifth Sunday of
Lent, such material may well be used during the week preceding Palm Sunday.

Invitations to Confession
Two forms, the first from the *CW* main volume for the season (Romans
5.7–8), the second based on 1 Peter 2.24. Both are from David Silk's *In Penitence and Faith*.

Kyrie Confessions
The first is based on Psalm 69.5, 17, 18, while the second is longer and focuses
on the desertion of the disciples and the kiss of Judas, adapted from *NPFW*
(original in the Church Pastoral Aid Society's *Church Family Worship*, 1986).

Gospel Acclamation
From the *CW* main volume, based on Philippians 2.8–9.

Intercession
The first form is adapted from *LHWE*, where in original form it is the Intercession for Palm Sunday, and is used in modified form for that day in TS (see
below). The second set is an adaptation from *ECY*. The third is adapted from
the same source, the original written by Trevor Lloyd, and is woven around the
participants in the Passion drama.

Introductions to the Peace
Both come from the *CW* main volume, the first, for the season, based on
Ephesians 2.13; the second, for general use, was formerly in the *ASB*.

Prayer at the Preparation of the Table
A single form, using the images of Jesus as bread of life and true vine.

Prefaces
The *CW* main volume provision, originally Series 3 and the *ASB*, and a preface
from *CWPE*, formerly in the *ASB*.

Extended Preface
The *CW* main volume provision, in short preface form in *ECY*, and ultimately
derived from the Roman Missal. It contains the striking phrases 'the whole
world is called to acknowledge his hidden majesty' and 'he is the victim who
dies no more, the Lamb once slain, who lives for ever'.

Blessings and Endings
The simple blessing is the *CW* main volume provision, from the *ASB*, where
it was an adapted version of that in Series 3. The solemn blessing alludes to
the Johannine 'God so loved the world' and the agony in the garden

('Christ, who accepted the cup of sacrifice'). Three short passages of Scripture are given.

The Liturgy of Palm Sunday

A complete liturgy, which incorporates the distinctive and customary elements of Palm Sunday, namely the procession of palms and the reading or singing of the Passion narrative, is provided. The procession has fourth-century Jerusalem as its origin, observed at Rome by the eleventh century and universally practised in Europe by the later Middle Ages as a blessing of branches of palm or of another plant (especially when palm was unavailable – willow and yew were and are alternatives), a reading of the Gospel relating the triumphant entry of Christ into the city, and a procession from the gathering-place to or around the outside of the church. The Roman observance of Palm Sunday originally had the singing of the Passion as the central feature – traditionally that according to Matthew. There is now relative flexibility, reflected in TS and the resources of other churches, as to the precise texts and choreography, although the principal elements remain constant.

The liturgy begins with the traditional text, 'Hosanna to the Son of David', preferably sung. There are several choral versions (for example by Orlando Gibbons), plainchant and more contemporary settings, some including the prophecy of Zechariah, given here as an extended alternative employing the 'Hosanna' as the antiphon. The *CW* authorized greeting is followed by the *LHWE* introduction verbatim, itself clearly based on the equivalent Roman Missal text, and the prayer of blessing from *LHWE*, slightly adapted. The procession begins after the palm Gospel. The liturgy continues with the rather old-fashioned sounding 'the Celebration of the Holy Communion'; it is not clear why the title is not 'the Liturgy of the Word', especially since the *CW* title 'the Liturgy of the Sacrament' is later used in its usual place. The Collect may be the original *CW* main volume version or the additional collect. The Passion reading may be heralded with an acclamation (the *CW* main volume provision). The different manner of announcing and concluding the Passion should be noted – there are no congregational responses.

The suggested prayers of intercession after the sermon are the *LHWE* form for the day, from the seasonal resources. The first seasonal introduction to the Peace is suggested, and the prayer at the Preparation of the Table (from the *CW* main volume alternatives). The extended preface and the first short preface of the season are given as alternatives. The words at the breaking of the bread are the alternative *CW* main volume form ('Every time we eat this bread . . .'), and so the similar acclamation should probably not have been used in the Eucharistic Prayer. The suggested words of distribution are the 'broken for you . . . shed for you' alternative from the *CW* main volume. The post-communion prayer is followed by an optional congregational text adapted from the Canadian *BAS*, where it is the post communion for Tuesday in Holy Week and said by the president alone. The blessing may be either the solemn seasonal form or another suitable text.

Resources for a Chrism Eucharist

Dioceses in the Church of England usually now have a Eucharist on Maundy Thursday (during the day) or another day of Holy Week at which oils are blessed and ministerial vows renewed or reaffirmed. TS gives a good historical note on both the use of oils and the emergence of the renewal of vows as introduced by Pope Paul VI, which does not need paraphrasing here. The form of the liturgy used on these occasions usually reflects the wishes and choices of the diocesan bishop and, often, the norms of the cathedral in which it takes place. This means that the resources given in TS can only be examples of what may be done locally. With regard the renewing of vows, TS makes provision for different combinations of ordained and authorized ministers: for example, it may be the case that only bishops, priests and deacons reaffirm their ordination vows, and that lay ministries are recognized and celebrated in some other way or on another occasion, such as the annual service at which new readers are licensed.

TS effectively gives a complete liturgy, with alternatives where local circumstances may require them. Most of the eucharistic material is from existing *CW* sources or their predecessors, including the *ASB* in the case of the collect. The prayer over the oil for the sick and dying is condensed from the longer form found in *CW Pastoral Services* ('A Celebration of Wholeness and Healing'). There are two special prefaces (short and extended) for use with an authorized *CW* Eucharistic Prayer. The short preface is from *CWPE*. Both refer to the anointing of Jesus by the Spirit as servant of all and the extended version emphasizes the royal priesthood of the whole people of God.

The Reception of Holy Oils during the Liturgy of Maundy Thursday

This is an increasingly practised element of the evening liturgy of Maundy Thursday, and the solemn arrival of the oils enables the parish community to share in what was done at the cathedral in the morning and associate itself with the ministry of the bishop and with the pastoral rites in which the oils will be used throughout the year. The accompanying prayers given in TS underline these associations.

The Liturgy of Maundy Thursday

Also called Holy Thursday, the liturgical celebrations of the day have their origin in fourth-century Jerusalem and the need for the reconciliation of penitents before Easter. The scriptural basis for the evening Eucharist is the Last Supper in the Upper Room. A single evening mass became the norm in the Middle Ages, and originally this included the blessing of the oils if the bishop presided. The foot washing on this day dates from about the seventh century, and was done by the senior figure present (e.g. bishop or abbot) to give visual expression to the Gospel account of the 'new commandment' or *mandatum* (John 13.34), hence the English name 'Maundy'. The evening liturgy came to be seen as the end of Lent and the beginning of the Easter Triduum. Since the Eucharist would not be celebrated on Good Friday, the Maundy liturgy developed to facilitate the removal and reservation of consecrated elements for use on the following day. This became a solemn procession of the sacrament to an 'altar of repose', decorated with candles and flowers, although the custom of burying or entombing the sacrament ceased with the end of the Middle Ages in England. The stripping (and formerly washing) of the altars completed the Western pattern at its full flowering. The modern Roman Rite retains the foot-washing, the procession to the altar of repose and the stripping, and many Anglican churches have revived some or all of the traditional ceremonial, for which TS gives resources or implied sanction for those who wish to observe them.

Unfortunately, and inconsistently, TS gives no specific introduction to the liturgy, nor are there any notes. The established pattern is followed, however, in that a complete order of service is given from which optional ceremonies may be included or omitted according to local custom. The *CW* main volume texts both seasonal and proper to the day are in the main suggested until after the Liturgy of the Word, supplemented by material from *NPFW*.

The washing of feet, if done, occurs after the sermon. The traditional accompanying chant, *Ubi caritas*, is supplied in the version by James Quinn SJ and found as *New English Hymnal* no. 512. This and the concluding prayer are the only texts given, since the impact of this part of the liturgy is chiefly visual. The intercessions which follow are those of *LHWE* adapted and extended. The *CW* main volume introduction to the Peace for the day is followed at the Preparation of the Table by the *LHWE* texts for use at this point. The *CW* main volume extended and short prefaces are reprinted, the short one recalling the *BCP* phrase 'these holy mysteries' in respect of the Eucharist. This preface is a modification of one for 'Eucharist' in *ECY*, itself adapted from the *ASB* Rite B. The extended preface underlines the Johannine character of the whole liturgy in also making reference to the washing of the disciples' feet and the new commandment. Texts up to and including the post communion are *CW* main volume resources, and except for the final prayer repeat the options suggested for Palm Sunday. For the stripping of the sanctuary a text from the Lamentations of Jeremiah (1.1–2a, 4, 5b, 12a, 13, 16; 2.15; 3.19, 22–31) interspersed with a response is suggested. This is a contemporary-language version of part of the medieval office of *Tenebrae*, formerly celebrated on Maundy Thursday and still used in some places.

The TS rubric concerning the Watch is presumably deliberately vague in order to cater for the different theological approaches to this part of the liturgy. Therefore there 'may be a procession', although the sacrament is not mentioned. The implication is probably the same as the directly stated assumption with regard to the traditional stations of the cross: those who perform the full procession to the altar of repose will already have the appropriate resources. The service may in fact end at this point with no Watch of any kind, in which case the *LHWE* ending can be read, a compressed text incorporating parts of Matthew 26.30, 39, 40, 45, 46.

The sequence of suggested readings from the Johannine Passion narrative interspersed with material from Psalms 113–118 is from *LHWE*, together with the option to conclude with Psalm 54 and the Gospel of the Watch (the synoptic texts given as years A to C variants).

The Liturgy of Good Friday

Historically speaking, the earliest parts of the Liturgy of Good Friday when celebrated in full are the solemn chanting of the Passion according to John and the veneration of the cross, originally a relic of the cross. Both occurred in Jerusalem in the fourth century. The liturgy has undergone expansion and enrichment, but these elements remain at its heart. The papal liturgy introduced solemn prayers, eventually nine in number. In Roman parishes, in addition to the Passion reading and the veneration, communion was received from the sacrament reserved the previous evening. Along with these practical elements, the mood became increasingly sombre in the Middle Ages, and as the TS introduction to the Passiontide resources reminds us, anti-Semitic overtones entered the texts. For these and other reasons, the cross and its veneration became the focus of the rite, accompanied by the singing of the Reproaches (*Improperia*), openly blaming the Jews for the crucifixion. Twentieth-century reforms removed most of the anti-Semitic material, although some would argue that the still-common singing of the Reproaches, even with modified text, continues to imply the opprobrium of former times. All this means the greatest of care must be exercised when planning and celebrating this liturgy, as TS makes clear.

The emphasis must be on simplicity if the focus on the Passion narrative and the cross rather than elaborate ceremonial is to be clear. The first spoken words are those of the Collect, immediately followed by the Old and New Testament readings. The Passion should be that according to John (18.1—19.42, or a sensible abbreviation if felt absolutely necessary; the power lies in the unfolding drama). Any sermon (the 'Preaching of the Passion' may have occurred before the liturgy) is followed by the Proclamation of the Cross, its entry acclaimed using one of two texts, both versions of the traditional form. 'Appropriate devotions' can presumably be taken to include the actual physical reverencing of the cross by an embrace or a kiss if that is the custom. It is perfectly possible to position the cross in such a way as to allow a variety of responses according to the devotional wishes of individuals, for example at the entrance to the sanctuary so that people may simply kneel at a communion rail if they so desire. Indeed, the Roman Missal says that 'the faithful may, where necessary, venerate the cross in silence, without leaving their places'. The devotions may include the *Crux fidelis* (e.g. *New English Hymnal* no. 517). There then follow a series of anthems. The first is similar to the traditional reproaches, interspersed with the *Trisagion*, with a version from the Canadian *BAS* and an alternative text, that of *LHWE*, both taking note of the associated sensitivities. Anthems 2 and 3 are the third and fourth options (scriptural) from *LHWE*. Anthem 4 is based on Psalm 67 enclosed by a traditional antiphon. The Acclamations which may conclude the veneration are responsorial in form and traditional.

The prayers of intercession (the 'Solemn Prayers') are not those in *LHWE*, but a revision of the text in the Canadian *BAS*. They are in traditional form, each section comprising a bidding, silence, response and collect. The language is rich, and many of the collects of ancient provenance. One matter for regret is that the fine prayer which begins 'O God of unchangeable power and eternal light' is used here and not in its original place during the Easter Vigil, as in the Gelasian Sacramentary and successive Roman Missals until the reform of Holy Week abbreviated the number of readings at the Vigil, resulting in its exclusion.

The Liturgy of the Sacrament may follow the solemn prayers if it was reserved for this purpose at the Maundy Thursday liturgy. TS does not envisage a full celebration of the Eucharist, a practice found in some places but without historical precedent and in danger of drawing attention away from the cross. The material for the distribution of communion is from the *CW* main volume. The post communions are either the Memorial of the Cross, which, in the words of Eric Milner-White in the introduction to his *Procession of Passion Prayers*, 'intertwined itself with the Office of our Lady' in the day hours, or a modification of the *LHWE* text. These prayers also conclude the service if there is to be no Liturgy of the Sacrament. An alternative conclusion is suggested which involves the reading of the Gospel of the Burial of Christ (John 19.38–42) and the carrying out of the cross, but if this is used the earlier Passion reading should end at John 19.37.

Further Reading

J. G. Davies, *Holy Week: A Short History*, Ecumenical Studies in Worship 11, Lutterworth Press, London, 1963.

Roger Greenacre and Jeremy Haselock, *The Sacrament of Easter*, Gracewing, Leominster, 1995.

Maxwell E. Johnson, 'From Three Weeks to Forty Days: Baptismal Preparation and the Origins of Lent', in *Living Water, Sealing Spirit: Readings on Christian Initiation*, ed. Maxwell E. Johnson, The Liturgical Press, Collegeville, MN, 1995, pp. 118–36.

Peter Jeffery, *A New Commandment: Toward a Renewed Rite for the Washing of Feet*, The Liturgical Press, Collegeville, MN, 1992.

Michael Perham and Kenneth Stevenson, *Waiting for the Risen Christ: A Commentary on Lent, Holy Week, Easter: Services and Prayers*, SPCK, London, 1986.

Joanne M. Pierce, 'Holy Week and Easter in the Middle Ages', in *Passover and Easter: Origin and History to Modern Times*, ed. Paul F. Bradshaw and Lawrence A. Hoffman, University of Notre Dame Press, Notre Dame, IN, 1999, pp. 161–85.

Kenneth Stevenson, *Jerusalem Revisited: The Liturgical Meaning of Holy Week*, Pastoral Press, Washington, DC, 1988.

Thomas J. Talley, *The Origins of the Liturgical Year*, 2nd edition, The Liturgical Press, Collegeville, MN, 1991, pp. 1–77, 163–225.

F. THE EASTER LITURGY

Although Easter was celebrated in one of two distinct ways by different groups of early Christians, attached either to the same day as the Jewish Passover or to the Sunday following the Passover, both seem to have associated themselves with the Passover in imagery and theology (see 1 Corinthians 5.7, a key text in both traditions). The long periods of fasting before (Lent and Holy Week) and rejoicing after (Eastertide) are later developments. In the third century emphasis on the celebration as being the 'passage' from death to life began to develop, and this may have led to the emergence of the Triduum (the three days of Good Friday, Holy Saturday and Easter Day) by the fourth century as a mirror of the death, entombment and resurrection of Christ. The Easter Vigil was the original single celebration, ending with the Eucharist at first-light or cock-crow, but this focus was later distorted both by the accretion of subsidiary celebrations during Easter Day itself (which became the only occasions in reformed churches, including the Church of England), and the eventual Roman practice of celebrating the Vigil during the day on Holy Saturday, which practice lasted until the reform of the Roman Catholic Holy Week in the 1950s, when the Vigil, although much curtailed, was restored to the evening or night. Liturgical developments since the 1950s have seen a further rediscovery of the primacy and riches of the Easter Vigil, with a corresponding multiplicity of resources. While many churches have chosen to make it at least part of their Easter celebrations, if not always the main focus, services during the day have remained important. TS reflects these developments in what is provided.

As a proportion of the book, the material given for this single day is greater than that devoted to entire seasons. The problem for many will be how to make the necessary choices intelligently and realistically. The resources are divided into two main sections: two alternative complete orders of service, themselves each containing options, and a series of appendices (greater in length than the two main orders of service put together) comprising a direc-tory of alternatives and additions, some further orders of service for use apart from at the Easter Vigil, and some practical instructions for particular cere-monies.

There is a comprehensive and helpful introduction to the alternative forms of the Easter Liturgy which establishes their historical basis and their differing balance. The main difference is the placing of the Service of Light in relation to the Vigil, that is before (Pattern A) or after (Pattern B). There is an implied preference for Pattern B as reflecting the earlier tradition and because it 'lends itself to an adventurous and creative approach'. An important piece of advice in respect of the alternative patterns is the importance of 'a conscious decision which one is to be followed [since] each of these structures has its own inner logic which makes them completely different services'. A third pattern is the 'Dawn Service', resources for which appear as Appendix H (see below).

There follows a clear setting-out of the four main elements of the Easter Liturgy: Vigil, Service of Light, Baptismal Liturgy, and Eucharist. The third might have been better called 'the Liturgy of Initiation' since it may incorporate confirmation. Notes follow as to timing and length, which will vary according to the needs and resources of each community, and the relationship between the Vigil and other services.

Pattern A

The Service of Light

The outline structure is followed by detailed practical notes, which should be read with care. The service itself begins with an introduction spoken by the president, the form of words being derived from the Roman Missal. The opening prayer is either the first text from *LHWE* or a 'Blessed are you . . .' form with its response. Attention is then drawn to the instructions for the optional marking of the Easter Candle in Appendix G. The words are to be said in any event, and are those of the Roman Missal, as in *LHWE*. The words which accompany each of the three stations with the candle are also the same as in the Missal. The *Exsultet* (lit. 'let him rejoice') or song of praise of God and blessing of the candle follows (alternative forms are given in Appendix E). There are many texts of the *Exsultet* available, and it is inevitable that individual preference will play a part in the selection. Here, the text of the first part, before the dialogue, is from the Roman Missal, although the invitation to pray for the minister, optional in the Missal, is not given at all in this form. The first part may be sung by all in the metrical form also given. The dialogue and subsequent text are traditional, but in a shorter form than the Roman Missal version and with considerable modification of what remains. It is not the *LHWE* text, although clearly based on it. Examples of optional interspersed responses are given, although correctly stating that these should not include 'Alleluia'.

The Vigil

This begins with the second part of the *LHWE* introduction to the whole liturgy, sensibly transposed here to mark more effectively the change of mood. Other suitable words may be used. Readings, psalms and prayer for the Vigil are given in Appendix A, and there is considerable scope for choice and variation. The number of readings used, and the nature and quantity of the material accompanying them, will be determined in part by consideration of the overall length of the liturgy and its timing, according to local circumstances. The Easter Acclamation follows, here the same as the *CW* opening greeting for Eastertide, and with an encouragement of appropriately joyful noise. The *Gloria in excelsis* or a suitable hymn begins immediately. The Collect of Easter (main volume or alternative form) is said after a special invitation and a period of silence. The New Testament reading is Romans 6.3–11, which may be followed by a psalm and, curiously, a repetition of the Easter Acclamation, since two Gospel acclamations in 'Alleluia' form are then suggested. The sermon after the Gospel may include individual testimony – this may be especially appropriate if there are baptisms and/or confirmations.

The Baptismal Liturgy

The introductory words are modified from *LHWE* to conclude with the opening words of the Decision. Thereafter the forms generic to a liturgy of initiation are those of the *CW Initiation Services*.

The Liturgy of the Eucharist

The introduction to the Peace is the *CW* text for Eastertide. A welcome detail is the direction that all greet one another with 'Christ is risen', as is the Eastern custom: this could be maintained throughout the season. Of the two prayers at the Preparation of the Table, the first is specific to the day, while the second is a *CW* general text, although entirely appropriate. The short preface is from the *CW* main volume and is based on that in the 1662 *BCP*, itself from the Latin text of one of the ten prefaces to which the English Church was restricted at a Provincial Council in 1175. Today it is also the basis for Easter Preface I in the Roman Missal. The extended preface is based on one in the Ambrosian Rite of the Church of Milan for Easter Wednesday, translated by Alan Griffiths and adapted here to include the phrase 'on this night of our redemption', which makes it unique to the Easter Liturgy. Another version from the same source is the extended preface for the Easter season. The phrase 'the mystery of his Passion' was once common in Western liturgy before the first millennium. A special form for use at the breaking of the bread recalls the 'eucharistic' self-description of Jesus in John 6. The invitation is the *CW* form for the season. The Easter Day post communion precedes a dismissal which repeats the Easter greeting and allows for either the *CW* main volume simple blessing or a solemn form from *NPFW*, previously in *ECY* and written by Michael Perham for St George's, Oakdale. The giving of a lighted candle follows when there has been a baptism. The final dismissal text is proper to the day, but may be used in the Easter season.

Pattern B

As with Pattern A, an outline structure and detailed notes are given. In contrast to Pattern A, the Vigil begins directly, the only light being that necessary for the readers to see the text. The first words may be those of Genesis 1.1, especially if the creation story is omitted from the Vigil readings. The light for illumination, although practical in nature, is nevertheless accompanied by one of two alternative prayers. The first is the contemporary-language version of the *BCP* Third Collect at Evening Prayer, while the second is a 'blessing of the light' prayer of the type found in the *DP* evening offices. The words of introduction are based on those of *LHWE*, this time continuing with those which relate to the Vigil, except that the presentation of baptismal candidates may come in between. The Vigil follows, with readings and other material selected according to local needs. The Service of Light is in form and texts as in Pattern A, but concludes with the Easter Acclamation, *Gloria in excelsis* and Collect. The Liturgy then proceeds as in Pattern A with the same texts and rubrics.

Appendix A: Vigil Readings, Psalms and Prayers

There is a great deal of material here covering many alternatives. Space does not permit an exhaustive commentary, but several general remarks may be made. Whereas *LHWE* simply gave suggested texts, TS provides notes on the practical implications of the Vigil, including location. If using Pattern B, the importance of not allowing a light by which to see to be confused with the Easter Candle is sensibly repeated. It is pointed out that the traditional Christ-focused collects associated with the readings (as in *LHWE*) are not the only possible form of prayer. They should be used with Pattern A 'where the Vigil readings are read by the light of the Easter Candle and therefore a more christological emphasis is appropriate', but 'Blessed are you . . .' type prayers are more suitable for 'the story-telling approach of Pattern B'.

The readings themselves are very varied, and some (but only some) possible thematic arrangements are given, with the firm direction that Exodus 14, the account of the crossing of the Red Sea, should always be included. There is therefore enormous scope here to explore the history of salvation by different routes in successive years. Issues regarding how the readings are to be read (single voice, dramatic reading, enacted reading, etc.) are dealt with in a further note. The full possibilities of the provision are certainly indicated by the fact that 'if the vigil is to last all night there could be specific points for eating and drinking that are related to the readings'! In common with the overall *CW* approach to liturgical celebration, silence is specifically mentioned as an essential element even with the most informal approach.

The prayers that accompany the readings are from a variety of sources, and many will be familiar from other contexts, such as the *CW* provision of collects and the *LHWE* selections. In using those which are also *CW* Collects for the Sundays through the year, TS appropriately conveys a sense of the whole liturgical year as a reflection on a single mystery: Lent is not the only season from which they are drawn.

Appendix B: Outline Service for a Mid-Morning Eucharist

The almost universal pastoral need for other liturgies on Easter Day should not be seen as a negative consequence of a rich and primary celebration of the

Easter Liturgy itself, but a reflection that for many years these services have been in many places the best attended at Easter, and that the requirements of mission alone call for them to be given as much attention to detail and careful preparation as what is liturgically the principal liturgy of the day. They offer gateways into the Easter mystery which new Christians and enquirers may otherwise find initially difficult to negotiate if confronted exclusively with the full Liturgy. Therefore the Outline Service for a mid-morning Eucharist on Easter Day using elements from the Easter Liturgy might be the best approach at first for a parish which has never before celebrated the full Liturgy, as a form of preparation for future developments. What it does not encourage, however, is the repetition of the ceremonies particular to the Easter Liturgy.

Appendix C: Outline Service of the Word
There will be many communities which need resources for a Service of the Word. This form assumes that the Easter Candle has not already been lit at an earlier service. It suggests a more responsive, metrical form of the *Exsultet* (included in Appendix E from where other examples may be chosen).

Appendix D: Welcoming the Easter Candle into the Church
A rite which might be used where there has been an earlier celebration of the Easter Liturgy in the same or another church, this form may therefore be particularly useful in multi-parish benefices or those with several church build-ings. It includes ceremonies and prayers which may be used in connection with an Easter garden: these could be used on other occasions in part or in full and so are also included in Appendix I. It ought to be said that there should not be more than one Easter Candle in the same church.

Appendix E: Alternative Forms of the Exsultet
Three alternative forms of the *Exsultet* are provided. Form 1 is metrical and includes a congregational response; form 2 is the same text with some entire verses sung by the congregation; form 3 is a non-metrical 'modern variant' by Gregory Jenks which is an interesting blend of traditional elements (reference to the 'happy fault' of Adam, omitted from the text in Patterns A and B) with very contemporary language ('all life forms'; 'the tribal taboos'). Finally in this section is material which refers to the bees, as providers of the wax, contained in some earlier texts of the *Exsultet* (although not the post-1570 or 'Tridentine' Roman Rite). TS observes that 'for those who wish to restore these references we offer this version for optional insertion into the main text of the Exsultet'. Other texts of the *Exsultet* not given here are of course available. There are locally adapted versions in circulation, published and unpublished, which makes it clear that, as in the Middle Ages and before, there is no universally agreed text.

Appendix F: Thanksgiving for the Resurrection

This rite is intended for use in different contexts throughout the Easter season, which suggests that it might have been better placed among the general resources for the season which follow those specifically for Easter Day. It provides material for use, for example, at the Eucharist (perhaps to lead into the *Gloria in excelsis*) and what might be called 'solemn' offices, for example Evensong on Easter Day. Section 1 is a cento of psalmody and other Scripture (for example, the acclamation of the enthroned Lamb from the Book of Revelation). Sections 2 and 3 are the *CW* Litany of the Resurrection, possibly for use in procession to the font, and perhaps in this way at the Easter Liturgy (although this is not suggested by the rubric), perhaps as an alternative to a Litany of the Saints, sung at that point in some places. The litany, whether used in full or in part, may conclude with the doxology suggested.

Appendix G: Instructions for Marking the Easter Candle

These have been available from other sources for many years, but it is entirely in keeping with the comprehensiveness of TS that they are included here: as such, they continue the practice which began with *PHG* of 'commended' resources giving considerable practical rubrics as well as selections of texts. The practice of marking the date comes from the Roman tradition. The other marks came to be added over the centuries, and in places were extensive. The making of the sign of the cross with a stylus and the insertion of incense grains in the form of nails are equivalents to blessing and censing, although the latter are often by custom also done.

Appendix H: The Dawn Service

This in actual fact is the third of the 'three forms' proposed by TS in the overall introduction to the Easter Liturgy, and is given in response to recent development in some communities in respect of the timing and location of a more informal, and sometimes ecumenical, Easter celebration. The structure is very loose, the possibilities many, and TS deliberately gives the minimum of liturgical resources. The notes do promote, however, the inclusion of the four elements of the Easter Liturgy, while full encouragement is given to use the precise location to guide the emphasis, and the arrival of dawn to underscore the lighting of the Easter Light, whatever form that takes.

Appendix I: Prayers at the Easter Garden

These could be used selectively or as a complete rite, perhaps as part of a major liturgy of Easter Day, as suggested in Appendix D, 'Welcoming the Easter Candle into the Church'.

Further Reading

Roger Greenacre and Jeremy Haselock, *The Sacrament of Easter*, Gracewing, Leominster, 1995.

A. J. MacGregor, *Fire and Light in the Western Triduum*, Alcuin Club Collections 71,
The Liturgical Press, Collegeville, MN, 1992.

Joanne M. Pierce, 'Holy Week and Easter in the Middle Ages' in *Passover and Easter:
Origin and History to Modern Times*, ed. Paul F. Bradshaw and Lawrence A.
Hoffman, University of Notre Dame Press, Notre Dame, IN, 1999, pp. 161–85.

Kenneth Stevenson, *Jerusalem Revisited: The Liturgical Meaning of Holy Week*, Pastoral
Press, Washington, DC, 1988.

G. EASTER

The earliest witness to the Easter season, a period of fifty days called by early
Christians 'Pentecost' and ending on the day of that name, appears to be Tertullian at the beginning of the third century. It may have originated by association
with the Jewish Feast of Weeks (*Shabuoth*), a fifty-day celebration of the
harvest, a 'week of weeks', beginning with the Feast of Unleavened Bread and
culminating in Pentecost. Early Christianity viewed the period after Easter as a
time of rejoicing in the presence of the Bridegroom, that is, the risen Christ.
Although the unity of the fifty days was later obscured by the emergence of the
Easter Octave and the period around the Ascension, the importance of the
single season, 'a single festival period', is now re-emphasized, as reflected in the
rubrics of *CW*. The resources for the Easter season therefore include a directory
of material for the Eucharist, an order for the 'Stations of the Resurrection', and
complete orders for Ascension and Pentecost. The Introduction to the Season
notes that in it 'all the resources of the church – music, flowers, bells, colours –
are used to celebrate Christ's resurrection'.

Seasonal Material

Invitations to Confession

The three alternatives draw on 1 Corinthians 5.7, 8 (the Passover Lamb: the
CW text for the season, from David Silk's *In Penitence and Faith*), Romans 6.4
(the new life of baptism) and Romans 6.10 (in *ECY* and from Silk, *In Penitence
and Faith*).

Confessions

The first form is a *CW* authorized text for general use. The other two are *Kyrie*
confessions from *ECY*, adapted from the Roman Missal, and a text recalling
the response of Mary, Thomas and the other disciples to the resurrection.

Absolution

This draws on the tradition of the *asperges*, or sprinkling with water at the
beginning of the Eucharist as a sign of new life and forgiveness, and is

especially appropriate for Sundays. The prayer over the water is linked with an authorized *CW* absolution (another may be used instead), before which there may be 'suitable' sung material, perhaps the *vidi aquam* (see the Eucharist for the Baptism of Christ).

Gospel Acclamations

Three of the five options are Johannine (John 6.35; 6.40; 11.25–26), while the fourth (from the *CW* main volume provision for the season), looks to Revelation 1.17, 18. The fifth text comprises statements about the victory of Jesus interspersed with 'Alleluia'.

Intercessions

The first set is based on *NPFW* (F60), there adapted from the Canadian *BAS*. The second is also in *NPFW* (F67), based on Easter-related titles of Jesus (light of the world, bread of life, etc.). The final option also uses relevant titles of Jesus (Son of Man, pioneer of our salvation, Lord over all things, etc.).

Introductions to the Peace

The *CW* main volume provision for the season (John 20.19, 20) is given along with alternatives based on 1 Corinthians 15.20 and Luke 24.35.

Prayers at the Preparation of the Table

These are either directly taken or adapted from the Canadian *BAS* (a baptismal prayer and a variant of the 'Roman' offertory prayers), *A New Zealand Prayer Book* (recognition in the breaking of the bread: given in Jonathan Priestland Young's *Enriching the Liturgy* for Easter 3), and the *CW* main volume ('be present, be present . . .', from the general resources).

Prefaces

Offered here are the *CW* main volume short preface (also given for the Easter Liturgy – see above), two further short prefaces from *CWPE* (*ASB* in origin), and a self-contained preface, not classified as 'extended', altered from the Roman Missal in *ECY*. The extended preface proper is the 'season' version of that for the Easter Liturgy, based on a translation from the Ambrosian Rite by Alan Griffiths. The final preface is responsive in form, and based on 1 Corinthians 15 (*NPFW* G78). In that it does not address God throughout, it is of a different order from any other *CW* preface, and indeed would seem to step outside the Western tradition for the genre in addressing 'death' rhetorically as Paul does.

Blessings and Endings

The *CW* main volume simple blessing is supplemented by the three *ASB* Easter blessings and one from *A New Zealand Prayer Book*. The solemn blessing is from *ECY*.

Alternative Dismissal

Following the form established in TS for other occasions, an acclamation (*NPFW* G37) is followed by a Dismissal Gospel (John 11.25–26), and the solemn blessing. There are three dismissal texts, but 'Alleluia' does not feature and the traditional 'Go in the peace of Christ, Alleluia, Alleluia' is not among the options: this might be used unvaryingly throughout the season.

Acclamations and Short Passages of Scripture

The acclamation used in the Alternative Dismissal and one based on 2 Timothy 1.22–13 (*NPFW* G44) are given. The passages of Scripture are all single verses apart from 1 Corinthians 15.20–21.

The Stations of the Resurrection

These provide a means of mirroring or balancing the traditional or scriptural Stations of the Cross with a structured devotion on the resurrection. The idea of doing so may, as the introductory text states, have arisen in Spain in the late twentieth century. As with the Stations of the Cross, what is given in TS is not the only form available (see, for example, Raymond Chapman, *Stations of the Resurrection: Meditations on the Fourteen Resurrection Appearances*, Canterbury Press, Norwich, 1998). This is recognized, and TS adds guidance to how such a devotion may be combined with the Eucharist. As noted above for the Stations of the Cross, care should be taken if proceeding with this option. The TS resources are drawn from the *CW* main volume collects and other material.

The Liturgy of Ascension Day

The liturgical celebration of the Ascension originates in the fourth century, although it did not always occur in the same place during the Easter season. The fortieth day became the norm, perhaps on account of the finalising of the canon of the New Testament.

In TS a complete order is given, with alternative texts, and it at its end assumes the beginning of a period of preparation for Pentecost. The response at the beginning of the Gathering, unique to the day (Psalm 47.5), may be replaced by an anthem depending on local resources. The optional Trinitarian invocation and a *CW* main volume greeting are followed by a suggested intro-ductory text, as with all the major liturgies of the year in the manner established by *LHWE* and *PHG*. The 'Ascension Reading' is then read, as if to mirror the 'Palm Gospel' on Palm Sunday, except that here it is Acts 1.6–11. The Liturgy of the Word includes a suggested canticle (Revelation 15.3, 4, from the *CW* main volume) and two alternative Gospel acclamations (Matthew 28.19–20 and Philippians 2.9–11). The first set of intercessions is *NPFW* (F61), by Michael Perham (adapted), the second a new composition with longer biddings and scriptural in resonance. The *CW* main volume intro-duction to the Peace is used, and a *CW* general prayer at the Preparation of the Table. The prefaces are both *CW* main volume seasonal provisions, the extended one based on the Roman Missal, the short form adapted from the 1662 *BCP*. Words at the breaking of the bread are from the Canadian *BAS*, and a special form of invitation to communion from *PHG* although in *ECY* for the Ascension. The *CW* Eastertide form is an alternative. There is a longer form of dismissal which looks forward to the gift of the Spirit at Pentecost, with no Gospel but a reading from Acts (1.12–14), a responsory, and the solemn blessing for the day from *CWPE* (written by Michael Perham and also in *ECY*), or a simple blessing. Variations of the traditional Easter Dismissal are given.

Pentecost

As indicated above, Pentecost (the 'fiftieth' day) formed part of the Jewish scheme of celebrating the harvest, and in this way became the end of the Christian fifty-day celebration of the resurrection from about the end of the second century. Following the Gospel of Luke, the fourth-century enrichment of liturgical feasts and their rites secured its place as the festival of the gift of the Holy Spirit, although originally the Ascension and the Spirit were celebrated on the same day. As with the Easter Octave, Pentecost came to be regarded almost as a season-within-the-season, thus undermining the unity of Eastertide, but liturgical renewal has brought a right rebalancing of Easter as a single season and a consequent enrichment of Pentecost as a distinctive day within it, while still closely linked with the Ascension. TS recognizes equally the context, the connection and the distinctions in the material that is provided, although does not follow the Roman Catholic practice of encouraging a Vigil of Pentecost, perhaps for reasons of the delicate balance.

Seasonal Material for use from Ascension to Pentecost

Invitations to Confession

Four alternatives are given: the *CW* main volume text for the period (1 Corinthians 2.9, 10), two selections from *NPFW* (B16: cf. John 16.18; and B18, from David Silk's *In Penitence and Faith*), and a text written by Nicolas Stebbing CR, recalling Psalm 68.17.

Kyrie Confessions

The first brief form is from the *CW* main volume general examples and based on the Roman Missal; the second is more expansive, written by Nicolas Stebbing CR.

Gospel Acclamations

These are drawn from the *CW* main volume, asking for the gift of the Spirit, and from Matthew 28.19–20, focusing on the mission consequent on that gift.

Intercession

The single set of intercessions is from *ECY*, written by Kenneth Stevenson for Holy Trinity, Guildford, and is woven around the attributes of the Spirit (power, wisdom, healing, etc.).

Introductions to the Peace

The *CW* main volume form for the season and its predecessor in the *ASB*.

Prayers at the Preparation of the Table

From the Canadian *BAS* (for Easter 7, adapted), and *A Prayer Book for Australia* (adapted).

Prefaces

The *CW* main volume short preface, effectively that of *ASB* Rite B in contemporary language, the *ASB* Rite A preface (also *NPFW* G125), and a preface from *ECY*, adapted there from the Canadian *BAS*.

Extended Preface

For the days between Ascension and Pentecost only (the extended preface for Pentecost itself is part of the TS complete order for that day) is the *CW* main volume provision, based on the Roman Missal.

Blessings and Endings

Two short blessings, the *CW* main volume form and one from *ECY*, both originally in the *ASB*. The solemn blessing is in *CWPE*, and was written by Michael Perham for St George's, Oakdale.

Acclamation

NPFW (G39), written by Michael Perham and in *ECY* for Ascension.

Short Passages of Scripture

All but one (Acts 1.10–11) are single verses, but including the lengthier Matthew 28.19 and Luke 24.50.

The Liturgy of the Feast of Pentecost

The distinctive features of this liturgy as TS conceives it are the Responsory, Reading and Prayer for personal renewal which form part of the Gathering, and the Blessing of the Light which is incorporated in the Dismissal. Apart from this, the liturgy follows *CW* norms in terms of structure and genre of texts. The optional Trinitarian invocation is followed by a *CW* authorized greeting and the Easter greeting (as in the main volume, they are not alternatives but must both be used). A *PHG/LHWE*-style presidential introduction precedes a Responsory asking for the gift of the Spirit, which might perhaps be replaced by the *Veni Creator* if desired. There is then a reading (Acts 2.1–13) in the manner of Palm Sunday and Ascension Day. In this there arises a contradiction between this liturgy and the directions given in the *CW* Lectionary. The latter states that Acts 2.1–21 must *always* be used as either the first or second reading in the Liturgy of the Word, whereas this order says that 'Acts 2.1–13 should *not* be included in the Readings if it has been used earlier in the service.' How this is resolved will be a matter for local decision. An obvious solution would be simply to omit the earlier reading and proceed directly to the Prayer for renewal, or to find another suitable reading for use in its place. There is nevertheless a sense that in the desire to mirror the pattern of Palm Sunday and Ascension Day the priority of the Liturgy of the Word has been overlooked.

The Prayer for personal renewal is optional and flexible in form. It may involve the oil of chrism or 'oil blessed specially for the occasion' using the prayer provided. The former is preferable if it has already been obtained and brought into the church on Maundy Thursday. The ministry of prayer may also, presumably, include the laying-on of hands, although this part of the service should perhaps not become so extended as to impede the flow of the liturgy as a whole – this ministry could, after all, be offered instead during the distribution of communion or after the service. In the Liturgy of the Word there is a suggested canticle from the *CW* main volume (Ezekiel 36.24–26, 28b), and two Gospel acclamations (*CW* main volume and 1 Corinthians 12.4, 5; 13.3). The intercession is the form from *ECY*, written by Kenneth Stevenson and included in the seasonal resources, and may be followed by Prayers of Penitence, presumably especially if the Prayer for renewal has been omitted or deferred. The extended preface, from the *CW* main volume, is by Michael Perham and in *ECY*, and may only be used on the Day of Pentecost itself. The short preface is also the *CW* main volume text, altered for *ECY* from *ASB* Rite B. The Easter form of invitation to communion is used on this day, for the last time. The prayer for the Blessing of the Light is adapted from *ECY*, the original being by Michael Vasey.

The rite then takes the form of a corporate commitment to live out what has been celebrated in the fifty days of Easter, and may include a symbolic 'going out' of the church, and the extinguishing of the Easter Candle, the latter only if there are to be no other services on this day. But if this is done, thought needs to be given as to whether it rather undermines the commitment that has just been made, unless the view is taken that it is now to be the 'light' in the whole people of God that shines in the world throughout the year, a point which the preacher or a rubric could perhaps address. The text inviting the Spirit to 'drive us out into the wild places of the world' must also be used with care, since in pastoral terms there may be those in the congregation who truly and already find themselves in the wilderness in their personal lives. The blessing is from among the seasonal resources, and for the last time the Easter Dismissal is given. Even if it is normally said it should if at all possible be sung on this occasion.

Further Reading

Paul F. Bradshaw and Lawrence A. Hoffman, *Passover and Easter: Origin and History to Modern Times*, University of Notre Dame Press, Notre Dame, IN, 1999.

Raniero Cantalamessa, *Easter in the Early Church*, The Liturgical Press, Collegeville, MN, 1993.

H. TRINITY TO ALL SAINTS

This section is not intended to provide resources for Ordinary Time, since these are readily available in the *CW* main volume and may be supplemented from such privately produced works as Jonathan Priestland Young's *Enriching the Liturgy*. Rather, TS provides directories of material for three major Festivals that occur in this period.

Trinity Sunday

Rather than being concerned with events in the history of salvation, Trinity Sunday is entirely focused on the theological mystery of the triune God. Unlike many of the historical feasts and seasons, it had a relatively late tenth-century origin and a very gradual increase in popularity and official approbation. Papal opinion was unfavourable until the fourteenth century. Popular in England, it gave rise to the custom of naming the Sundays between Pentecost and Advent 'after Trinity' in the Sarum use, a form adopted by the 1549 *BCP* and its successors. While the *ASB* chose to adopt the original Roman Sundays 'after Pentecost', *CW* has reverted to Sundays 'after Trinity'.

Most of the resources for Trinity Sunday are drawn from the existing *CW* seasonal provision and the plentiful material for the day in *ECY*. The latter provides two of the three alternative invitations to confession (written by Trevor Lloyd, based on Isaiah 6.5, 7 and by John Townend, based on Matthew 23.37) and the third, new composition warns against idolatry. The *Kyrie* confessions are two of those of *ECY*, both written by Michael Perham for Oakdale (the second based on Isaiah 6.5, 7). The intercession, also from *ECY*, is by Trevor Lloyd and based on William Cowper's (1731–1800) hymn 'Father of heaven, whose love profound'. The first short preface (from the *ASB* and ultimately Series 3) and the extended preface (with echoes of the *Te Deum*, a modified version of that by Michael Perham in *ECY*) are the *CW* provisions. Another short preface is given which adopts the phraseology of the Collects of Epiphany 4 and the Sunday before Lent. There is one simple blessing, from the *CW* main volume, and two solemn blessings, the first in *CWPE*, from *ECY* and ultimately *PFW*, based on the Aaronic blessing in Numbers 6.24–25; the second is also from *ECY*, and is by Michael Perham, based on a prayer of Bishop Thomas Ken (1637–1711). There is an 'ending' from *ECY* also based on words of Thomas Ken. Two Acclamations (one altered from the *CW* main volume and based on Revelation 4.11; 5.9b, 10; the other a cento of Isaiah 6.3 and verses from Psalm 29) and some short passages of Scripture are provided.

**The Day of Thanksgiving for the Institution of Holy Communion
(Corpus Christi)**

CW restored this day to the status of a Festival (it was a Commemoration in *ASB*) for those communities who wish so to observe it, in recognition of the fact that such had been the practice in many places for many years. The use of the name 'Corpus Christi' recalls the medieval title of a celebration originating in Liège in 1246 that was first given papal approval in 1264, and which came to include a procession of the Blessed Sacrament. More recent Roman Catholic practice has renamed it the 'Body and Blood of Christ'. TS provides only texts for the day in the standard directory format, not rubrics, sensibly leaving local custom to determine which additional ceremonies, if any, will accompany the Eucharist.

The invitation to confession based on the 1662 *BCP* and in the main text of Order 1 is given, with two shorter alternatives, the second of which is based on 1 Corinthians 11.27–29. The *Kyrie* confessions are from the 'Eucharist' material in *ECY* (composed by David Stancliffe for Portsmouth Cathedral) and from the Roman Missal. John 6.51 forms the basis of the Gospel acclamation. The intercession is also by Michael Perham from *ECY*, with references to the Eucharist as fellowship meal, as the presence of Christ, as indelibly linked to the Passion, and as worship 'with the whole company of heaven'. The prayer at the Preparation of the Table is Johannine in feel (cf. John 6.34–35). Five alternative short prefaces are suggested, beginning with the *CW* main volume text which recalls the Last Supper and is based on the Maundy Thursday preface in the *ASB* Rite B. The second preface is the *ASB* text for Maundy Thursday. A preface for Epiphanytide in *PHG* is the source of the third, which makes the connection between baptism and the Eucharist, 'that mystery in bread and wine'. The fourth text is altered from the Roman Missal (as in *ECY*). The extended preface is an altered text from the Roman Missal, where it is the Preface of the Holy Eucharist II for Corpus Christi and votive Masses of the Holy Eucharist. The language is very rich. The simple blessing is from *CW* supplementary texts for general use. The solemn blessing is by Michael Perham, from *ECY* and given in slightly different form in *NPFW* (J106). There is an alternative ending from *ECY* by Michael Perham, based on Proverbs 9.2, 5, 6 and Psalm 43.1. This psalm verse supplies the antiphon to Psalm 43 in the rite of preparation in the Latin Mass, and in the 'Devotion before the celebration of Holy Communion' in the 1928 *BCP*. The acclamation is by Michael Perham from *ECY* (John 6.33, 34, 54, 63), and is followed by four short passages of Scripture.

Dedication Festival

Since at least the fourth century in many places the date on which a church building was consecrated has been celebrated as a Festival, not to be confused with the Patronal Festival of the saint to whom it is dedicated. In *CW*, if the actual date is not known, the Dedication may be observed on either the First

Sunday in October or the Last Sunday after Trinity. *ECY* provided a directory of material for the day, from which much of the TS provision is drawn. The invitation to confession (*ECY*) is by Trevor Lloyd and based on 1 Corinthians 6.19–20. The *Kyrie* confession (*ECY*) is by Michael Perham (Psalms 69.9; 84.10; 121.8). The Gospel acclamation adapts Psalm 26.8. The intercession is adapted from *ECY*, in which it was an altered version of a text in the Canadian *BAS*. *ECY* supplies the introduction to the Peace, from a traditional text for the blessing of a house. The two short prefaces are both in *CWPE*, the first from the *ASB* and in *ECY*, the second also in *ECY* and adapted from the *ASB* Rite B. The extended preface is adapted from *ECY*, the original source being the Roman Missal. A simple blessing is by Michael Perham from *ECY*, and the solemn form is altered in *ECY* from *PFW*. There is an alternative ending from *ECY* in the form of an old Scottish prayer for a church and parish. A full alternative rite of dismissal is provided, comprising the Dismissal Gospel (John 4.23–24), the solemn blessing and words of dismissal for the day. There is an acclamation from *ECY*, written by Michael Perham and echoing John 6.33, 34, 54, 63, and the usual selection of short passages of Scripture.

Further Reading

Martin Dudley, 'Liturgy and Doctrine: Corpus Christi', *Worship* 66 (1992), pp. 417–26.

Nathan Mitchell, *Cult and Controversy: The Worship of the Eucharist outside Mass*, Pueblo, New York, 1982.

Miri Rubin, *Corpus Christi: The Eucharist in Late Medieval Culture*, Cambridge University Press, Cambridge, 1991.

I. ALL SAINTS TO ADVENT

The feast of All Saints seems to have originated in Syria in the fifth century, although the first mention of the title is in 609 in connection with the translation of relics of martyrs to the Pantheon in Rome. It has been observed on 1 November since the time of Gregory III. All Souls dates from the seventh century, when Isidore of Seville observed a commemoration of the dead on the day following Pentecost. Observance on 2 November is owed to Odilo of Cluny in 998.

TS follows the *CW* convention in regarding the period from All Saints to Advent as a quasi-season, a period in which the liturgy takes on a particular flavour with the juxtaposition of All Saints and All Souls at the centre and the kingship of Christ as the conclusion. In the Introduction to the Season (an indicative title) TS admirably summarizes the difference between All Saints and All Souls in the life of the Church and of the individual Christian and sets the scene for the ending of the liturgical year which will begin again at Advent. The resources draw heavily on both the *CW* main volume and inevitably *PHG*, which first introduced the notion of this period as a distinct season, and include material for Remembrance Sunday.

Seasonal Material

The first invitation to confession is from the *CW* main volume for the season (Matthew 3.2), accompanied by two from *PHG*, where they appear in the Eucharist of All Saints and the order for Remembrance Sunday. *ECY* provides the first *Kyrie* confession, by David Silk from his *In Penitence and Faith*. The second one by David Stancliffe is also in the seasonal material for Advent, and in *PHG* was indeed for more wide use between All Saints and Christmas. A congregational confession by Stuart Thomas from *NPFW* (B48, for 'Lament', echoing Psalm 51) is also suggested. The Gospel acclamations are the *CW* main volume text (Luke 19.38) and three further options (Matthew 5.3; Colossians 1.18; Luke 21.36). The first intercession is woven around Isaiah 61.1–3, and is adapted from *NPFW* (F72). The second set focuses on the priesthood and kingship of Christ, and might even be used at Ascensiontide. The final set, from *PHG*, is especially suitable for use on All Saints' Day. The introductions to the Peace are the *CW* main volume provisions for the season (Colossians 3.14, 15; 1 Thessalonians 5.23; 3.13). The prayer at the Preparation of the Table has the whole company of heaven as its particular focus, anticipating the final words of the preface. The two short prefaces are from the *CW* main volume, echoing the *Te Deum*, and from *NPFW* (G143), emphasizing fellowship with the saints. The extended preface is that of the *CW* main volume for the season, and looks to the heavenly Jerusalem and the healing of the kingdom. There are three simple blessings, from the *CW* main volume, *ECY* (from *A New Zealand Prayer Book*), and *PHG* (by Michael Perham for All Souls' Day). The solemn blessing is in *CWPE* (from *PHG*, for the Eucharist of All Saints), and an ending is an adaptation of *NPFW* (J119), based on 1 Chronicles 29.11.

The Eucharist of All Saints

This is a full order of service, as *PHG* provided, using some of the same material and resources from the seasonal directory, from the *CW* main volume and from *ECY*. The president's words of introduction should include the short exhortation to rejoice from *PHG*. The *CW* invitation to confession is accompanied by the first seasonal *Kyrie* confession (as an example). It is suggested that the main-text authorized absolution be used. *Gloria in excelsis* is made alternative to the Beatitudes – it may be felt that the latter would be more suitable as a canticle between the first and second reading if it is not to be read as the Gospel (as it must be in Year A). The Gospel acclamation is the *CW* main volume text for the day (not in the TS seasonal material). The intercession is the third option of the seasonal material, with a different ending (i.e., the unadapted *NPFW* text). The *CW* main volume introduction to the Peace is given, and the prayer based on the *Didache* for use at the Preparation of the Table, a *CW* general resource. The *CW* main volume short and extended prefaces are given, the longer text quoting the section of the *Te Deum* concerned with apostles, prophets and martyrs, adapted from *PHG*. There is an alternative dismissal on the established TS pattern: acclamation (from the Canadian *BAS*, altered), Dismissal Gospel (John 17.6–9), solemn blessing (*CWPE*, from *ECY*, written by Michael Perham), and unique dismissal words. Finally, there are the usual short passages of Scripture.

The Eucharist of the Commemoration of the Faithful Departed (All Souls' Day)

The *PHG* invitation to confession (alluding to the Collect of Epiphany 4) is accompanied by the *CW* congregational confession, 'Father eternal, giver of light and grace . . .', originally in the *ASB* and written by David Frost. A *Kyrie* confession and two alternative absolutions, from the main volume, precede the collect (*CWPE* only, with no short alternative). The Gospel acclamation uses John 6.38. The intercession is *NPFW* (F74), and was in *PHG*. It is also included in *CW Pastoral Services* among the resources for funerals. The Peace is Johannine, in *CWPE*, and the prayer at the Preparation is a *CW* text for general use but which appropriately refers to 'the frailty of our praise'. Two short and one extended preface are all in *CWPE*, the first adapted from the Roman Missal, the second from the *ASB* as a preface of the resurrection (also in *PHG* for the day), the latter altered here from its *CWPE* form (based on 1 Peter 1). The invitation to communion is from *PHG*, a text from the Canadian *BAS*.

The Commemoration of the Faithful Departed follows the distribution, and begins with the responsory from *PHG* (the canticle 'Glory and honour'). Any names may then be read, and the rite continues in either of two forms, which essentially divide between them the equivalent *PHG* material. Thus Form A begins with the short Johannine response, which is followed by two prayers adapted from Silk, *PUAS*. Form B uses the Russian *Contakion* of the Dead (in *PHG* as a congregational prayer and now also in *CW Pastoral Services*), continuing with the adaptation of a prayer of Bishop John Cosin (1594–1672) from his 'Prayers at the Hour of Death' (in *PHG* and *CW Pastoral Services*). The post-communion prayer is in *CWPE*. The two simple blessings are both in *CWPE*: the first is by Michael Perham (for *PHG*), and the second is an Easter text, as is the solemn blessing, also in *CWPE*. The dismissal forms are the *CW* main text option for Order 1 and the final *PHG* option without the Alleluias.

Remembrance Sunday

The resources for Remembrance Sunday are only for use in the context of a Eucharist or at Morning or Evening Prayer or a Service of the Word, and are not intended to supplant the service commended in 1968 (revised 1984) by Anglican, Roman Catholic and Free Church authorities and included in *PHG*. These texts would therefore lend themselves to the principal Eucharist when there is a Civic Remembrance service at another time of day, or to an earlier said service when the ecumenical form is to be used in place of the usual principal service, bearing in mind that the Holy Communion must be cele-brated each Sunday in every parish church. This said, the material in TS is in fact drawn from the ecumenical order that was reprinted in *PHG*, with the exception of the short passages of Scripture.

Christ the King

This Feast dates from 1925, when it was approved by Pope Pius XI. Originally celebrated on the last Sunday of October, it is now on the final Sunday before Advent and thus the last of the liturgical year. It completes what *PHG* called the 'kingdom season'; its authorized adoption by the Church of England (as opposed to the commended *PHG* provision) in the *CW* Calendar in 1997 followed the practice of many other provinces of the Anglican Communion.

The *CW* main volume provides material proper to the day, from which is included here the invitation to confession (Matthew 3.2), the first Gospel acclamation (Luke 19.38), the introduction to the Peace (Colossians 3.14, 15, also *NPFW* H35), the extended preface adapted from the Roman Missal, and the first simple blessing. To these are added a *Kyrie* confession and a congrega-tional text (from Isaiah 6) from the *CW* supplementary material. The alternative Gospel acclamation uses a phrase from the *Te Deum* ('You, Christ, are the King of glory . . .'). The intercessions are from Gail Ramshaw (ed.), *Intercessions for the Christian People* (Liturgical Press, 1999, p. 138). A unique prayer at the preparation of the table is provided which refers to 'the royal wine of heaven'. The short prefaces recall Christ's anointing as priest and king and his priestly sacrifice on and reign from the cross. The second short preface uses some of the phraseology of the extended version. The post-communion prayer was the Collect of the Sunday next before Advent in the *ASB*, but now has this function in the *CW* main volume. The second simple blessing was the *ASB* blessing for the Ascension, although entirely appropriate here, and also in *NPFW* (J89). The solemn blessing is in *CWPE*, written by Michael Perham for the Ascension in *ECY*. The Acclamation is based on Psalm 24, and there are the usual short passages of Scripture.

Further Reading

Adolf Adam, *The Liturgical Year*, Pueblo, New York, 1981, pp. 228–30, 237–40.

Michael Perham, *The Communion of Saints*, Alcuin Club Collections 62, SPCK, London, 1980.

Michael Perham and Kenneth Stevenson, 'All Saintstide' in *Welcoming the Light of Christ: A Commentary on 'The Promise of His Glory'*, SPCK, London, 1991, pp. 21–37.

N. T. Wright, *For All the Saints? Remembering the Christian Departed*, SPCK, London, 2003.

Chapter 4

New Patterns for Worship

A. HISTORY

Background

In January 1644 the *Book of Common Prayer* was replaced by the *Westminster Directory for the Public Worship of God*. This contained instructions for each service, about how to assemble, how to read the Scriptures, how to pray (with an example of the latter three pages long). As Ian Breward says in the introduction to his edition of this text (Grove Books, 1980), 'It was the first attempt after the Reformation to combine order and freedom in a way that demonstrated how reform and liturgy could be profoundly unitive because it was faithfully biblical.' The Liturgical Commission in 1986 was also grappling with the problem of how to combine common prayer with local freedom, and used 'The Directory' as the working title for what we now know as *Patterns for Worship* (= *PFW*) right up to the eve of publication. The word had been used before – but more recently. When *Lent, Holy Week and Easter* was published in 1984, Douglas Jones, Chairman of the Liturgical Commission, wrote in the Introduction: 'We are providing a directory from which choices may be made. We think of this book as a manual to be used with selectivity, sensitivity and imagination.' That book also included an outline service, consisting only of rubrics, for the Agape with Holy Communion. This was one of the solutions considered by the Commission in looking at combining local freedom with the tradition of common prayer, a solution trailed (with the directory name attached) in the Commission's 1985 end of quinquennium report *The Worship of the Church*.

While the problems facing the Church – and therefore the Commission – were nowhere near as great as the conflicts of the seventeenth century, they were potentially far-reaching and should not be minimized. In August 1986 Nigel McCulloch, then Bishop of Taunton, had written in the Bath and Wells Diocesan News: 'I have just been to a marvellous service. The church was nearly full . . .' It was the monthly 'Family Service', the best attended act of worship in the village. He expressed his concerns about the content ('theologically, they can be very imbalanced, and their liturgical framework is often somewhat quirky') and conduct ('Often the lay people who give the addresses are absolutely on the right wave-length. But the fact is that most of them do not have the authority of the Church of England to get up and deliver what is . . . the main sermon of the month.'). This got on to the agenda of both the House of Bishops and the Liturgical Commission, which was already beginning to consider both 'family services' and the needs of churches in Urban Priority Areas (UPAs).

The Commission had before it *For the Family*, the 1985 report of the Bishop's working party in the Diocese of Chelmsford on non-statutory worship, and the massive report of the Archbishop of Canterbury's Commission on Urban Priority Areas, *Faith in the City* (1985). That report asked for worship to 'emerge out of and reflect local cultures'; to 'be more informal and flexible in its use of urban language' and 'reflect a universality of form with local variations'. It wanted services which promote a greater involvement of the congregation in worship, and which could be embodied in short, functional service booklets or cards. 'The formal liturgies so beloved of the wider church' were to be 'complemented in UPAs by more informal and spontaneous acts of worship and witness'.

The Church of England Board of Education report, *Children in the Way* (National Society/Church House Publishing, 1988), asked the Liturgical Commission to 'examine the need for new liturgies to serve all-age worship'; there had been similar requests to successive Liturgical Commissions since at least 1965. The answer of the Commission in the 1960s was that it was not possible to produce set forms of service because the needs were so diverse, but that it might be possible to produce a selection of suitable structures, with a wide choice of material to go with them. The only tangible result of this was an excellent booklet which the Commission asked John Wilkinson to write on *Family and Evangelistic Services* in 1967.

In 1986 the Liturgical Commission approved a paper drafted by David Silk and Trevor Lloyd, which they took to the House of Bishops in June, seeking approval for the compilation of a 'Directory' which would 'provide some indication of different ways of doing liturgy, taking into account sociological, architectural and churchmanship differences; indicate where advantage might be taken of notes and rubrics in the ASB . . . ; [and] provide outline structures and mandatory sections for some main services which would provide greater freedom for those who wish either to enrich or to shorten the services (including "Family" services and worship in UPAs)'.

So in October 1986 the first meeting took place of a Commission sub-group looking at whether the needs of both the UPAs and 'family services' could be met by similar structures and resources. Chaired by Trevor Lloyd and including Jane Sinclair, Brian Spinks and Kenneth Stevenson, the group became responsible for a vast amount of material which helped to change many people's approach to worship. The first meeting discussed the relationship of 'family services' to Morning Prayer and Holy Communion, future patterns of Sunday worship, alternative structures and 'How to DIY', the lectionary, levels of language and meaning, symbols, mission and evangelism, and methods of research and consultation. Though very large amounts of liturgical text were being produced (and some of this very imaginative and creative, as in the four new eucharistic prayers in the first edition of *PFW*), the group was also well equipped academically to pursue its interest in structures, liturgical theology and education.

Inevitably, some of the group's work foreshadowed some of the issues to be handled and methods of dealing with them that emerged in the progress towards what became *CW*. For instance, formative work was done, starting with an academic historical paper by Brian Spinks, on the question of the interchangeability of Morning Prayer and the first part of Holy Communion (the simplified version is still there in *NPFW* on p. 27 as a historical background handout!). This led eventually to the flexibility of the *CW* Service of the Word and A Service of the Word with a Celebration of Holy Communion. Different members of the group took on responsibility for different areas, so Jane Sinclair took on psalms and canticles, remaining involved with that area of work right through to the eventual synodical approval of the *CW* Psalter. She, with Brian Spinks and Trevor Lloyd, joined Michael Vasey as a Commission delegation to the Roman Catholic Institute of Liturgical Formation in Ireland. One result of this was the formation of PRAXIS; another was the determination to use whatever volume resulted from the group's work as an educational tool. The first edition of *PFW* included not only a long introduction on issues around the nature of the family, reading the Bible, and constructing eucharistic prayers, but something called a Commentary. Largely compiled by Trevor Lloyd and Jane Sinclair, this provided, mainly by telling stories and without being prescriptive, some hints and tips and formational material for those who prepare worship.

Another area in which the group's work set something of a pattern for the future was that of consultation. In June–September 1988 they went to pairs of UPA parishes of differing traditions in five urban areas (Southwark, Birmingham, Newcastle, Manchester and Liverpool), observing the use of one of their experimental texts, conducting a survey and receiving comments from a wider group. The response sheets show the wide range of topics raised – alternatives to books, language levels, use of visuals, drama and symbols, and of story, shorter eucharistic prayers, simple structures. Someone in inner-city Newcastle commenting on the bland 'praise and glory' phrases of the *ASB* asked for more explicit reference to the pain of the cross, because that reflected where they were.

In this way, and through meetings with diocesan liturgical committee representatives, the texts they were working on were extensively leaked and commented on. Other people attended meetings of the group, including for several meetings the late Michael Perry, well known for his work with the Jubilate group in hymn-writing and the production of books such as *Church Family Worship* and *The Dramatised Bible*. Ecumenical input from the Roman Catholic observer on the Commission, Geoffrey Steel, resulted in the inclusion of the new Roman introductory phrases to the Lord's Prayer long before they were officially published. There was also consultation with ethnic minority leaders and those in the Board of Education who had worked on the report *Called to be Adult Disciples.* In the General Synod debate on this in November 1987 the Chairman of the Commission, Colin James, the Bishop of Winchester, said the Commission was already working on the report's request for 'material that values and celebrates the daily lives and experience of lay people' through its UPA group. Colin James was unvaryingly encouraging – in his self-confessed role of 'non-playing captain' – of the creative work going on in the Commission, and after one appallingly badly managed meeting of some members of the UPA group with the House of Bishops, involved the Bishops of Bath and Wells, Leicester and Oxford in meetings with the group. They warmly commended the work when it went to the House of Bishops for a second time in 1989: 'There is a great deal of material here which will be of real benefit to the Church.'

When the Commission's report was published in November 1989 as *Patterns for Worship* the *Daily Mail* at least recognized its radical nature, though it was the section in the introduction about Bible reading that caught its imagination: 'All those dull old Bible readings . . . aren't you sick of them? Okay swingers, let's put the snap, crackle and above all pop back into gospelling. Little Jackanory-style stories from your cosy, cuddly vicar. Nothing too long. Nothing too solemn . . .' But much more radical than the comments on reading the Bible were the Commission's proposals for outline services for the Service of the Word and for Holy Communion, Rite C, backed by a massive selection of resource texts, including four new experimental eucharistic prayers and a range of responsive thanksgivings or long prefaces.

After the General Synod debated *PFW* in February 1990, the House of Bishops was content to let the proposals for A Service of the Word (together with the creedal and penitential material which was thought to require authorization) go into the Synod process, but had doubts about Rite C, which delayed the introduction of any eucharistic material to Synod for over four years. What the Commission wanted was a structure in which to test out its approach to the Eucharist and to eucharistic prayers, alongside the continuing *ASB* provision, in sufficient time to gauge reactions before embarking on the revision of the *ASB* eucharistic material. The 1989 edition of *PFW* presented its thinking on structure not just in Rite C but in introductory material and in the 'Instructions for the Eucharist', which survive in *NPFW* as 'Planning and Preparing Holy Communion' and set out the 'deep structures' of the eucharistic prayer and its Trinitarian pattern, with only a single, post-narrative, epiclesis. It was this Trinitarian, Eastern pattern which the Commission wanted to test: all four of the new prayers were on this plan, and Trevor Lloyd's speech, eventually introducing the new prayers to Synod in 1994, made clear the difference between this and the Western pattern of the *ASB* prayers. The section in *NPFW* picks this up.

In the end, largely because the Final Approval vote was taken in a newly elected Synod which had not participated in the earlier debates, the new prayers were lost, but much else survived. Rite C re-emerged as a note to A Service of the Word and is in *NPFW* and the *CW* main volume as A Service of the Word with a Celebration of Holy Communion. And *NPFW*, like its predecessor, contains a large number of eucharistic prefaces, both long and short, with instructions on specially composed prefaces which imply that the president might begin and end the preface, with others contributing in between. There are also words for the Peace and for blessing non-communicants, and eight sample eucharistic services – more than enough to indicate that *NPFW*, like its predecessor, is not just about Services of the Word.

Patterns for Worship

The 'commended' edition of *PFW* was published in 1995 ('commended' because, as well as the volume being published with the approval of the House of Bishops, the liturgical texts were all either authorized by the Synod or commended under Canon B4 by the House). It immediately sold out, went into a number of reprints, and sold over ten thousand copies in under two years. It was remarkable in a number of ways. Superficially, it was unlike any other official worship book. The idea for its white, red, blue and yellow cover came from a Mondrian reproduction on the wall of the office of Church House Publishing manager Alan Mitchell, and captured the patterns idea well. Its sixteen Sample Services had illustrations by the cartoonist Taffy. Packs of colour off-prints of these, providing all that a congregation needed on a white A4 folded card, sold out rapidly and are still to be found in use. It also set the pattern to be followed later in *CW* of combining in one book both authorized and commended material, with no obvious distinction between them on the page. And bound up with the liturgical text was a large amount of educational material, in the section entitled 'The commentary'. There had been educational material in the service introductions in both *LHWE* and *PHG*, but this was far longer, more deliberate in its less academic approach, and capable of being used independently of the texts.

But the other remarkable thing was the way the book was organized, living up to its working title of 'The Directory'. After the Introduction, similar to that in the Synod edition, making a case for what the Liturgical Commission was doing in relation to UPAs, 'family services', common prayer and the lectionary, comes the authorized text of A Service of the Word (which has its own authorized introduction and notes), followed by instructions and guidelines for putting flesh on the bare rubrical bones of the Service of the Word skeleton. At the end of the book comes the Commentary already referred to, and Sample Services which illustrate how the material in the book can be used, as well as providing off-the-peg services for local use. In between are over a hundred and fifty pages of resource material, in sections which are in the same order as a service outline, beginning with introductions and concluding with blessings and endings. Each of these texts has a distinctive number. This may not sound revolutionary, but as well as making it possible to access and refer easily to individual texts, for example via the extensive biblical index, or to make lists of them in the order in which they might come in a service being compiled, it marked the beginning of the establishment by Church House Publishing and the Liturgical Commission of an electronic database of liturgical texts. *Electronic Patterns for Worship*, a simple text disk of the liturgical contents, easily searchable because of the numbering system, came out eighteen months later, in the same year as the first version of the Church's service compilation programme, *Visual Liturgy*, which contained material from *PFW* as well as the whole of the *ASB*, lectionary material and nearly three thousand hymns and songs. The link between *PFW* and electronic publishing had begun in a series of conversations back in 1988 between Trevor Lloyd and Dick Douglas and Tim Anderson of Hodder and Stoughton, with a view to co-publishing *PFW*, in both paper and electronic formats. In the event this came to nothing, apart from Hodder and Stoughton helping with the design work for the service cards, but resulted in the development of the computer programme *Worshipmaster* by Tim Anderson, the forerunner of the present *Visual Liturgy*.

Preparing a New Edition

Four years after publication, with the main texts for *CW* falling into place, there were still people wanting reprints of *PFW*. The Liturgical Commission discussion in late 1999, agreeing that 'it might not be helpful simply to go on reprinting the present edition when some of it (e.g. the authorized material) is out of date' considered some of the features of *PFW* to be retained in any future edition: 'the combination of teaching/training material with liturgical text, the combination of authorized and commended material in one volume, the organising of texts in a notional service item order, rather than seasonally and thematically, the provision of sample services demonstrating the principles, the provision of a substantial cross-referencing and indexing system, and a language level which is slightly simpler, more UPA and "Family Service" than some of our material'. At that point it was thought that a Times and Seasons volume, replacing *LHWE, PHG* and *ECY*, would appear at the same time, share some of the same texts and that the two might be on one CD, as well as being in *Visual Liturgy.*

After further discussion, a year later the Commission set up a sub-group to prepare a new edition of *PFW*, just as biased towards an educational approach as the earlier group. Trevor Lloyd chaired the committee responsible for delivering adult education and Reader training in the Diocese of Exeter; Andrew Burnham was about to leave the staff of St Stephen's House, Oxford, to become Bishop of Ebbsfleet; and Mark Earey was the PRAXIS National Liturgical Education Officer, later Vicar of Morley in Yorkshire. They were later joined by Peter Craig-Wild, Vicar of Mirfield, who had been responsible for planning worship at a number of major charismatic events, with Liz Simpson, who had just completed a Diploma in Higher Education and was soon to be vicar of five rural parishes in Buckinghamshire, as secretary, and Kathryn Pritchard as Editor for Church House Publishing. In keeping with the electronic expectations, most of the detailed textual work, on both commentary and liturgical text, was done by circulating texts round the group using Microsoft Word's 'track changes', with successive changes highlighted and notes added arguing for the change made: these, rather than any paper record, should probably be deposited in an archive somewhere! There was consultation with potential users (though not on the massive scale of the first edition), including letters in the church press which brought in a surprising number of replies. Those involved with ministry with children and with the deaf community, as well as people from different ethnic backgrounds, saw and commented on the text, as did the Church's Communications Unit.

Some of the major changes from the previous edition to which the Commission agreed, apart from the detailed work in conforming the liturgical texts to those in *CW,* were:

- Re-organizing, revising and supplementing the commentary, educational material so that instead of being one-third of the book it was divided up to come at the start of each of the resource sections of texts. A new major section, 'Planning for Worship', now came at the start of the book and included new material on music and on children and worship. Some of the old introduction was revised to become Parochial Church Council discussion starters and handouts, for example those on All-Age Worship on p. 43 and on Reading the Bible on p. 101.
- The Sample Services were thoroughly revised, new topics introduced from the 'Secular Calendar' the Commission was discussing (e.g. St Valentine's Day, Fathers' Day, A Service of Lament for those facing pain), and an introductory page of hints and tips for each service was provided. The services were now on two levels, some fully worked-out examples which might be used as they stand, some outlines with a few suggestions for material to insert. And one service was provided in three formats, a text for the congregation, a structure for those taking part (musicians, etc.), including the 'proper' texts for this service, and a complete text for the leader. Changing between these formats is now easily done with one mouse click for those using *Visual Liturgy.*
- Making the whole book much more user-friendly, so for instance page 1 starts 'How to use this book' and asks (like a good computer program) 'What do you want to do?' The organization of the book and the layout were far clearer, the reference numbers more discrete, and the red page edges marking the start of each section made it easier to find one's way around.
- The Resource Section themes, now appearing just inside the back cover as well as at the start of the Resource Section, were thoroughly revised and better explained, as well as being accessible though the index.

The group's interim report in early 2001 led to a Commission discussion about the relationship between this work and the emerging Times and Seasons material. It was agreed that *NPFW* should contain as much as possible of the basic resource material in Times and Seasons so that people did not have to look in two places, hoping there might be different material in one or other of the two volumes. It was important to avoid any impression that *NPFW* was a more 'low level' provision, or for evangelicals rather than catholics, or for the less literate. If part of the purpose of *NPFW* is to make liturgical material more easily accessible for those who organize family services, for example, this should introduce them to the full range of material, including material which is richer in language. *NPFW* would include secular themes such as society, family, healing. Times and Seasons focused on the nature of the liturgical season and how to celebrate it, whereas *NPFW* was about how to structure worship.

B. COMMENTARY

Planning Worship

The core of the educational material is a series of stories in each section about four imaginary churches with the initials A, B, C and D: St Anne's, a large suburban probably evangelical church, St Bartholomew's, a collection of rural villages, and St Christopher's, inner urban, nineteenth-century neo-gothic probably catholic. In the previous edition the letter D (standing for 'disaster' or 'Don't do it this way') was assigned to St David, but there were representations from the Church in Wales and churches dedicated to St David. A search revealed a suitable name: St Dodo was an eighth-century Belgian Benedictine abbot, and so far there have been no comments from our European friends. There are not many official Church of England worship books intended to produce laughter, but those leading diocesan teaching events using this material know when participants have reached St Dodo by the suppressed chuckles. People often identify with the stories, many of which are true.

As well as the stories, there is a wealth of other material, including two diagrammatic examples, showing how to construct services. There are discussion starters on the nature of worship and of common prayer, and information on the canon law relating to worship. There is more emphasis on music, both throughout the book and in the four pages beginning on p. 35, some of it written by Professor John Harper, Director of the RSCM, one of the Liturgical Commission's consultants. There is also more material on children in worship, on pp. 39ff. and elsewhere, the result of consultation with diocesan children's officers, and including material submitted by them. The section 'Preambles before the Eucharistic Prayer', containing Jewish-style questions and answers about why we are doing this, comes from the document produced by a joint Liturgical Commission–Board of Education group to introduce the draft prayer for use with children, which was one of those lost in 1996.

Resource Sections

The texts are arranged in ten sections, each preceded by commentary, notes and other material designed to improve the presentation of worship. The contents of this part of the book are clearly set out on pp. 56–8.

Gathering and Greeting, the first section, sets out the wide variety of different ways of beginning a service and helps readers understand what is going on underneath the words: 'greetings convey unspoken messages'. All of the thirty-four texts are responsive; not all of them require worshippers to have the response in front of them; and some are more clearly for all-age services:

> God is good
> **all the time.**
> All the time
> **God is good.**

Ten opening prayers conclude the section.

The introductory material to *Penitence* looks at the location of this section within the service, and how to introduce it. In response to the question 'Can forms of confession and absolution be written for special occasions?', it counsels against going beyond the twenty-two authorized forms but gives clear instructions about how to write new penitential sentences for insertion into the *Kyries*. A set of thematic invitations to confession is provided, and the suggested pairing of confessions with particular absolutions of a similar style (which was in the original edition of *PFW* but got dislocated by the synodical process) is restored. Appropriate themes and seasons are suggested and there are more examples of the *Kyrie* confession genre.

Liturgy of the Word examines the nature of the sermon, as redefined by Note 7 in A Service of the Word, and looks at ways of bringing more life into the reading of the Word. A chart makes clearer than any of the Notes in *CW* the periods of the year for which authorized readings should be followed, which vary according to whether the service is a Word Service or Holy Communion. But the meat of this section lies in the lectionary modules provided for the 'open season' when authorized readings need not be used. Mark Earey was one of the team who worked with Michael Vasey on the alternative lectionary modules which appeared in *PHG* (and in a more truncated form in *PFW*), and so when it was decided that the modular lectionary material would appear in *NPFW* rather than in Times and Seasons, it was obvious that he should take the lead in drafting this section. There are now forty-six sets of readings, some thematic (Passover and Deliverance, Time for a Feast), some focused on people (Noah, Women in the messianic time), some providing an opportunity for an in-depth study of a book or part of a book of the Bible. Each module lasts from four to eight weeks and provides Old Testament, Psalm, New Testament and Gospel, together with a response on the theme, which might be used as a greeting or part of a responsory during the course of readings.

Psalms and Canticles has some good imaginative material in the stories, and also for example in the section on saying the Psalms. As the Notes make clear, there is no attempt to provide a complete set of psalms and canticles, which would simply have duplicated what is available elsewhere in *CW*. Rather, in keeping with the book's educational intent, they have been chosen to demonstrate a variety of style and presentation, and to open the door of the imagination to local creativity. So for Psalm 34 and for three of the canticles a number of different versions are included. Some are excerpts with responses (including dialogue as well as refrain), some are metrical paraphrases in a variety of styles – hymn, folk song, Celtic style, chorus. This is all designed to help and encourage those who wish to see the use of the Psalter, in whatever version, kept at the heart of Anglican worship.

Creeds and Affirmations of Faith has some suggestions about which creeds or affirmations to use on what occasions, and some discussion on the role of creeds in worship. The texts, as in the 1995 edition, are those which went through the 1993 Service of the Word and Affirmations of Faith Revision Committee, subsequently conformed to *CW*. They fall into two groups. First the historic creeds, including a responsive version of the Nicene Creed where the responses get shorter as it builds towards a climax, and the question and answer version of the Apostles' Creed used when the Pope visited Canterbury Cathedral in 1982. Second, authorized Affirmations of Faith, including the shorter alternative responsive baptismal creed, a translation (originally drafted by Michael Vasey) of the christological portion of the Athanasian Creed, and several creedal excerpts from Scripture which had appeared in a similar form in *Church Family Worship*, edited by Michael Perry, in 1986. The one from Ephesians 3 was added by the Revision Committee. The Liturgical Commission in 1989 had some discussion about creedal hymns and felt that none were close enough to the text to be considered for authorization, and so Trevor Lloyd commissioned Bishop Timothy Dudley-Smith to write a metrical version of the Apostles' Creed, and 'We believe in God the Father' was duly written at Ruan Minor that August.

The section on *Prayers* includes clear instructions on how to construct and lead the intercessions, how to compose a collect, and reproduces the guidelines on language followed by the Liturgical Commission in working on this material since 1987. The UPA and all-age worship background to some of this occasionally created differences of opinion with those who preferred a more traditional, classical liturgical style, and the Commission had some detailed textual discussion on some texts (not only in this section) which appeared both in this volume and in the drafts of Times and Seasons. The Commission concluded:

> In variant readings of 'tree' or 'cross' . . . 'rule' or 'kingdom' the appropriateness of the text for 'Patterns' and 'Times and Seasons' would reflect the different ethos in which the two books would be used. The principle of

allowing variation of translation and phrasing of the same text . . . was endorsed.

An interesting side issue here was the increased sensitivity to issues of inclusivity, which led to a change to an authorized *CW Pastoral Services* text, in the litany beginning 'Jesus, bread from heaven', which says 'you gave the man born blind the gift of sight and opened the eyes of his faith; bring those in darkness . . .', and in *NPFW* now says 'you gave the man born blind the gift of sight: open the eye of faith and bring us from darkness . . .'

The section includes sung responses, with music from Taizé and Iona. The Liturgical Commission had wanted more music in the Psalms and Canticles section, but that proved impossible to do without making the book even more expensive. The thoroughly revised section of responsive intercessions and litanies illustrates how to start from different bases, from Scripture or the sayings of Jesus, from the Church's year, or from the world situation:

In a world of change and hope,
of fear and adventure:
faithful God,
glorify your name.

The *Praise and Thanksgiving* section includes short acclamations (with instructions on how to use them and how to invent more), praise responses (with alternate lines sung or spoken by the congregation), short prefaces and longer thanksgivings. Many of the latter are eucharistic in style, and there are instructions both about how to use them as longer prefaces according to which eucharistic prayer is being used, and also about using specially composed thanksgivings.

The stories in the section on *The Peace*, and the paragraph on what it is for, show that there is still more for many congregations to explore, theologically and spiritually, about what, superficially, might seem a simple action. And many will welcome the paragraph on 'How to stop the Peace'! Forty-two sets of introductory words on a wide variety of themes follow, almost all with Bible references.

Action and Movement includes discussion about symbols, processions and the distribution of communion, with some suggestions for training those authorized to do so and the words of the relevant Canon and Regulation. Texts are provided for dedicating church officers and leaders.

Conclusion indicates how to follow the rubric in A Service of the Word, 'The service should have a clear ending'. There is more new material here, with a clear distinction between closing prayers for a Word Service and those for the Eucharist, sets of final acclamations, and sixty blessings. Some of the latter are solemn three-part ones, and some come from *CWPE*.

Sample Services

The final section of the book is 140 pages of services using the outlines and the resource material, illustrating the principles discussed earlier in the book. Some are eucharistic, some are Services of the Word, some are for regular use, some seasonal, some for single occasions such as St Valentine's Day. Interesting issues in compiling services abound. Do you major on Valentine or the theme of love (and how are we to be realistic, earthy and spiritual about that without offending)? How justified are we in simply going along with the secular calendar culture? The slightly tongue-in-cheek 'words of introduction' suggested for this service are: 'This is the day when we celebrate the martyrdom of St Valentine . . . There is nothing to connect his death with the choosing of a "Valentine" of the opposite sex, other than that it coincided with a rather jolly Roman pagan festival in mid-February.' How do you put a service for Mothering Sunday together and avoid on the one hand accusations of sexism, unreal expectations of the role of a wife in marriage today, and implying that you can put things right with (necessarily!) cheap gifts, and on the other, of ducking these issues and offending another range of people by focusing on the Blessed Virgin? Any ideas for a range of suitable liturgically symbolic gifts for fathers in a Fathers' Day service? And how do you organize occasions like this without excluding the single and the bereaved from worship?

This is where the page or so of introduction for each service comes into its own with creative suggestions. One thing the sub-group discussed (and the Liturgical Commission agreed) was the need for an interactive website associated with the book, where issues like these could be discussed, and a range of further services could be made available. It is hoped that *Visual Liturgy* and its website will provide the way forward for this in the next few years. The *Visual Liturgy 4* database contains practically the whole of *NPFW*. Individual resource items can be found by typing the *NPFW* code number into the browser. The sample services and the entire resource sections are all available in the list of templates. And all the introductory and educational material is easily available under the help menu, to encourage its use in local training courses.

David Stancliffe, Bishop of Salisbury and Chairman of the Liturgical Commission when *NPFW* was being produced, reviews in his Preface to the book the needs which have remained the same through all the changes in worship since work began on this in 1986:

> the need to explore different ways of recognizing and celebrating the presence of God in worship, the need to maintain the unity of the Church while doing so, the need to train more people to share in the planning and preparation of worship, and the need to enjoy God in worship in such a way that others are attracted and join in.

Further Reading

Colin Buchanan and Trevor Lloyd, *Six Eucharistic Prayers as Proposed in 1996,* Grove Worship Series 136, Grove Books, Cambridge, 1996.

Mark Earey, *Producing Your Own Orders of Service,* Church House Publishing, London, 2000.

David Hebblethwaite, *Liturgical Revision in the Church of England 1984–2004,* Alcuin-GROW Joint Liturgical Study 57, Grove Books, Cambridge, 2004.

Trevor Lloyd, Jane Sinclair and Michael Vasey, *Introducing Patterns for Worship,* Grove Worship Series 111, Grove Books, Nottingham, 1990.

Trevor Lloyd, *A Service of the Word,* Grove Worship Series 151, Grove Books, Cambridge, 1999.

Michael Perham (ed.), *The Renewal of Common Prayer,* SPCK/Church House Publishing, London, 1993.

Michael Perham, *New Handbook of Pastoral Liturgy,* SPCK, London, 2000.

Tim Stratford, *Using Common Worship – Service of the Word*, Church House Publishing, London, 2002.

Visual Liturgy 4.0 for Common Worship, Church House Publishing, London, 2003.

John Wilkinson, *Family and Evangelistic Services,* Church Information Office, London, 1967.

Chapter 5

The Additional Collects

The Liturgical Commission constituted in 2000 did not have revision of the collects in its original brief. However, it was widely known that the collects in *CW* were unpopular in many circles. Their compilers had attempted to use the original *BCP* collects as a starting basis wherever possible. This had resulted in a collection that preserved much of the syntax of the original. In particular, the compilers had decided to restore the use of the relative clause, which the *ASB* had removed. Traditional collects had tended to begin with a relative clause referring to God before continuing with a petition, as for example, 'O Almighty God, who alone canst order the unruly wills and affections of sinful men: Grant . . .' (*BCP* Collect for the Fourth Sunday after Easter). Thus, although the vocabulary of the *CW* collects was contemporary, its use of syntax was not.

In fairness to the *CW* compilers, much of the criticism levelled at the language of *ASB* had focused on its collects. In particular, the removal by the *ASB* of the relative clause from collects that had originally contained one was regarded as both brutal and unnecessary. So in restoring instances of the relative clause and by adopting a conservative modernization of the *BCP* originals, the compilers of the *CW* collects had intended to correct an infelicity. However, they probably had not reckoned with the effect of twenty years of using the *ASB* in public worship. The *CW* collects were authorized from the First Sunday in Advent, 1997. The Collect for that Sunday was little changed from its *ASB* predecessor, being closely akin to the *BCP* original. However, the following Sunday rendered this:

> O Lord, raise up, we pray, your power
> and come among us,
> and with great might succour us,
> that whereas, through our sins and wickedness
> we are grievously hindered
> in running the race that is set before us,
> your bountiful grace and mercy
> may speedily help and deliver us;
> through Jesus Christ your Son our Lord,
> to whom with you and the Holy Spirit
> be honour and glory, now and for ever.

This language jarred in a number of contexts. Many parishes had become used to the contemporary style of the *ASB*, so felt this to be an unnecessary relapse into archaism. Inner-city parishes that had criticized the language of the *ASB* as being inaccessible to those of a non-book culture regarded the language of this and other collects in the collection as complete gobbledegook. To the ears of many, a linguistic miscalculation had been made. Rendering a sixteenth-century prayer into contemporary language must involve a shift of syntax, not merely of vocabulary, or the result risks sounding like the literary equivalent of mock Tudor architecture.

As further parts of the *CW* corpus were produced and authorized, it was clear that the collects (and perhaps the Psalter) were the only parts of the new material to suffer from this tendency. So just over eight months after the complete authorization of *CW*, the General Synod found itself debating a Diocesan Synod motion from Wakefield, which stated: 'That this Synod, in the light of criticisms of the new collects for *Common Worship*, request the House of Bishops to commission additional collects for each Sunday and Feast Day in the Liturgical Year in a worthy contemporary idiom.' Although various features of the collects were aired during the debate, the archaic syntax (and the use of the relative clause in particular) came in for most criticism. The motion was carried comfortably, so the Liturgical Commission found itself having to produce an alternative to liturgy that was barely three years old.

Each year the Liturgical Commission meets with members of the various diocesan liturgical committees to consult and communicate with those who run training programmes at local level. In the autumn meeting of 2001, Mark Earey, then Liturgical Training Officer for PRAXIS, circulated a questionnaire aimed at compiling the various criticisms being levelled at the existing *CW* collects. This was later published by *News of Liturgy*, and provoked a flurry of respondents. Although this was not a scientific piece of fieldwork, it provided the framers of the new compilation with much useful anecdotal evidence of the kind of criticisms being levelled. Once again, the archaic syntax of the *CW* collects came in for chief criticism, although their vocabulary was also regarded as inaccessible. Some people regretted the passing of the 'thematic' collects of the *ASB* throughout the year. These had disappeared with the adoption of the Revised Common Lectionary, which is largely non-thematic.

The Liturgical Commission was duly asked by the House of Bishops to draw up additional collects according to the Synod motion. The Commission established a sub-group to produce a draft text for consideration. Their first task was to clarify in what ways the new collects were to be different from those already in existence. It was here that the questionnaire proved most useful. Clearly there was a need for collects that used more contemporary vocabulary and syntax. There was also a desire that the new collects should be shorter in length, as the decision to include the full doxology at the end of all the *CW* collects had been heavily criticized, both in the Synod debate and in the questionnaire. The group examined a number of possible texts that could have acted as sources. These included the existing Roman Catholic Sunday collects, the recently produced Joint Liturgical Group collection *Opening Prayers*, and the collects recently authorized for the Anglican Church in Aotearoa/New Zealand. The last collection, in particular, was of interest as it contained three collects for each Sunday, each with a different linguistic register. The job of producing liturgy becomes much simpler if existing sources can be either used directly or adapted.

However, after much consideration, the sub-group decided that none of the possible texts available exactly suited the task that was emerging. The Roman Catholic collects were regarded as too terse for an Anglican context. The Joint Liturgical Group's collection tended to use the *ASB* method of rendering the relative clause as a direct statement about God addressed to God ('O God, you . . .'). This had been a much criticized aspect of the *ASB* collects, so there was a reluctance to re-adopt this approach in a new set. The New Zealand collects often came closest to what seemed to be needed, but sometimes the language was so terse and direct that there was a risk it would reduce the breadth of appeal. For example:

> God our light,
> make your Church like a rainbow
> shining and proclaiming to all the world
> that the storm is at an end
> there is peace for those who seek it
> and love for the forgiving.
> (Second Collect for Lent 3)

As we can see, it was possible to learn from the New Zealand collection how to use scriptural language and imagery with imagination. However, for some, the result was too concrete in comparison to the more allusive language of classic Anglican collects. There is a danger in collects (and all short prayers) that concrete references can end up in prescriptive moralizing or rather vacuous didacticism, such as occurs in the following example:

> Jesus, as we travel far and fast,
> lead our minds back to the wise men following your star,
> and forward to the day
> when all will see your shining star.
> (First Collect for the Feast of the Epiphany)

Of course, there is a place for troubling, questioning and challenging language in prayers. However, the Collect, which concludes the Gathering of the Eucharist and is repeated in the offices throughout the week, is probably not the right place for this.

The sub-group also had to struggle with the more typical linguistic issues that surround collects. Should they always have the recognizable collect structure, including the relative clause? Should there always be a Trinitarian doxology to conclude? Despite one or two questionnaires to the contrary, the voices raised against the doxology were overwhelming. The *CW* collects had printed it in as an attempt to encourage its use, even though it was never mandatory. This grew from a renewed commitment to reflect Trinitarian theology in contemporary liturgy. However, it could conversely be argued that if this was merely a case of representing the Holy Trinity as a liturgical formula, the job had not really been adequately attempted. Indeed, merely using a formula was in danger of undermining the possibility of expressing a dynamic view of the Trinity through the language of contemporary prayer. The sub-group experimented with a number of approaches to the relative clause (including complete removal). Only with time, and many redrafts, was it possible to achieve some kind of consensus of policy, and then one that reflected a compromise between various competing concerns.

The sub-group's work was complete by May 2002 as it submitted a draft to the Liturgical Commission. It was clear that further redrafting was necessary at that time as the style of the collects varied widely, depending to some extent on the author of the original. However, the sub-group had performed a vital function in helping the Commission to determine the trajectory of the project. The key decision was to compose from scratch. This made the task much more difficult than one of revising from existing sources, but on the other hand it avoided the pitfall of having to evaluate the fidelity of the text in reference to some kind of benchmark (for example, the *BCP*). With totally new collects, it was possible to evaluate them as they stood. In addition, by incorporating a wide range of stylistic approaches, the sub-group's draft helped the Commission to get a clear idea of the parameters (stylistic and structural) within which it was prepared to work.

Given the scale of the task of writing entirely from scratch, it was decided that the Commission should interpret the House of Bishops' mandate to include Sundays and Principal Feast Days in the *temporale*, but not to embark on additional collects for Saints' Days. To do so would have protracted the task considerably, and it was felt that the Synod would prefer to have the new collects available for Sundays earlier than to wait longer for a fuller set.

It took a further year of revision by members of the Commission before a text was ready for submission to the House of Bishops and thence to the Synod. By this time, the parameters shaping the composition were clear, and were summarized in the introduction to the Synod text (GS 1493) thus:

- the collects are, in general, significantly shorter than those contained in *Common Worship*
- on the occasions when the relative clause is used, attention has been paid to the need for brevity
- use of the vocative case (O God . . .) has been avoided

- use of archaisms in both syntax and language has been strongly avoided
- the use of a closing Trinitarian doxology has been dropped except in a few significant cases, but the use of an essentially Trinitarian framework governing the structure of the prayer has been used in a number of instances
- contemporary imagery and directness of language has been encouraged and adopted in many cases, without the concomitant pitfall of being so over-direct that the prayer fails to apply 'across the board' and so to perform its function as 'collecting' the prayers of all the people
- when direct language is encouraged, there is a related need to avoid sermonising or moralising in the prayer.

It was equally important to state what was different about the new set. These new collects were to be:

- short
- simple in their syntax
- vivid and interesting in their themes and imagery
- accessible in the kind of language they use, and
- to end up by saying something which is clear and distinct.

One linguistic issue that surfaced in the writing of the collects was the use of the vocative case ('O God', 'O Christ'). When God is addressed at the start of a collect, the classic approach is to use the vocative. However, many had objected to this tendency in the *CW* collects as another example of archaism. In the main, *CW* makes little use of the vocative elsewhere, although, interestingly, it was reintroduced at the Gospel acclamations of the Eucharist, where the *ASB* had none. Modern worship has not entirely eschewed the use of the vocative. Many contemporary worship songs use it in abundance, although it is very common to see it spelt 'oh' on many locally produced OHP slides and computer projections, so it could be that its significance is being increasingly misunderstood. Given that the *CW* collection was not being replaced by the new collects, the Commission was at liberty to adopt a more rigorously contemporary approach with the new set, and so use of the vocative was avoided. This policy added somewhat to the complexity of how to compose the opening of a collect. The creative example set by the Church of Aotearoa/New Zealand assisted in this regard.

The Synod overwhelmingly welcomed the approach adopted in the Commission's draft, passing it through to revision stage. The Revision Committee had to tackle a number of suggestions. One important point, made by the Revd Dr Peter Williams, was that there was insufficient emphasis upon the atonement in the Commission's draft. This involved the insertion of two new collects, and the revision of some others. A suggestion from the Revd Tim Stratford for a single collect to mark a season was also accepted (he had previously raised this possibility in a Grove booklet: Colin Buchanan, Mark Earey,

Gilly Myers and Tim Stratford, *Collects: An Alternative View*, Grove Worship Series 171, Cambridge, 2002, p. 21).

An amusing discussion centred on the use of the term 'Magi' in the Collect for the Epiphany. After some discussion, the Liturgical Commission had decided on this term rather than the traditional 'Wise Men'. This was primarily due to advice received from the Revd Dr John Nolland at Trinity College, Bristol, who had pointed out that the use of the term 'Wise Men' in the Authorized Version of the Bible was inventive and not supported by contemporary scholarship. 'Wisdom' was not implied by the Greek title *magoi*, nor was it the point being emphasized by the Gospel-writer. In addition, although in all probability the *magoi* in question were very likely to have been men, inserting it seemed a somewhat unnecessary emphasis of male roles, rather against the spirit of the Commission's report *Making Women Visible*. (Perhaps it was a case of 'making men unnecessarily visible'.) After much discussion, 'Magi' won the day. However, the somewhat tongue-in-cheek summary of these discussions in the Revision Committee's report (GS 1493Y, paragraph 33: 'The Committee has retained "Magi" on the grounds that the visitors were not necessarily wise and not necessarily men') was seized by the media when the collects gained final approval in February 2004.

Of more interest and concern was the way a number of conservative Evangelical members of the Synod took issue with the use of imagery that made use of 'liturgical time'. This was particularly the case in the draft text of the Collect for Advent 4, which had originally run:

> Eternal God,
> as we wait with Mary for the coming of your Son,
> bring us through the birth-pangs of our present age
> to see, with her, our great salvation
> in Jesus Christ our Lord.

This was a bit too close to the Marian bone for some. However, there also seemed to be a difficulty in accepting the double horizon of eschatological expectation that is intrinsic to the focus of Advent. It would appear that for some in the Church, 'reliving' is not something one considers doing in liturgy. This was an unfortunate line for the Committee to take, as it can be a powerful way of utilizing the biblical imagery in a collect to forge a link between what was done then and what is being done now. The collect was rephrased to make more explicit what was being done, but at the expense of some didacticism creeping in:

> Eternal God,
> as Mary waited for the birth of your Son,
> so we wait for his coming in glory;
> bring us through the birth pangs of this present age

to see, with her, our great salvation
in Jesus Christ our Lord.

Other Synod members clearly took issue with the approach to liturgy that emphasizes metaphor and trades on the ambiguity of some biblical imagery. A number of submissions tried to 'tie down' scriptural allusions to a clear meaning by adopting a 'this means that' approach. In general, the Revision Committee resisted this, as all the suggestions for rephrasing lengthened the collect considerably. The issue at stake was the degree to which the Church is prepared to allow the language of prayer to retain simplicity and ambiguity permitting this to be food for the spiritual imagination. It would appear that for some, prayer used in liturgy should permit no variation of possible meaning or flexibility of interpretation. What sort of spirituality this approach would engender in the long run one can only imagine.

A number of the Synod responses indicated a concern to iron out any form of language that could be considered archaic. However, the Revision Committee made very few changes to the original text. There is a difference between an archaic form of language considered as an entire linguistic register (such as the *CW* collects chose to use) and instances of individual words which in some contexts seem archaic. Contemporary language sometimes uses archaisms for emphasis or to enhance imagery. Examples of words that were retained, despite submissions for a change, were 'kindle', 'banish', 'estranged', 'crooked' and 'hosts'; but the Revision Committee correctly altered 'tokens' and 'keep us mindful'.

The Committee's discussions of these kinds of submission show how fine the line is between language which is contemporary yet beautiful and language which is contemporary and flat. Beauty in language requires the willingness to risk both ambiguity and archaism in the interests of conveying something powerful with precision and brevity. The collects are probably the most demanding of all prayers in this respect, especially given the desire that these should be prayers which 'collect' the general intentions of everyone without succumbing to blandness or 'genericization'.

The revised text was debated by the Synod in July 2003 and received Final Approval in February 2004. The Church of England now has a choice of four authorized collects for each Sunday and Principal Feast Day. These are the *BCP* collects, the *CW* contemporary language and *CW* traditional language collects, and the Additional Collects. These cover a huge range of linguistic styles and registers. The choice of which collect to use in a service from *CW* is at the discretion of the minister. The Additional Collects are perhaps one of the most extensive exercises in original composition for the Liturgical Commission to embark upon in recent years. As such they provide a useful historical marker in the development of the language of English liturgy at the start of the second millennium.

Chapter 6

Rites on the Way

A. HISTORY

As the history of initiation rites in general has already been outlined in the relevant chapter of the first volume of this work, this account will note only those aspects that relate directly to the background of Rites on the Way.

The Early Church

The catechumenate is the name given to the process of formation and discipleship, moving a new follower of Christ from initial belief, through a period of probation, to full participation within the worshipping community. It focuses on the development of discipline, in prayer, study of Scripture, and in leading a godly life. It is not clear from the New Testament whether the first Christian believers expected new converts to undertake a period of preparation prior to baptism, but Acts 8.35 and 19.5 imply some exposition of the Scriptures before a profession of faith in Jesus as Lord, followed by baptism. Certainly by the beginning of the third century in many places the Church had developed an extended process of proselytizing and making new disciples that involved instruction and frequent prayer, fasting and vigils prior to baptism.

By the fourth century the period of final preparation for baptism coincided with the season of Lent, and in addition to regular instruction it included a liturgical rite at the initial enrolment of the candidates and periodic ceremonies, including exorcism, during the weeks leading up to baptism at Easter, which had now become the normative occasion for its administration. In the baptismal homilies that have survived from this era, several principal catechetical themes can be discerned. Among them was Jesus' obedience to God in receiving the baptism of repentance from John the Baptist. By this obedience, Jesus was enabled to conquer sin and changed the nature of baptism by his anointing with the Spirit. Another was the transformation wrought by the beginning of a new life in Christ through the waters of baptism (Romans 6.2–5). This brought about an indelible mark and a changed life. Fourth-century teaching also saw the waters of baptism as a cleansing bath of regeneration. Finally, cognisant faith was the prerequisite for baptism, which, as a gift from God, led to the adoption of the candidates as children of God.

Sadly, however, the high ideals of the preaching were to some extent compromised by actual practice. Less rigorous scrutiny was commonly made into the motives and conduct of potential candidates for baptism than had been the case in earlier centuries; and many would delay their baptism almost indefinitely, becoming in effect perpetual catechumens, so that they could still retain the opportunity of receiving through baptism forgiveness for any sins they might commit, at least until serious illness caused them to fear missing their chance altogether and dying unbaptized.

Medieval Developments

From the fifth century onwards a transition gradually occurred from adult initiation to the baptism of children as the norm. The same fear that had caused people to hold back from receiving the forgiveness from sins until later in life now caused people to seek baptism for infants lest they die without the sign of salvation. Because of the high risk of infant mortality, this led to baptisms taking place throughout the year, often within days of birth. As a result, the catechumenate as such disappeared, although many of its ceremonies were retained and incorporated into the baptismal rite itself. In the West, the practice of the Church of Rome, whereby the final post-baptismal anointing was reserved to the bishop alone and performed at a later date in cases when he himself was not present at the baptism, became universal. Known as confirmation, this could happen weeks, months or increasingly commonly years after baptism in the vast dioceses of northern Europe, where the difficulties of travelling and the distraction of other episcopal responsibilities made parish visitations infrequent.

Because children were still admitted to communion immediately after baptism, even when confirmation was separated from the baptismal rite, parents often neglected the duty of presenting their children for confirmation. Attempts were made by various church councils to set a maximum age by which it had to be done – often five or seven years – and they imposed penalties on parents who failed to comply. However, this resulted in that particular age being regarded as the norm, and the tendency to defer confirmation until then was encouraged by the emergence of a theology of confirmation which regarded it as a rite conferring additional grace on the candidates, who were thereby strengthened in their faith to face the uncertainties and temptations of the sinful world as they grew older. In the late Middle Ages scruples over babies being able to consume the eucharistic bread reverently led to their being communicated from the chalice alone, and the subsequent withdrawal of the chalice from the laity as a whole, because of similar scruples about drops of the precious blood being spilled, had the consequence of young children generally being denied communion at all at least until they reached what was regarded as 'the age of discretion', which might be before or after confirmation.

The Reformation

Although some of the sixteenth-century Reformers abolished confirmation altogether because they judged that it lacked any scriptural warrant, others retained it as a rite in which children could 'confirm' for themselves the faith in which they had been baptized as infants. The Church of England took the latter course and, in common with other Reformed traditions that retained confirmation, required instruction in the faith as a prerequisite participation in the rite, creating in effect a kind of post-baptismal catechumenate. At the end of the baptism service the godparents were charged to take care that the child was brought to the bishop to be confirmed as soon as he or she could recite the Creed, the Lord's Prayer and the Ten Commandments and be instructed in the Catechism; and the confirmation service included the direction that the clergy were to provide instruction in the Catechism on Sundays and Holy Days in conjunction with Evening Prayer. The medieval English practice of only admitting children to communion once they had been confirmed (which had been introduced at the Council of Lambeth in 1281 in order to encourage candidates to come forward for confirmation) was retained in the *BCP*, although with a concession introduced into the 1662 version that they might be admitted if they were 'ready and desirous to be confirmed' – reflecting the situation in the period of the Commonwealth when there had been no bishops to conduct confirmations.

Modern Developments

The most developed form of liturgical material for the catechumenate currently available is the Roman Catholic Rite of Christian Initiation of Adults (RCIA), which has its origins in French missionary work in India and West Africa. Recognizing the disparity between those enquirers exploring Christianity for the first time and those who regularly met for worship on a Sunday morning, the missionaries developed small groups to accompany new disciples, and special liturgies for the journey from conversion to baptism. A European conference on the catechumenate was first held in 1969, drawing together representatives from many European countries, including Anglicans. The RCIA was published in English in 1974 and proved an inspiration, not just for missionary and catechumenal work in the Roman Catholic Church, but also for Christians around the world. The Lutheran Church, particularly in the USA and Canada, the Anglican Church in Australia and ECUSA have been among those active in forming catechumenal networks and publishing resources to accompany the Way of Christ.

As church membership declines, knowledge of Christianity derived from the educational system decreases, and the pool of 'returners' to the Church shrinks, there has been a growing recognition in the Church of England that mission and faith development must be resourced more fully. Alpha, Emmaus and other courses have proved very effective in making Christians, but there is a further task, once people have declared their faith, of making disciples who are integrated into church. The absence from the *ASB* of a revised Catechism had been noted, and the task of drafting a possible text was remitted to the Board of Education of the Church of England (with representation from the Liturgical Commission). The resulting *New Revised Catechism* (1990) met with much criticism, and this underlined the need for a new approach. Following the debate on *Christian Initiation Matters* (GS 983) in July 1991, the Board of Education, the Board of Mission and the Liturgical Commission met together to prepare a paper on patterns of nurture, including the catechumenate. This was published as *On the Way: Towards an Integrated Approach to Christian Initiation* (GS Misc 444) in 1995. This report saw sacramental rites not as isolated transactions but rather as integrated within a series of stages of faith development. It proposed that rites which would support the spiritual journey of individuals and enable the church community to support and learn from their journey should be made available for optional use.

Draft rites prepared by the Liturgical Commission for baptism and confirmation were published as GS 1152, *Initiation Services: A Report by the Liturgical Commission* (1995), and preliminary proposals for supporting rites in 1998 as GS Misc 530, *Rites on the Way: Work in Progress.* The untimely death of the primary drafter of these latter rites, Michael Vasey, left the process in limbo, and further work on *Rites on the Way* was not taken up by the Liturgical Commission until the next quinquennium of the General Synod, 2000 to 2005. *Rites on the Way* was brought back to the Synod in revised form in July 2004, and commended by the House of Bishops in January 2005.

In preparing the present texts, the Commission was informed by the experience of those who had made use of the drafts contained in GS Misc 530, and consultation on the texts was extensive. It profited from discussions with those engaged in work with children and with those working on forms of the catechumenate within the Church of England. The texts also draw on material from other parts of the Anglican Communion and other churches, especially the RCIA.

Admission to Communion before Confirmation

During the twentieth century, the commonly received understanding that confirmation was the precondition for receiving communion gradually changed, initially in other Christian Churches and in other parts of the Anglican Communion, beginning with ECUSA. In 1968 the Lambeth Conference asked the Provinces of the Anglican Communion to examine the theology of initiation and admission to communion. There was clearly some disparity in practice, particularly around confirmation and the giving of communion to the baptized. In England, the 1971 Ely Report, *Christian Initiation: Birth and Growth in the Christian Society,* moved the discussion further, stating that baptism was complete sacramental initiation, and recommending that adults and children should be admitted to communion on that basis. In 1982 the Faith and Order Commission of the World Council of

Churches meeting in Lima reported: 'Those churches which baptise children but refuse them a share in the Eucharist before such a rite (i.e. confirmation) may wish to ponder whether they have fully appreciated and accepted the consequence of baptism.'

In the Church of England the Knaresborough Report in 1985, *Communion before Confirmation*, returned to the subject and concluded that regulations should be approved to permit the admission of the baptized to communion before confirmation. The General Synod took note of the report, but did nothing more. However, many dioceses, including Manchester, Peterborough and Southwark, had already been experimenting with admission to communion for the baptized but unconfirmed. Research by the Knaresborough working group found that a substantial majority of the parishes concerned were convinced of the positive value of admitting children to communion before confirmation. Following a debate on *Christian Initiation Matters* (GS 983) in July 1991, the General Synod affirmed the 'traditional sequence of Baptism, Confirmation, admission to Communion as normative', but 'accepted that within that sequence Confirmation can take place at an earlier age when it is deemed appropriate by the parish priest and the bishop'. An amendment seeking to discontinue the experimental admission to communion before confirmation was, however, defeated.

The International Anglican Liturgical Consultation had affirmed its support for the admission of all the baptized to communion in the report arising out of its first meeting in Boston, Massachusetts in 1985 (*Nurturing Children in Communion*, ed. Colin Buchanan, Grove Liturgical Study 44, Nottingham, Grove Books, 1985). When it met in Toronto in 1991 to discuss Christian Initiation, it debated whether the traditional Anglican sequence had encouraged baptized children to be treated as if they were only catechumens, and whether cultural factors could continue to be used to exclude children from the Eucharist. Its Statement, 'Walk in Newness of Life' (published in *Christian Initiation in the Anglican Communion*, ed. David Holeton, Grove Worship Series 118, Nottingham, Grove Books, 1991), put forward seven principles of Christian initiation, including the following:

> baptism is the complete sacramental initiation and leads to participation in the eucharist. Confirmation and other rites of affirmation have a continuing pastoral role in the renewal of faith among the baptised but are in no way to be seen as a completion of baptism or as necessary for admission to communion.

A step forward was taken in the Church of England with the publication in 1997 of the *Guidelines Agreed by the House of Bishops on the Admission of Baptized Persons to Holy Communion before Confirmation* (GS Misc 488). These encouraged parishes to review their patterns of initiation and consider various options, including admitting children to communion at an earlier age while reserving confirmation as an adult commitment at around the age of eighteen, but not precluding the continuation of confirmation at a younger age. These guidelines represent the current position of the Church of England on this issue, although there are signs of possible further debate.

Because a number of parishes had been experimenting with the admission of children to communion prior to confirmation for quite some time, a wide diversity of practice, of mixed quality, had been developing. In response to this, the Liturgical Commission offered draft texts for the Admission of the Baptized to Communion before Confirmation in *Rites on the Way*, 1998. These included resources for use at the greeting, the intercessions, a collect, proper preface, post communion and dismissal. However, because of the untimely death of Michael Vasey, who chaired the group, these texts were not finished. The Liturgical Commission resumed work on the texts in 2001, and wide consultation was made among the experimenting congregations before the texts were included within Rites on the Way.

B. COMMENTARY

An editorial decision was made to publish *Rites on the Way* not only as a separate booklet but also interspersed within the new edition of *CW Initiation Services* in 2005. The rites are therefore divided between those that are intended to be used either with children, their parents or with adult catechumens before the sacrament of initiation, and those that follow initiation. The new initiation volume follows this chronological journey from Thanksgiving for the Gift of a Child through the Welcome, the Call and the preparatory material for learning groups and individuals. Guidance for using *Rites on the Way* in a seasonal pattern for those who can answer for themselves is included, followed by Baptism and the seasonal material that accompanies it. The Frequently Asked Questions from the initial Initiation volume of 1998 are also included, and then the rite of Admission of the Baptized to Communion, since that follows baptism, but precedes confirmation. The episcopal rite of baptism and confirmation and the seasonal and supplementary texts which accompany that are as printed in the 1998 *CW* Initiation volume.

The concluding texts of Rites on the Way include a Celebration and Thanksgiving for Baptism or other rites marking initiation or Reception into the Church of England. Affirmation of Baptismal Faith and Reception into Communion with the Church of England may be led by local ministers, and are placed after the primary rites of baptism and confirmation, as rites that appropriate the blessings of baptism. The final part of the book, rites recovering baptism, concludes with rites of reconciliation, the healing services from *Common Worship: Pastoral Services*, and a commentary.

Three themes in particular are central to the ethos underlying Rites on the Way: journey, story and way. They are taken from those particular themes identified in *On the Way*, and were also central in the development of the initiation services. The telling of that story is strongly encouraged within Rites on the Way, not just in the rites themselves through testimony, but also within learning groups. The success of small groups as a means to adult learning is well documented, and the formation of groups in which new disciples can learn from one another and from others in the Christian community is a natural extension of evangelistic programmes such as Alpha. Thanksgiving for Baptism is suggested as the natural time for the learning group to finish or to change its emphasis.

If these rites offer a framework to help new disciples find their feet in our shared Christian life, they also aid all God's people in exploring the identity and calling that are ours in Christ. If they are used well, the Church as a whole will learn from the lives of those who are new to the Way. For many churches this will require a change in ethos: no longer do we expect new disciples to come and sit at our feet, but there is an expectation that we all journey together. For some churches with a dearth of new disciples, Rites on the Way may never be used; other churches may find the challenge implicit within the rites is too threatening to their traditional model of being church.

Using Rites on the Way

The interspersal of the Rites on the Way between the other authorized and commended initiation services is intended to encourage a sense that they should be used to accompany the journey of faith, from initial exploration to commitment. They celebrate in the formal setting of a church service or learning group the deepening relationship between the new disciple and God. They also acknowledge the emergent relationship of trust and love that is developing between the new disciple and the church community. While as Christians we share a common Way, the journey is different for every believer, and the rites should be used judiciously with that in mind. The experience of those using the Roman Catholic catechumenate RCIA material has been that when a church adopts the ethos of the model, and lightly adapts it within the local context, it is of enormous benefit.

The need for sensitivity in our ecumenical relationships is explored briefly in the Rites on the Way commentary material. The out-working of the Anglican–Methodist Covenant is not yet so clear that the Church of England understands how to handle the requirement for episcopal confirmation. Thus for some who approach the Church of England for initiation, the use of Rites on the Way would be inappropriate. However, while the new member may already be a committed and educated Christian, there may still be some instruction needed on Anglicanism. For that, these rites will need to be suitably adapted.

Seasonal Patterns of Initiation for those who can answer for themselves

Possible timetables are included for using Rites on the Way within the seasonal life of the church, according to the historic pattern. Where initiation takes place at Epiphany or the Baptism of Christ, at Easter (with the possibility of confirmation following at Pentecost) and on All Saints' Day, timetables are set out to encourage the congregation to support the new disciples as they learn about the church year, and place the life story of Jesus within the context of the church calendar. It is recognized that the process of initiation is likely to be drawn out over some months, and those preparing new disciples for initiation will need to plan their catechumenate over the period of up to a year before the sacrament of initiation.

Notes

Unlike many liturgies, all the Rites on the Way texts are optional. The concept of rites accompanying a catechetical journey is still new to much of the Anglican Church. These are provided for those churches that have begun, or would like to begin, exploring a process of introducing new disciples to church and encouraging their own communities to join in that exploration. Each part of every rite, though carefully crafted to work within the whole, can be used alone or in another configuration. To the making of liturgies there is no end, and it may be that some of the resources to be found here inspire others to produce resources for those aspects of the journey of faith not yet recognized and resourced.

The title 'Enquirers', used in the RCIA for new disciples to the Christian faith, was used in the 1998 draft *Rites on the Way*. However, it was felt that the language as well as the rites of the RCIA needed to be simplified, and the term 'new disciples' was felt to be more inclusive. The term 'catechumenate' is not used within the texts, as it was seen as technical language and therefore inappropriate for those new to the Christian faith.

In *Common Worship: Initiation Services*, Notes particularly pertinent to Rites on the Way include those on Godparents and Sponsors, Testimony and the Giving of Gifts and the Bible. These Notes contain explanation about those terms used in the texts that were felt to need clarification. In particular, prayers are given in each of the Welcome rites for the commissioning of Godparents and Sponsors. It is also suggested, in a somewhat quirky note, that it may be appropriate, particularly at the Welcome and the Thanksgiving, to give the new disciple a gift to express the welcome and support of the church community. Depending on the recipient and the nature of the church community, a book, for example a prayer book, may be appropriate. However, in some communities a picture or icon, a cross, carving or sculpture or some other symbol of Christian faith may be a more suitable encouragement for the new disciple.

Obviously, a Bible should be given at some point in the initiation process, though there is a great deal of freedom as to when that is most appropriately done. So long as some common sense is used, the options are wide. A prayer on the giving of a Bible is included in the Resources section.

The French catechumenal tradition that developed during the twentieth century made significant use of lay leadership in the learning groups. The note on Preparation and Ministry encourages those leading these rites to share both the planning and the leadership of the rites with new disciples and their sponsors: 'Participation in the preparation of worship and inclusion in its leadership will be valuable in helping those who are still learning about Christian worship to understand and own it.'

Rites supporting Disciples on the Way of Christ

1 Welcoming of Those Preparing for the Baptism of Children

This short rite is both an encouragement and a promise to families that they are welcome in the church and that it offers them and their child support on their journey of faith. It is common practice to meet with parents who wish their children to be baptized to prepare them theologically and pastorally for the christening. Some of those coming for baptism preparation may have little regular contact with the church into which their child is being initiated, and this rite could be used as a liturgical preparation. This rite may therefore be used during baptism preparation, or as part of the Sunday service when the child is first brought to church.

The relationship between this rite and the Thanksgiving for the Gift of a Child is made somewhat confusing in the *CW* main volume, where it is suggested that Thanksgiving might be used as a preliminary rite to baptism. While that rite may certainly precede baptism, it may do so by some weeks or months, and thus the Welcome will then function more specifically as the immediate preparation for the sacrament of baptism. This rite also includes the possibility of a commissioning of godparents and sponsors. This reflects the commissioning in the RCIA material, where the sponsors and godparents take a significant role in the catechumenate. In churches that use sponsors, it could be appropriate to commission both the godparents, chosen by the family, and the sponsors from the local church. This might be confusing, or supportive, depending on the context.

2 Welcome of Disciples on the Way of Faith

This Welcome is an important part of the formation of learning groups, recognizing as it does those whom God is calling to discipleship. It is an opportunity for those adults embarking on a period of exploration of their faith and the faith of the church to declare this publicly. It is not intended for initial enquirers, but for those who want to commit themselves to continuing the journey. It is also important for the church community, allowing acknowledgement by the congregation and solidarity with those who are also on the Way. This rite recognizes a changing relationship between the Christian community and the individual, and involves the shared decision by the church and a new disciple that the latter is ready to proceed to a period of commitment to the community and to study of the Way.

The church community acknowledges that relationship and makes a commitment to support, pray and learn with the new disciples, and the sponsors also make their own commitment to the journey. Sponsors may be commissioned during this rite. The sponsors may join the minister of the rite in making the sign of the cross on the forehead of each new disciple, and words of protection are used, which differ depending on whether the disciple has been baptized already or not. This echoes the purification and enlightenment material in the RCIA, which has been simplified and incorporated into the Welcome for Anglican use.

3 Affirmation of the Christian Way

The RCIA identifies four aspects of Christian discipleship which should be explored in seeking faith in Jesus Christ: the Scriptures, the worship of the Church, personal prayer and Christian service and witness. Building on this, the report *On the Way* proposed four elements to the Christian Way: discipleship means learning to worship with the Church; to grow in prayer; to listen to the Scriptures; and to serve our neighbour.

The original draft of the Affirmation of the Christian Way did not include a call to communion, nor to mission. Both these have become pertinent to the church agenda, and have therefore been added. Each part of the Affirmation includes the call, a sentence of Scripture and a prayer addressed to Jesus which can be said together. Two or more voices could be used to lead a congregation or group in using this text. Scripture verses are taken from different English translations of the Gospels. The call to worship includes a verse from Matthew 18.20 (NRSV); the call to prayer from John 15.4a (NIV); the call to share the Scriptures from Luke 24.15–17, 27 (NRSV adapted); the call to share communion from Luke 22.19 (NRSV); the call to service from Matthew 25.40 (NRSV adapted); and the call to share the good news from Matthew 28.19. It remains to be seen how the Affirmation of the Christian Way is actually used within the church community.

4 Call and Celebration of the Decision to be Baptized or Confirmed, or to Affirm Baptismal Faith

The Call and Celebration of the Decision to be Baptized or Confirmed, or to Affirm Baptismal Faith is intended for those who wish to continue on the Way, following a period of exploration and regular involvement in the Christian community. It marks the beginning of a period of more intense preparation for the rite of initiation. The role of the sponsors in discernment should not be underestimated. Through prayer and listening, they have made the journey of faith with the new disciples to this point of commitment, and their continuing support, friendship and wisdom will help both the candidates and the congregation grow in the Way.

Like the other Rites on the Way, there is an expectation that this rite will take place in a public act of worship, so that the regular worshipping community is aware of the new disciples and can support and learn from them. There may be some concern about using oil to sign a candidate for baptism at this Call and Celebration, since this rite is separated in time from the baptism itself. However, neat attempts to apportion grace to particular elements of any rite fall foul of history as well as theology. As the Notes make clear, the signing with oil prior to baptism as part of the preparation over a more extended time frame is consistent with the historical traditions of the Church. The use of oil as preparation for baptism reflects the cleansing and healing purpose of the anointing, such as an athlete might have used in ancient cultures in preparation for competition. Using oil to anoint a candidate for baptism in no way negates the use of the oil of chrism after baptism. Both the theology and tradition of using oil are complex, and it was felt that therefore a generous provision should be made for those who choose to use symbolism to the full.

The rite ends with intercession, adapted from the RCIA. As those who have decided to be baptized embark on a period of more intense learning and formation, it is appropriate that they should be included in the intercessions, both here and in the forthcoming weeks leading to initiation.

5 The Presentation of the Four Texts

For the new disciple, the period following the Call marks a transition from learning about the life of Jesus to formation in the Christian life and learning about the faith, worship and witness of the Church. Traditionally, those preparing for initiation are given the Apostles' Creed on the Third Sunday of Lent and the Lord's Prayer on the Fifth Sunday of Lent. The report *On the Way* proposed that all Christians should be encouraged to make four core texts their own, the Summary of the Law, the Lord's Prayer, the Apostles' Creed and the Beatitudes, in order to give fuller shape to their discipleship, the two additions representing the Old and New Testament Scriptures. The Presentation of the Four Texts offers liturgical provision for the handing over of these core texts in the learning group and/or in church.

Each rite includes suitable readings from the Old and New Testaments, and an introduction to the text. These words place the text in its theological and pastoral context, and would be suitable for use with adults or older children. The biblical texts are taken from the NRSV translation, and already occur in the *CW* main volume. Each of the giving of the texts ends with one of the *CW* Additional Collects.

Jesus' Summary of the Law is printed in the *CW* main volume as part of the Form of Preparation (p. 163). The Collect is the Additional Collect for the First Sunday after Trinity. The text of the Lord's Prayer itself is not printed in Rites on the Way, but the *CW* main volume contains four versions, including the text for suitable occasions from the International Commission on English in the Liturgy (p. 106). The Collect that follows the giving of the Lord's Prayer is the Additional Collect for the Tenth Sunday after Trinity, and the Collect that follows the Apostles' Creed is the Additional Collect for Trinity Sunday.

Although the Matthew text is given for the giving of the Beatitudes, there is an option to give the Luke 6 text where that is deemed more suitable, as some catechumenal material does. It is also used in the *CW* main volume as part of A Form of Preparation (p. 164). The Collect is the Additional Collect for the Thirteenth Sunday after Trinity.

6 Prayers in Preparation for Baptism

This material is for use when initiation becomes imminent. It could be useful for learning groups, for a baptism preparation evening, or as part of a principal service on the Sunday or the night before baptism. The prayer of thanksgiving at the beginning of the service and the Collect were written specifically for this rite. Some of the material is new, but the Trinitarian prayer 'Lord God, in the beginning . . .' is adapted from *Using the Catechumenate Process in Australia* (1999).

7 Celebration after an Initiation Service outside the Parish

Parishes increasingly join others both in preparation for confirmation and to celebrate various rites of initiation, perhaps within deaneries or at the cathedral church. In that situation it is important, both to the disciple and to the church, that the sacrament that has been performed outside of the parish be recognized and celebrated within the principal act of public worship. A pastoral introduction is included, to help the congregation to put the welcome and celebration into the context of their communal life as the people of God.

It would be appropriate for the newly initiated to be included in the intercessions, and introduced to the congregation by name at the Peace. As with the other rites in this series, it is important to personalize the service as appropriate, with welcome and recognition as the main features. The Welcome and Peace from the *CW* baptism service follow, texts well known to most regular churchgoers, and which link the rite directly to the liturgy of baptism.

8 Thanksgiving for Holy Baptism

RCIA recognized that after the sacrament of initiation a period of post-baptismal catechesis is valuable. This rite is designed for use with adult disciples, although it could be adapted for use with children and young people. It is based on the Thanksgiving for Holy Baptism attached to the *CW* forms of Morning and Evening Prayer, and it includes the Commission from the CW baptism service. This reflection on the event and process of initiation may include an opportunity for testimony, and the congregation may also want to reaffirm its commitment to mission and service within the local community. The Affirmation of the Christian Way is optional after testimony.

There is a feeling of celebration to this rite, with encouragement to look beyond the church to the world and its needs. Just as the end of a sacrament of initiation encourages the church to look beyond its own concerns to the wider community and to the mission of the church, so at the end of a period of catechumenal learning, the church as a whole is encouraged to re-engage with mission to the world. The Notes suggest that this may also be an appropriate time for the learning group to end or begin a new phase of meeting, for example as a house group.

9 Admission to Communion before Confirmation

The Notes highlight the House of Bishops' 1997 *Guidelines* mentioned earlier. Without the agreement of both the PCC and diocesan bishop, individual parishes may not introduce communion before confirmation. There is also a reminder that this rite should not be conducted in isolation, but that the church community should be made aware that people are being prepared for it. In an effort to distance this rite from confirmation, the Notes advise that the bishop should not normally preside at this rite, and that it should be set in the context of the normal family Eucharist. Every element of the rite is optional, and there is some encouragement that those being admitted should share in the leadership of parts of the service, but that the primary focus of the service should be the reception of communion by the whole baptized community.

A Pastoral Introduction is included at the beginning of this rite, written in the same form as those accompanying other pastoral rites including baptism. This offers theological explanation for admission after baptism, and affirms the centrality of learning from one another, whether old or young, as 'we journey together on the Way of Christ'.

The Welcome was written by the consultative group who met in 2003 under the leadership of the Liturgical Commission. It was felt that an optional Welcome should be included in a style that would echo the most accessible language for children. The Intercessions, Proper Preface and the Prayers at the Dismissal are little changed from the 1998 *Rites on the Way*. Other texts are taken from the *CW* baptismal rite, from the Prayer at the Preparation of the Table in the *CW* main volume (p. 292), and from *NPFW* (p. 296, J33).

Because of the divergent practice that has grown up around this rite, it was felt appropriate to include optional questions for those who needed them. Although it is clear that it is through baptism that people are fully initiated, there is a residual feeling that admission to communion should include some element of catechetical learning. Following the pattern used by the Church in Wales and in Guildford Diocese, questions to the congregation and those to be admitted are included at the end of the rite, which, if used, replace the Welcome.

Resources

The resources were compiled on the 'knapsack' model recommended by *On the Way*: 'the purpose of the knapsack would be to provide the individual with a core of devotional material which could inform his or her private prayer' (p. 102). As well as the Four Texts in the main part of Rites on the Way, Prayer During the Day is particularly commended as a tool for new disciples. The

Collects from Prayer During the Day are printed as a resource for individuals or for learning groups. Most of the other resources are taken from the *CW* main volume or from *NPFW* (see Notes 8 and 9). However, the prayer at the giving of a Bible was written by the working group, and created more discussion than most other parts of the rites. Taking its lead from 2 Timothy 3.15 and Psalm 19.10, it was worked and reworked by the Liturgical Commission, House of Bishops and General Synod. It is interesting that one of the shortest texts in the series generated the most work.

Further Reading

Episcopal Church in the USA, *Book of Occasional Services*, Church Hymnal Corporation, New York, 1979.

Evangelical Lutheran Church in America, *What Do You Seek? – Welcoming the Adult Enquirer* and *Welcome to Christ: Introduction to the Catechumenate, Rites for the Catechumenate, Catechumenate Guide*, Augsburg/Fortress Press, Minneapolis, 1997.

Maxwell E. Johnson, *The Rites of Christian Initiation*, The Liturgical Press, Collegeville, MN, 1999.

Donald A. Withey, *Adult Initiation*, Alcuin/GROW Liturgical Study 10, Grove Books, Bramcote, 1989.

Chapter 7

Wholeness and Healing

A. HISTORY

Old Testament

The concept of wholeness begins in Genesis with God's creation, in the picture of life as good and in God's perfect provision for all that he has made. However, the early chapters of Genesis then quickly describe the Fall, and the Old Testament puts human suffering and sin into the context of God's creation being marred, explaining what we recognize as the common experience of humanity – that life is a mixture of blessing and suffering. Health is associated with the restoration of God's order, for the individual, society and all creation. Every aspect of being is to be drawn into this order, for therein lies peace and harmony, which brings blessing and true health.

The covenantal relationship of God with his people is foundational to any understanding of healing in the Old Testament, for they are uniquely placed both to experience and to demonstrate God's well-being, expressed as *shalom*. Their God is the God who heals (Exodus 15.26). The commandments, the Law, and the call of the prophets, all seek to draw them into harmony with God, with their family, their community and their nation, and bring them victory over those nations who do not fear God. In the calls to a wayward nation to return to God and his ways, healing is associated with repentance and reconciliation. For example, if God's people turn back to him, then the land will be healed (2 Chronicles 7.14), and there will be healing of disloyalty, faithlessness and broken relationship (Jeremiah 3.22; Hosea 14.4). This is seen supremely in the prophets' promise of healing that comes with full and lasting atonement, epitomized in Isaiah's picture of the Suffering Servant (52.13—53.12). Such corporate promise of well-being and blessing is primary in the Old Testament. Stories of individual healing are illustrative, or occur at crucial points in Israel's history, or to validate the ministry of God's chosen instruments.

Although this underlying theme is dominant, too simple a correlation between obedience and well-being is challenged. If it were this simple, we would all be 'good'. In the Book of Job, the questions that we continue to face today are explored. As well as the relationship between God and his people, his calling them into a life of *shalom*, and the effect of a sinful disobedience, there is the work of Satan at large in the world. Job's friends express many of the ways by which we try to understand what is happening when a righteous person suffers. In their effort to help him they tend to increase his distress as he struggles to relate his experience to his knowledge of God and his personal faith. It raises questions for a theology of wholeness and healing, and the related ministry of the Church. Suffering falls on the righteous and unrighteous alike, and can be a terrible dark valley but also a place of unexpected learning and grace. We cannot tame it into a neat, tidy, rational theology, or see it as vindication of what can sometimes seem like God's impotence in the face of evil or his own arbitrary actions. Yet we can see God's power, love and grace within it. Job takes us to the heart of the human experience of suffering, and the confusion and pain of not being able to understand 'Why?' and whose fault it is.

The Old Testament background to the laying on of hands and anointing reflects the focus on God's wider plan and purpose, rather than a concept of ministry to individuals. Both were used in acts of blessing, or consecration and dedication. For example, Jacob laid hands on his sons for their blessing (Genesis 48.14) and Moses laid hands on Joshua to commission him to take on his ministry (Numbers 27.18–23). The act connotes transference, whether of blessing, gifting or of sin. So it was used to transfer sins on to the scapegoat (Leviticus 16.20–22), and onto an animal about to be sacrificed (Exodus 29.10–21). In Numbers 8.5–14 we see hands laid on the Levites to consecrate them for their priestly ministry, and the Levites lay hands on the animals to be sacrificed for atonement for their sins. There is no laying on of hands for healing in the Old Testament, although Elisha put his palms on the child's palms when he was reviving him (2 Kings 4.34) and Hezekiah's boil was rubbed with a cake of figs (Isaiah 38.21).

Oil is used in the Old Testament in anointing priests and kings and, less frequently, prophets. These anointings signify a consecration of the person to God's purpose. In 1 Kings 19.15–18 Elijah was instructed to anoint Elisha as prophet and Hazael and Jehu as kings. David is anointed as king by Samuel and the elders of Israel (1 Samuel 16.11–13; 2 Samuel 5.1–4) and Aaron is anointed as priest, together with the tabernacle, altar and related items, both ordaining people and consecrating objects to God's purposes (Exodus 29.7; Leviticus 8.10–13). Oil was also generally valued for cooking and burning in lamps and for its medicinal properties as balm. It is associated with nourishment, soothing and with celebration. So there are many references to oil in passages which tell of God's blessing. It also has links to atonement, being used in cleansing as in purification after infectious disease (Leviticus 14.14–20). The promise of the Messiah as the 'Anointed One' therefore has rich significance, which is later expressed in Jesus' ministry.

New Testament

Wholeness and healing in the New Testament are part of Jesus' mission. God incarnate brings in the new order of God's kingdom, which is attended by signs of God's power and his authority over all things, physical and spiritual. Jesus' ministry expresses his authority over Satan, demons and spiritual forces, bringing restoration to those under their influence. He has God's authority to forgive sin and bring reconciliation. He is Lord of creation, stilling wind and waves, multiplying bread, turning water into wine, reversing the effects of disease and disability, and raising the dead to life. Wholeness is about the restoring of all things in Christ, now and into eternal life, and healing and rec-onciliation are part of this ministry. Jesus is the longed-for Messiah who was expected to bring in such a time of blessing. When John the Baptist enquired whether Jesus was the 'one who is to come' (Luke 7.19–23), the answer was that John's disciples were to report back all they had seen and heard. In Jesus' reply there is a clear reference to the realization of Old Testament hopes and promises, as in Isaiah 29.17–24; 35; and 61.1–3 (the passage with which Jesus directly associated himself when in the synagogue in Nazareth at the outset of his ministry, taking on the identity of the Anointed One; Luke 4.16–21).

Jesus' ministry was holistic, and attentive to matters of spirit and body and to people's relations within the community and society. The Greek words used for healing reflect this broad understanding: salvation and healing can be used interchangeably (*sozo*); waking from sleep, standing up and resurrection all come from the same root (*egeiro*, and similarly *anistemi*); restoration can be restoration from a state of sin as well as of body (*iaomai*, and similarly *apokathistemi*). *Therapeuo* is frequently used for Jesus' ministry, giving the sense of service. So there is an overall intimation of Jesus' work in a person's life being much broader than just the outward act with its visible results.

The use of verbal command demonstrates authority in healing (Luke 7.11–17). Rebuke of illness suggests an identity to sickness similar to demons, a link that we see picked up repeatedly in the early post-apostolic Church (for example in Luke 4.39 the fever afflicting Simon's mother-in-law is rebuked by Christ and 'it left her'). Christ's words also convey a sense of gift such as 'receive your sight' (Luke 18.42), or instruction such as 'rise' or 'come forth' in raising the dead (Luke 7.14; 8.54; John 11.43). In the early Church the authority of Jesus is invoked for healing through use of his name (e.g. Acts 3; 4; 9.32–41).

Jesus used touch in healing. Sometimes he used the laying on of hands (Mark 6.5; 8.22–26; Luke 4.40–41; 13.10–17). Sometimes he just touched the person (Mark 1.29–31; Matthew 8.1–4; 9.27–31; 20.29–34), and some-times healing happened when people touched him (Mark 3.10; 5.25–34; 6.53–56). The laying on of hands was also used in the early Church (Acts 9.17–19; 28.7–10), as was touch generally (Acts 3.7; 14.19–20; 20.10).

The temporary roles for which kings, priests and prophets (less frequently) were anointed in the Old Testament are all fulfilled in the coming of the Anointed One – Christ (the title sharing the same Greek root as 'chrism'). Oil was used for medicinal as well as religious purposes in New Testament times, and this common use becomes invested with more meaning in ministry that ushers in the Kingdom of God. No record is given of Jesus using oil himself or commanding its use by his disciples. However, he anointed with spittle (John 9.6; Mark 7.33), he refers to anointing with oil and wine in the story of the Good Samaritan (Luke 10.34), and when the twelve disciples went out to minister 'they cast out many demons, and anointed with oil many who were sick and cured them' (Mark 6.13).

With regard to the relationship between healing and faith, healing some- times acts as a catalyst to new faith, discipleship and witness (John 9.17, 27–38; Mark 5.18–20). Healing is also given as a reward for faith, giving rise to Jesus' frequent words 'your faith has healed/saved you'. So in the New Testa- ment we see that faith is present, but not necessarily that of the recipient, or prior to healing.

In Acts and the Epistles the early Church continues ministry of a holistic nature. It follows on from Jesus' commission to preach and to heal with his authority and with power from on high. The good news is proclaimed with accompanying signs. Each story in Acts has significance geographically and illustrates how the kingdom is spreading from Jerusalem, through Samaria, to the ends of the earth. Any attempt to separate physical healing from the rest of ministry is untenable, both in the recorded instances of it taking place, and in the teaching and references to gifts and ministries exercised by the Church. All the 'charismata' are gifts to be used by the Church and they cover a wide range of ministry, including healing (1 Corinthians 12.4–11, 27–31), with love being primary.

In the Letter of James (5.13–16), it is said that prayer should characterize the Church's response to suffering, sickness and sin, along with the use of oil by the elders. Here we have words for a range of suffering that includes physical and spiritual affliction, persecution, weakness and the general infir- mity of old age. The healing that comes is also comprehensive – bringing healing/salvation, raising up and forgiveness, with a promise of the Lord's action now and an implicit understanding of the eternal perspective.

It is clear that suffering and sin continue despite the breaking in of the kingdom. We await the final consummation, and live with pain, frustration and hopeful longing for total restoration (Romans 8.18–25). This future hope is a corporate promise in the coming of a new heaven and new earth (Revela- tion 21), and a promise for individuals, as in Jesus' promise in John 14.1–4 and Luke 23.43. In 1 Corinthians 15 death is recognized as an enemy (v. 26), but the predominant theme is that it is only through death that we are able to come to life everlasting, after Christ who has been raised from the dead as the firstfruits, in whom 'all will be made alive' (15.20–23, 42–56). Consequently Paul desires 'to depart and be with Christ, which is better by far' (Philippians 1.23). Such a view of death alters the perspective on what constitutes recovery and healing.

The Early Church

The liturgical evidence for ministry to the sick in the patristic period relates to the blessing of oil, rather than forms for its use. We also have some indication of how those who were sick were cared for and what the Church did when they visited, which included taking communion to those absent from the celebration. Although little survives by way of forms of service, it is nevertheless evident that the early Church in the West had provision for prayer for healing and laying on of hands, with expectation of recovery. It was administered by the bishop and his presbyters. Frequent attendance at church for prayer was encouraged, as in the *Canons of Hippolytus* (*c.* mid fourth century), and daily prayer in the home was advocated for the seriously ill. Irenaeus testifies to the healing of the blind, deaf, those with demons, those who were weak, lame and paralysed, and even to the raising of the dead (*Against Heresies* II.xxxi.2; xxxii.4) by lay people as well as church ministers. Anointing was used (Tertullian, *c.* 200, *To Scapula* 4), and it became frequent practice by the fifth century. The taking of communion from a celebration to those who are at home is attested as early as Justin Martyr (Rome, *c.* 150), and it seems to have become common practice. The prime focus is on the gathered community, but importance is attached to receiving if unable to attend.

Oil was primarily used in baptismal rites, reflecting the dominance of baptism as the context for understanding the Christian faith. In baptism the believer turns away from all that is past, renounces Satan and begins a new life in Christ. Oil is used in marking this new start: in exorcism – renouncing evil and expressing Christ's power, victory and continuing protection; in preparation to do battle – as an athlete or competitor would be anointed with oil, with associations of health and vigour; and in identification – being sealed in assurance of being in Christ (the Anointed One) who is the fulfilment of hope as true prophet, priest and king. The use of oil at baptism becomes more widely recognized as of value for the whole life of the baptized, spiritual and physical, while living out the Christian hope, especially when in need. The blessing of oil for use with the sick has much in common with baptism, with a holistic view encompassing remission of sin, rebuke of illness and restoration to health.

The oil was often, but not invariably, previously blessed by the bishop. The earliest liturgy we have for this appears to be that in the *Apostolic Tradition* attributed to Hippolytus (though the true date and provenance of this are uncertain). This picks up the Old Testament background of the anointing of kings, priests and prophets, with a prayer that its use may bring strength and health, and the understanding that this would be to the spirit as much as to the body. After the service the oil was taken home and could be used both to anoint and as a medicine. Oil was commonly used externally and internally for health reasons, so self-administration of consecrated oil would have been seen as offering particular benefit. In the *Apostolic Constitutions* (Syria, *c.* 375, VIII.4 and 29) there were prayers for the blessing of oil, water and bread and the sick person's bed, asking for power to bring health and drive out demons. The water was used both for sprinkling and drinking.

The prayers of consecration of oil in the Gelasian Sacramentary (pre-seventh century) and Gregorian Sacramentary (composite from seventh and eighth centuries) pick up similar ideas to those seen in the *Apostolic Tradition*, with a holistic view of healing. Evidence of the tradition of consecrating the three oils of catechumenate, chrism and healing on Maundy Thursday can also be traced back to the Gelasian Sacramentary, although it was not universal practice as consecration could take place whenever required and be done by priests as well as bishops.

The link between prayers for healing and exorcism is strong in the early Church. Part of the expectation of healing comes from the belief that a person needs to be freed from illness, with the illness rebuked and the person fully reconciled to God, as we see in Justin Martyr. We have prayers for blessing the sick and for exorcizing those who were considered to be possessed in Origen (Alexandria, d. 254) and the Sacramentary of Serapion (Egypt, *c.* 350). John Chrysostom (Antioch, d. 407) understood healing as spiritual, with prayer for reconciliation, mediated through the ministry of the Church. From *The Apostolic Constitutions* (Book VIII) and the *Canons of Hippolytus*, we know that at the ordination of presbyters and bishops there were prayers that they would be given the necessary power for forgiving sins, exorcism and healing. Deacons were authorized to exorcize, and exorcists were also recognized as a separate ministry, but only under the authority of the bishop, who was the principal minister for both healing and exorcism.

The Gregorian Sacramentary gives an account of a service which shows how Western practice developed. It began with exorcism and sprinkling with holy water, prayers for recovery, then the laying on of hands by the priests and their assistants (under the authority of the bishop), with the sick person kneeling. This was followed by anointing in which the oil was applied liberally. There were three prayers for anointing, recalling its use with kings and prophets in the Old Testament, praying that no unclean spirits might hide but that Christ and the Holy Spirit would dwell within, and for the remission of sins and restoration spiritually and physically. This was followed by communion. The rite could be repeated for seven days and was complemented by sung services twice a day by the sick person's bedside.

Apart from liturgical textual evidence in this early period, there are many stories recorded of healing involving oil and the laying on of hands. However, it is difficult to discern factual evidence in what are often accounts of a hagiographical kind, especially when associated with miraculous healing, even at the point of death.

The Medieval Period

The early Church had emphasized the connection between prayer for healing, accompanied by anointing, with the hope of recovery. Lay people as well as clergy were able to administer anointing. Both these were to change as the medieval period dawned.

Two significant factors in the theological and intellectual climate in which the medieval Church found itself might be mentioned. The first is the gradual absorption of Neoplatonic ideas into the Church's thinking. Although the Neoplatonist philosophers were hostile to Christianity, because of its material-ism and emphasis on incarnation, their Christian readers (notably Augustine, whose writings they influenced) were attracted by the importance given to Intelligence and Soul, both of them seeking union with an ultimate and unknowable source of all that exists. Such a doctrine inevitably devalued the well-being of the mortal body in favour of concern for the immortal soul.

Ecclesiastical politics also had a significant effect on the healing ministry and at the beginning of the twelfth century the growing power of the monas-teries was becoming a concern for the Church. This issued in legislation that ultimately restricted various spheres of activity, including the involvement of the clergy in medical healing. The first General Council in the West – the First Lateran Council of 1123 – banned monks from holding public Masses and from offering penance. They were also forbidden to consecrate oil, administer unction (anointing) or visit the sick (Canon 17). However, most religious orders continued these practices.

One of the strongest objections to the monastic practice of medicine was that the monks studied medicine and law in order to generate extra income. This was condemned by the Second Lateran Council of 1139, which deter-mined that the monks were neglecting the cure of souls and concentrating instead on treating bodies. Certainly, some members of itinerant orders were practising surgery profitably. The Council of Tours addressed this forcefully in 1163, and barred church people from practising surgery for the reason that 'the church abhors the shedding of blood'. A consequence of this legislation, together with the medieval Church's ban on human dissection, was a severe limitation on the development of anatomical knowledge. Medicine and surgery thus became separated, with the latter falling to barber surgeons.

As for the institutional practice of the healing ministry, two elements deserve special attention, namely communion of the dying, and anointing (unction). Over time, receiving communion became the most important act of preparation on the part of the dying. Known as viaticum, it embodied notions of food for the final journey, assurance of forgiveness and therefore assurance of eternal life, bringing a source of comfort and hope throughout Christian history. In the Eastern Church, anointing has always been part of the ministry to the sick. By the sixth century, however, the Western Church had begun to associate the remission of sin with unction, and by the time of Charlemagne (742–814) unction for healing was beginning to be transformed into unction in readiness for death. The sequence of penance, anointing and viaticum became the norm; their administration ceased to be associated with the expectation of healing and came to be seen as preparation for death. In the twelfth century the original order changed to penance, viaticum and anointing. As the final act, anointing came to be known as extreme unction and its proximity to death made it something to be feared rather than welcomed.

These developments lent weight to the view that the act of anointing should be reserved to the clergy and in 813 the administration of unction was limited to priests by the Council of Chalon-Sur-Saône. This ruling represented a strong statement of the professional church's control over the passage from life to death. It also served to reinforce a growing association between sickness and sin in the mind of the Church. This relationship received official expression when, in 1215, the Fourth Lateran Council insisted that physicians treating the sick must first send for the priest to hear the afflicted person's confession. Excommunication resulted if this ruling was disobeyed. Such thinking persisted well into the early modern period.

Medieval theologians of the first half of the twelfth century did not always observe the changes in the interpretation of anointing, and there are divergent accounts of unction as extreme unction, as the anointing of the sick and as the anointing of the sick with viaticum. There are also varying views on the repeatability of unction, perhaps most systematically summed up by Peter Lombard (1100–60) in his *Sentences*. He endorses Hugh of St Victor's support for subsequent anointings, on the grounds that the effect of this sacrament is to cure the sick, although he opposes the reconsecration of the oil used in unction. Where he stands alone is in insisting that the bishop should be the sole minister of unction.

In the English liturgical tradition there are many canons governing the visitation of the sick from the Anglo-Saxon age to the fifteenth century. Provision is made for this ministry, for example, in Archbishop Theodore's *Penitential*, and in the *Excerpts* of Archbishop Edgar of York there are instructions for making oil for anointing available to the sick. The Canons of King Edgar (AD 960) contain two instructions concerning housel (communion) and unction for the sick. In 1287, the Synod of Exeter specified a penalty for the neglect of these orders, and priests could be suspended from their office for failure to comply. The Canons of Aelfric also provided for housel and unction, but noted that some sick people were fearful of being anointed because they associated this with the departure of all hope of recovery. Aelfric refutes this in an epistle probably written for clergy on Maundy Thursday.

Any attempt to trace the formative influences on Anglican liturgical approaches to ministry to the sick must pay careful attention to the Sarum *Ordo ad Visitandum Infirmum*. This was the prototype for the Visitation of the Sick in the First Prayer Book of Edward VI in 1549. The texts in it probably date from the mid fourteenth century, rather than from the Salisbury material assembled by Bishop Richard Poore in the thirteenth century. There is a strong emphasis on recovery, present both in the texts of the rite itself and in the rubrics. While the normal expectation was that anointing would be administered to those whose illness was likely to result in death, the Sarum rubrics allowed the act of anointing to be repeated in cases where the sufferer made a recovery but succumbed at a later time to an illness that appeared to be terminal. While death was the terminus of every life, the Visitation Office, and anointing in particular, were explicitly part of a *managed* progression towards death. For that reason, anointing was not to be conferred on those going to war or to fight a duel or embarking on a pilgrimage or a sea voyage.

The Reformation

Although the Sarum Visitation of the Sick conveyed a relatively confident view of God's ability to heal, in its practice it had become extreme unction, prayer and anointing for remission of sins and the healing of the soul in preparation for death. Much of the Reformation reaction was against the practice of extreme unction, recognizing no biblical basis for the sacrament as it was defined at the time. The Reformers did not necessarily object to the use of laying on of hands and anointing for the sick. Luther did not condemn either, as long as the oil was not understood to be a sacrament or to hold supernatural power. Calvin did object to its practice, as miraculous healing was only required for the period of the early Church and now that the Church is established it is God's word and reliance on the Holy Spirit that is needful, not 'mere hypocritical stage-play' (*Institutes* IV.19.18).

The 1549 Prayer Book

It is notable that the *BCP* ministry to the sick in general continues to be in expectation of death. This may reflect the reality of poor prognosis in illness in the sixteenth century or the loss of confidence in the healing ministry of the Church, or the service may have been seen as a direct substitute for extreme unction and therefore for ministry to the dying. Thus the tone of the 1549 Prayer Book, although including a note of hope of healing, is paradoxically less confident than the Sarum Rite had been. It contained two services: The Visitation of the Sick and The Communion of the Sick.

The 1549 Visitation of the Sick used much from the Sarum *Manual*, but in a selective manner which conveyed a distinct theology. It begins with a greeting of peace and Psalm 143, then an antiphon 'Remember not, Lord, our iniquities . . .', the *Kyries*, the Lord's Prayer and a set of versicles and responses. It then has two of the nine prayers of the Sarum rite, which had been predominantly hopeful of recovery. These two ask for restoration of health, but end with 'or else give him grace so to take thy correction, that after this painful life endeth, he may dwell with thee in life everlasting'. The minister then delivers an exhortation that spells out a theology of sickness as God's visitation, correction and chastisement, for demonstration of patience and trial of faith, that the sick person may share in Christ's suffering and then in his resurrection, so deriving profit from his illness. Some of the first part of this was in the Sarum *Manual*, to which was added material from the 1547 Homily against the Fear of Death, with the option of leaving out the second part if the person was very sick. The exhortation is followed by a responsive form of the Apostles' Creed as used at baptism. The rubric then directs that the sick person shall be examined on his state of life, to discern any areas where he is out of charity with the world, or where he has offended anyone or done wrong which should be redressed. A will should be made, if not already done, debts should be discharged and encouragement is given to donate to the poor. This is followed by a personal confession and a declaratory absolution: 'by his [Jesus Christ's] authority committed to me, I absolve thee from all thy sins'. A further collect for mercy precedes Psalm 71, followed by an antiphon and prayer.

An option of a simple anointing is provided, and the fact that it is optional suggests a lack of commitment to its use. There is no provision for a form of consecrating oil by the bishop on Maundy Thursday, as was the custom of the time, or even by a local priest. The rubric directs anointing on the forehead or just on the breast, with the sign of the cross, much simplifying the sevenfold anointing of Sarum with its associated psalms. There is a prayer, more hopeful and holistic in tone than the rest of the service, for restoration of health and strength to serve God, relief of pains and troubles in body and mind, pardon for sin and victory and triumph over the devil, sin and death, ending with Psalm 13.

The introductory rubric to Communion of the Sick begins with encouragement that because of the uncertainties of life, and especially in times of plague, all parishioners should attend the Communion Service regularly. In the event of sickness the sick person is to give notice overnight, or early in the morning, that he is too ill to come to church. He must also say how many will communicate with him at home.

> And if the same day there be a celebracion of the holy Communion in the churche, then shall the priest reserve (at the open communion) so much of the sacrament of the body and bloud, as shall serve the sicke person, and so many as shall Communicate with him (if there be any). And so soone as he convenientlye may, after the open Communion ended in the churche, shall goe and minister the same, first to those that are appoynted to communicate with the sicke (if there be any), and last of all to the sicke person himselfe.

Alternatively this form of service can be celebrated in the sick person's home, if there is no church service, if the curate attends before noon and if there is a place in the home where the Communion can be celebrated reverently. It is a brief service to be used with the Visitation, with Introit, the *Gloria Patri*, *Kyries* and salutation. A collect presents sickness as God's visitation for correction, to be borne patiently until there is either recovery or death. The Epistle is Hebrews 12.5–6 which refers to suffering in time of persecution, and is used to give a strong reminder that the sick person requires rebuke and correction by God. The Gospel is John 5.24 on the need to have faith in Christ in order to have everlasting life. The regular Communion Service is then picked up with a salutation, the *Sursum Corda* and eucharistic prayer. The rubrics give the desired order for reception, and state that if several home communions are being done in one day, then sacrament from the celebration in the first house was taken from there to the others. The next rubric affirms the principle of receiving communion spiritually, even if not physically, if someone is too ill to receive, or if criteria allowing a home communion have not been fulfilled, providing there is true repentance, belief in Christ and his redemptive death and evidence of a thankful heart.

The 1552 Prayer Book

The reaction to the 1549 Prayer Book included Bucer's *Censura,* a critique written from a Reformation standpoint. Bucer's main criticism was of the optional provision for anointing, for which he felt there was insufficient justification. For him the use of oil and ministry of healing in Mark and James were limited to the time of the Apostles and the early Church. The lack of biblical and early church evidence to validate its use, combined with the abusive practices of his own time, made Bucer call for this part of the rite to be abolished. In his view the Eucharist was sufficient for ministry to the sick. Consequently he affirmed the rite of Communion to the Sick, apart from wanting a change to the introductory rubric to exhort people to a practice of receiving communion weekly.

The 1552 Prayer Book Visitation of the Sick notably omits Psalm 143 and the optional order for anointing, perhaps heeding Bucer's advice. The 1552 Communion of the Sick has simplified rubrics. The sick person must again give notice, telling the curate how many will communicate with him. Immediately after that, comes the rubric 'And haulinge a convenient place in the sycke mans house, where the Curate maye reverently minister, and a good nombre to receyve the communion wyth the sycke personne wyth al thinges necessarye for the same'. There is no mandatory confession before communion is received. A new rubric is added giving the curate permission to communicate a single person in time of plague and infectious disease. Apart from the rubrics, only the collect and readings are provided, which are unchanged from 1549. As it stands, it has omitted so much that it is open to wide interpretation.

1662 and After

The form for The Visitation of the Sick in the 1662 *BCP* reinforces the theological and pastoral message of the 1552 Prayer Book, that sickness is a visitation by God and has a corrective and positive role, for the Lord chastises those whom he loves. It is mainly a preparation for death, although there is a door for recovery if God wills it. Some of the few references to hope of healing and positive prayer for recovery that 1552 had contained have been edited out. In the prayer before the exhortation the reference to Peter's mother-in-law and the Centurion's servant have gone, as have the verses that express refreshment, comfort and praise at the end of Psalm 71. The Creed is given in full, still in an interrogative form. As in 1552 there is no order for anointing, with the more holistic view of healing that accompanied it in 1549. Instead there is the addition of the Aaronic blessing, and the provision of some further optional prayers for specific pastoral situations, which are useful additions but do not redress the somewhat pessimistic balance. In the Communion of the Sick there are only some relatively minor changes to the rubrics.

The Reformation reaction to extreme unction, and the deletion of any liturgical provision for anointing from 1552 onwards, meant that the laying on of hands and anointing of the sick generally ceased being practised in the Anglican Church until the beginning of the eighteenth century, apart from the limited practice by the monarch called 'Touching for the King's Evil'. This included laying hands on the sick with prayers for recovery, with an expectation of healing. It originated as early as the eleventh century and was practised by many British kings and queens from Edward the Confessor to Queen Anne. Forms were included in some editions of the Prayer Book.

It was the Nonjurors who challenged the status quo. Those who refused to swear allegiance to William and Mary in 1689 were deprived of their livings and some of them set about revising the 1662 *BCP*, reverting to 1549 or to ancient liturgies. Consequently, some called for a reinstatement of the practice of anointing. They produced two forms, in 1718 and 1734, not without controversy among themselves. Basically these were the 1662 Visitation of the Sick with anointing of the sick for recovery. Thus, this was not extreme unction, but a positive embracing of James 5, including a reading of James 5.14–16, and a form for the blessing of oil. However, it did not become standard Church of England practice.

In the mid nineteenth century, the Tractarian Movement again challenged the established practice of the time. Discussion over the nature of the sacraments inevitably raised questions concerning unction in ministry to the sick and the use of personal sacramental confession, with the focus on the latter. The 1662 services of Visitation and Communion of the Sick continued to be the norm, but there was some limited call for restoring the anointing. Edward Pusey in *Eirenicon* (1865) noted the problem caused by anointing of the sick being connected to remission of sin by the Council of Trent and in subsequent Roman practice. Later Tractarians such as Forbes (in 1867), Pye (in 1867) and Grueber (in 1881) called for the restoration of anointing, concerned that the Church of England had lost the benefit of this ministry and expressing a holistic understanding of its nature. They proposed that it was legal to use it, as its absence from the *BCP* meant there was no prescribed form for it, rather than that it was prohibited. Unofficial forms were consequently produced. The form found in *The Priest's Book of Private Devotion* has its origins in this period (1872) and was widely used into the 1960s, along with forms in other similar books.

As the debate continued over the years, the full range of theological and practical issues was raised: whether healing is for the Church in this age or belonged only to the early Church; whether the ministry was to soul or body or both; the place of anointing; at what stage in an illness it should be given; who should anoint; and what form of service should be used. Concurrently, as a renewed centrality of the Eucharist emerged, there was a growing recognition of the desirability of communion for the sick. This also increased the practical and pastoral need for reservation of the sacrament, with renewed concerns both from those who opposed the practice and those who opposed its restriction. The reintroduction of the continuous reservation of the sacrament has been traced to J. M. Neale in East Grinstead in 1855, in response to pastoral needs, and other instances can be found in the following years. As part of the process leading towards the revision of the Prayer Book in the early twentieth century, it was proposed that provision be made for the elements to be kept when it was impossible to take them directly after a communion service to the sick person, and for no other purpose. Significantly, by 1924 this proposal included others unable to attend a communion service. The final, more detailed proposals in the abortive 1927/8 revision included rules about use of an aumbry for the reservation of the sacrament.

The Twentieth Century

A number of factors contributed to raising the profile of the healing ministry in the twentieth century, and while several of them lie outside the strictly liturgical brief of this commentary, mention should at least be made of developments in the study of psychology, which invited a much wider consideration of the causes of illness; the Church's response to the growth of Christian Science at the beginning of the century; the establishment of various healing movements or guilds; and the Pentecostal and Charismatic Movements.

The guilds began in 1904 with the Guild of Health, which was still active in 1992 when Holy Rood House in Yorkshire was founded. While the inheritors of these movements cater nowadays for a broad constituency, embracing the psychological, pedagogical, therapeutic and charismatic strands in Christian healing, the Guild of St Raphael has retained a distinctive position in the Anglo-Catholic wing of the Church. It was founded in 1915 when the Guild of Health became an interdenominational organization. High Church members, concerned about sacramental authority for anointing and laying on of hands and prayer, as well as maintaining close links with the medical profession, withdrew to form the new guild. Today, the Guild of St Raphael continues to encourage the sacramental side of the healing ministry and performs a valuable function in encouraging local members to meet and pray regularly for the sick in the parish situation.

Writers on the healing ministry in the early twentieth century have pointed to certain powerful issues which drew attention to the frailty of the body and to the need for spiritual healing. One of these was National Service, hailed by some as an antidote to soft living, but for others representing selection of the fittest, thus excluding about 43 per cent of the population. Wartime experience caused many young ministers and clergy to take an interest in the practical and spiritual effectiveness of psychology, and the urgings of individuals such as James Moore Hickson (founder of the Guild of Emmanuel in 1905) led to a discussion of the healing ministry at the Lambeth Conference in 1920. As far as theological trends were concerned, the view that human life and the human body were a legitimate object of concern for the Christian Church was powerfully reinforced by that theology of the incarnation which dominated Anglican thinking for at least the first third of the twentieth century. The subject of the healing ministry was raised at successive Lambeth Conferences in 1920, 1958, 1978 and 1988.

The liturgical response of some, but not all, of the Church of England to the questions and doctrinal points that were being raised about ministry to the sick found expression in the forms for the Visitation of the Sick and the Communion of the Sick in the Proposed Prayer Book of 1928. These services sought to address perceived inadequacies in the forms provided in the 1662 Prayer Book. Percy Dearmer, a keen proponent of revised provisions for ministering to the sick, wrote in *The Parson's Handbook* of the misrepresentation in 1662, which suggested far too close a causal link between sin and sickness. He also drew attention to the persistent misunderstanding of the parish priest's visit to the houses of the sick as a certain presage of death. Instead, he urged a recovery of this ministry in a form which strengthened and healed, rather than which prepared sick people to die.

A telling footnote to the 1928 Order for the Visitation of the Sick observes that 'the Order in the Form of 1662 is not reprinted here, being, for the most part, contained in the Order following'. In reality, the whole tenor of 1928 is very different. The Order is divided into five clear sections: the Visitation; an Exhortation to Faith and Prayer; an Exhortation to Repentance; an Act of Prayer of Blessing; and Special Prayers to be Used as Occasion May Serve. References to 'the enemy' and to the 'fatherly correction' of God are omitted, and the possibility of recovery is at least admitted ('whatsoever the issue that thou shalt ordain for him . . .'). The Exhortation to Faith and Prayer departs noticeably from 1662: the Creed is in the declarative rather than the interrogative form, and is prefaced by a reminder of baptism. The third section includes a reminder about a rule of life and prayer, and offers a more elaborate form of examination and confession. The fourth section prays explicitly for the recovery of the patient ('O Almighty God, who art the giver of all health . . .'), and makes provision for the laying-on of hands. The fifth section provides a richer choice of prayers than its predecessor. By 1935, there were liturgical forms available for anointing and blessing. (In fact, Dearmer had printed an adaptation of the rite of anointing in the Nonjurors' Liturgy in the 1907 edition of *The Parson's Handbook*.)

The 1927/28 Alternative Order for Communion of the Sick consists of a series of rubrics and instructions for the reservation of the sacrament for this purpose, a practice so controversial that pleas for its inclusion were largely responsible for the defeat of the proposed Prayer Book in the House of Commons. Vigorous arguments were advanced both for the legitimacy of this practice in the tradition of the Church of England and for its practical value, especially in emergencies when a priest had to meet the needs of the sick or dying with very little time to spare. Anglo-Catholics who were anxious to see reservation given an official place saw this as a way to allow the sick to continue to make their communion frequently, while at the same time solving the dilemma of fasting communion for the clergy, as well as the difficulty of celebrations after noon, for the *BCP* directs that when communion is celebrated in the home of a sick person, the priest is to receive first. By contrast, in good 'catholic' practice, the president was bound to receive at a separate celebration, but did not receive when distributing reserved elements.

No further efforts towards official provisions were made until the early 1960s, when a promissory note included with the Series 1 rites for most other services in 1965 affirmed that forms of service for ministry to the sick were in preparation and would be published shortly. In the event, these did not appear until 1983. Several practical problems retarded progress as well as the controversial matters surrounding rites for the sick – reservation, blessing of oils, and the form of absolution. As work on material leading to the *ASB* developed, it was envisaged that rites for initiation, healing and reconciliation would all be related. In 1980 *Services for the Sick* (GS 471) was published at the same time as *The Blessing of Oils and the Reconciliation of a Penitent* (GS 472). Both of them received General Approval in 1981, and *Services for the Sick* continued on to receive Final Approval as the 1983 *Ministry to the Sick* referred to above. It was decided to send Reconciliation of a Penitent and Blessing of Oils through the process separately. However, prayer for blessing oils, to be used on Maundy Thursday, was blocked by the House of Laity, as was the absolution derived from the 1662 Visitation of the Sick: 'I absolve you from all your sins . . .' Thus, these latter services were never authorized.

The 1983 forms of service include orders for the Communion of the Sick (Rite A and Rite B); an Order for the distribution of the elements to those not present at the Celebration (again, in Rite A and Rite B forms); Orders for the Laying on of Hands with Prayer, and Anointing, both at the Holy Communion and at Morning or Evening Prayer; a Commendation at the Time of Death; and Prayers for use with the Sick. These services mark a decisive change in attitudes to ministry to the sick: 1928 had come a considerable way from the austere provisions of 1662, but in 1983 the divine image in humanity is asserted, particularly in the eucharistic prayers, and the emphasis is on surrounding the sick person with the comfort of the scriptural tradition and the Church's faith. The prayers for laying on of hands and anointing are Trinitarian, and are open to the healing of the physical and the spiritual aspects of the patient, with a renewed emphasis on wholeness. A rich selection of Prayers for Use with the Sick develops this trend, and also reflects the more sophisticated medical resources of its time. Thus the mentally ill are explicitly mentioned; a prayer is provided for those facing surgery; and the need for some assurance of the protection of the divine presence is recognized.

There is no Order for the Visitation of the Sick, either in this collection or in the *ASB* itself. Instead, the provisions emphasize personal preparation and the importance of the celebration of Holy Communion in the presence of the sick. The pastoral sensitivity exercised in the drafting of the Communion Orders can be seen in the short eucharistic prayers that omit the *Sanctus, Benedictus* and Acclamations, and therefore demand less of those who are ill. The suggested Scripture readings reinforce the notion of God's care for humanity. This is in marked contrast to the lections in 1662 (Hebrews 12.5 and John 5.24). While the Notes make clear that anointing should be in accordance with Canon B37, there is, anomalously, no rite given for the blessing of oil.

An important part has been played in twentieth-century discussions of healing by the Charismatic Movement. While its origins lie in late-nineteenth-century Revivalism, and the early-twentieth-century Pentecostal Movement, it achieved prominence through the Charismatic Renewal from the 1960s onward, which affected all denominations. Most recently there has been renewal in what has been termed 'The Third Wave', primarily initiated by the evangelistic work of John Wimber and the Vineyard network of Christian Churches, which began in California. Wimber made particularly influential visits to England in the 1980s and 1990s. His teaching called for 'power evangelism' and for ministry to be exercised by the whole body of Christ in the spreading of the kingdom of God. In contrast to a celebrated individual who is recognized as a 'healer' able to 'perform miracles', this approach seeks to show how accessible God makes himself and how ready he is to be active in our lives and situations, demonstrating the kingdom in power. Although it has been caricatured as a 'signs and wonders' ministry, the reality is subtler. It encourages a positive view of what God can do, although Wimber readily acknowledged that 'cure' or 'recovery' may not be the outcome of prayer for healing. Despite some excesses and difficulties associated with this outpouring of the Spirit, many Anglicans have experienced God's power at work in their own lives and been used in ministry themselves. This, along with other influences of postmodern culture and current theological developments, has influenced *CW* liturgical provision. Ministry for wholeness and healing must now allow for variety of style, flexible patterns of ministry and lay participation.

B. COMMENTARY

The *CW* material comprises a Theological Introduction; A Celebration of Wholeness and Healing (intended for a diocesan or deanery occasion); Laying on of Hands with Prayer and Anointing at a Celebration of Holy Communion; Supplementary Texts; Prayers for Individuals in Public Worship;

provisions for the Ministry to the Sick; and finally Prayers for Protection and Peace.

Theological Introduction

This roots the ministry firmly in the context of biblical patterns of healing and their dependence upon a baptismal context. Christ is bringing in a new order, of which healing is a part and a sign. He is the one who has shared and knows our suffering and weaknesses and has taken them on himself. The concept of Christ sharing in our suffering has the corollary of our sharing in his suffering. In the *BCP*, suffering was seen as a means to be drawn closer to God, to strengthen faith or bring us to repentance having been corrected and chastised, and sickness should therefore be borne patiently and with an understanding that it will be for our profit. In *CW* the emphasis is more on sickness and adversity being part of our vulnerability and powerlessness 'in the face of the dominion of sin and death'. The reality of being influenced, if not overcome, by principalities and powers makes us look to Christ's victory and recognize that we are in a battle zone, facing our suffering with trust and hope as we look to Christ for deliverance. Both these emphases can be supported by Scripture and therefore both have their place in understanding how suffering should be met by the Christian. The Introduction in *CW* shows a discernible shift from the *BCP* approach, as 'healing, reconciliation and restoration are integral to the good news of Jesus Christ', building further on the developments seen in 1983.

The ministry offered is to be comprehensive and open to God's touch in all areas of life, as physical wholeness is not the only way Christ meets human need. The broad salvation that Jesus brings encompasses the physical, emotional and spiritual aspects of life and, beyond that, the relationship with the social order and the whole of creation. The Introduction points to possible simplifications or misunderstandings. It holds the tension between acknowledging God's love and power and desire to bring us to wholeness 'as part of the proclaiming of the good news and as an outworking of the presence of the Spirit in the life of the Church', and understanding that 'healing has always to be seen against the background of the continuing anguish of an alienated world and the hidden work of the Holy Spirit bringing God's new order to birth'. We will know frustration as we await the final accomplishment of the new heaven and new earth. But we will also have glimpses of what is to come and the love, power and authority of God, in Christ, through his Spirit, in instances of the kingdom breaking in.

A Celebration of Wholeness and Healing

The main rite (for a diocesan or deanery occasion) is intended normally to be non-eucharistic, although there are the necessary pointers which enable it to be combined with the Eucharist where that is desired. It is envisaged as an occasional gathering on a fairly large scale, and not as part of the regular life of a particular worshipping community. Provision is made in the Notes for an extended celebration occupying several hours or most of a day, and times of silence and reflection can be given greater emphasis in such a setting. The Notes also distinguish between the administrants of laying on of hands (who need not be ordained) and administrants of anointing (who must be in priest's orders).

The Gathering

The model greeting is markedly different in style from the forms in the *CW* eucharistic rites or Services of the Word. The source (1 Peter 2.9) announces the deeply scriptural trend that is evident in the texts. There are two possible positions in the service for one of the forms of introduction, either as part of the Greeting, or prior to the Prayers of Intercession. Again, they rely on New Testament sources, though working out the scriptural teaching in an accessible and refreshingly unhomiletic form. Other suitable words may be used, and therefore the suggested formulas may indicate a style and tone, rather than prescribing a set form. The Dialogue is the penultimate phase in the Gathering, and an opportunity both to draw the congregation into the rite and to direct its intention towards joy and thanksgiving. This is made especially clear in the last versicle and response, based on the acclamation of the four six-winged creatures in Revelation 4.8. The Collect, based on Acts 10.38, seeks in Christ's ministry, empowered by the Spirit, a model for the continuing ministry of the Church. In the context of the healing ministry, the transition from suffering to victory to preaching the gospel of salvation sets out a pattern that is capable of addressing both the hope of Christian healing for suffering individuals, and the calling to the whole Church to share in Christ's life, death and resurrection. It is to be noted that at A Celebration of Wholeness and Healing, this prayer replaces the Collect of the day. At other more regular services, it may be used, although the Collect of the day will normally be the first choice. This assists in rooting the healing ministry in the regular worship of the Church.

The Liturgy of the Word

The table of readings is helpfully classified by season and by theme. The sermon is an important, but also sensitive, part of any service with ministry for wholeness and healing. The expectations of those who attend will be varied and many will be emotionally vulnerable. How the Scriptures are treated can bring comfort, hope, faith and openness to God's healing touch, but the problems of false expectations, disappointment and confusion are considerable.

Prayer and Penitence

There are several advantages to intercessions in litany form. The Litany of Healing may be used in the relatively general terms in which it appears here, or be adapted without strain to accommodate particular petitions. Some of the conventional areas of concern (Church, world, local community) are treated via the central concern for the sick, suffering and dying. Prayer for 'all who minister to those who are suffering' covers the medical, clerical, psychological and voluntary categories without danger of omission. The Litany has been criticized for its juxtaposition of the words 'disabled' and 'whole', and it should be emphasized that there is no suggestion that physical impairment militates against the petition for wholeness as understood in these rites. If an alternative form of intercession is chosen, care should be taken to maintain the balance of the service and not to anticipate the laying on of hands and anointing which come later.

The call to penitence sticks closely to biblical words in its versicle and response form. Its emphasis is on peace and trust. The first of the two forms of confessions that follow is a *Kyrie* confession, a pattern originating in the Roman Catholic Church. It effectively emphasizes themes of new life, pardon and light in darkness, all in the context of God's mercy. The alternative form is drawn from the material for Remembrance Sunday in *The Promise of His Glory*. It focuses starkly on the breach of the commandments which Jesus identified as the greatest – love of God and love of neighbour (Matthew 22.37–39) – yet holds out the hope of remedy in the strength of God. The end of the confession is based on Micah 6.8–10, which offers a picture of a wholesome relationship with God and with the world.

The absolution begins in the confidence that we have already been reconciled to the Father through Christ, a reconciliation that is sustained by the Holy Spirit. This condition is mediated by the Church which is Christ's body. The phrase 'ministry of reconciliation' might cause some confusion to those who know it as the title of a distinct rite, but its occurrence here is brief, and will probably pass without comment on most occasions. The text is one of a number of authorized absolutions in *CW*. It was not accepted by the General Synod when originally presented in 1981, but later appeared in *Lent, Holy Week and Easter*. It found authorization subsequently under the provisions for 'A Service of the Word'.

Laying on of Hands and Anointing

The laying on of hands and anointing are an active and visible focus for prayer. Christ's touch, as the Gospels attest, carried with it the assurance of blessing and a strong sense of love and power. That this often involved a physical sensation testifies that Christ's actions ministered to the whole person. The early Church adopted Christ's own practice and it is continued by his Church now in his name.

The prayer over the oil begins as a thanksgiving prayer, on the model of a eucharistic prayer and of the prayer over the water in baptism. As in the Eucharist and baptism, there is a brief dialogue between president and people; here this calls the congregation to pay particular attention to the action of God as creator, helper and promise-keeper. In the prayer the story of salvation is told in terms of Christ's deliverance of his people from weakness and sin. This ministry continued through the Apostles and is alive in the Church today. The third paragraph opts for an invocation of the Spirit that is sufficiently broadly phrased to be taken as an epiclesis with reference to the oil or as a more general prayer that the Spirit may be present as the agent of God's blessing. Reasons for this understated drafting might be found in a desire to accommodate the widest spectrum of views on the sacramental status of anointing. At root, however, it reflects the disagreement in General Synod over the blessing of inanimate objects. Yet the oil is clearly much more than an accompanying gesture. The same prayer is recast in a responsive form in the Supplementary Texts, which is unprecedented and acknowledges a more assertive desire on the part of contemporary worshippers to be overtly involved in liturgical action. A similar pattern exists for the Prayer over the Water in the *CW* baptismal rite. Both came into the provisions at the revision stage, and were not offered originally by the Liturgical Commission. In the Supplementary Texts there is also a short prayer over the oil, which is quite definitely a blessing and setting apart for a particular purpose.

A prayer for wholeness of body, mind and spirit accompanies the action of laying on of hands. It is essentially a form of intercession, in which an allusion to the importance of touch in Jesus' earthly ministry of healing becomes a metaphor for God's ongoing activity in the lives of all sick people who seek his healing. A fuller form of the prayer is provided for use during the Ministry to the Sick (pp. 92 ff.).

The oil is set apart and blessed for this ministry, and the prayer over the oil asks, among other things, that those anointed will be blessed, made whole and 'restored in your image, renewed in your love, and serve you as sons and daughters in your kingdom'. Anointing is performed in the name of God, bestowing Christ's forgiveness and healing. While not exorcistic in tone, the prayer picks up echoes of baptismal theology, with the history of its use in the catechumenate for exorcism.

Drawing on Proverbs 18.10, Philippians 2.9–10 and Ephesians 1.21, the prayer after the laying on of hands and anointing reaffirms that Christ alone is the source of health and that the tradition of the Church is founded on trust in him.

The Sending Out

Versicles and responses constructed out of 2 Corinthians 4.6–7 preface a short Gospel reading. They strike a note of confidence that we have been entrusted with the knowledge of God revealed in Christ. The greeting of Peace is delayed until this part of the service, where it may be expressed and shared to reinforce the fact that the people are sent out reconciled 'in the joy and peace of Christ'. The text reminds worshippers that they are marked by Christ (a baptismal allusion) for eternal life and that until that life comes the Spirit lives within them. It derives from 2 Corinthians 1.22, Ephesians 1.13–14 and Ephesians 4.30, and is also found in the *CW* confirmation service.

Laying on of Hands with Prayer and Anointing at a Celebration of Holy Communion

The structural outline of A Celebration of Wholeness and Healing provides for the celebration of the Eucharist. The Laying on of Hands with Prayer and Anointing at a Celebration of Holy Communion is not a variant of this provision. Instead, it envisages a different set of needs, for example the regular healing service which might form part of a parochial pastoral strategy. The Notes recommend that the president of the Eucharist also lay hands on and anoint those who come forward. Holy Communion may be celebrated according to any authorized rite, though incorporating the special provisions offered in this section.

There are certain structural differences from the Celebration of Wholeness and Healing to be noted. These include an earlier position for Prayers of Penitence, and a change of rhythm, with Laying on of Hands and Anointing leading into the Liturgy of the Sacrament. The laying on of hands and anointing have integral affinities both with the intercessory prayers that precede them and with the eucharistic liturgy that follows. The relationship between healing and reconciliation is appropriately summed up in the Peace, and the association of oil with joy leads logically to acts of presentation and thanksgiving in the Preparation of the Table and the eucharistic prayer.

The comments that follow deal only with elements that differ from those in A Celebration of Wholeness and Healing or from the normal eucharistic rite.

The theme of healing can be introduced after the Greeting by using one of the introductory paragraphs given as Supplementary Texts or other suitable words. The suggested form for the Prayers of Penitence, derived from the *Kyrie eleison*, enables this part of eucharistic liturgy to be retained, while linking a confidence in God's mercy to a trust in Christ the healer, evidenced in the Gospels. It is appropriately followed by a simple and familiar form of absolution. Confession and absolution in the eucharistic model of this service fall more naturally in this position than in the later position in the non-eucharistic model. At a service of this kind, the readings set for the day will normally take precedence and if the ministry of healing is to be offered at the principal Sunday Service, then the readings of the day must take priority. The impact of the Peace in its normal eucharistic position will be different from its impact as part of the Dismissal in the Celebration of Wholeness and Healing.

Three of the Short Proper Prefaces provided cover general use and concentrate on incarnational themes. In particular, they express Christ's sharing of our human nature in all its weakness, and the healing and salvation achieved through his death and resurrection. The fourth, although for general use, is inspired by Luke 7.22–23, which itself demonstrates how Jesus becomes the fulfilment of the prophecy of Isaiah (see Isaiah 35.3–6 and Luke 4.16–21).

The fifth preface takes the image of the tree whose leaves are for the healing of the nations from Revelation 22.1–2. An extended preface based on the parable of the Good Samaritan (Luke 10) is also provided. The christological interpretation of the figure of the Samaritan has patristic origins and is used on several occasions in the sermons of Augustine. The Prayer after Communion is a reminder that Christ feeds us towards the total healing of eternal life, a theme found notably in John 6.35, but present in many contexts, notably in the Lord's Prayer. At the dismissal the invocation of the Trinity makes a powerful statement in a form of blessing that recognizes the need for healing of body, mind and spirit. The notion of belonging to another country is deeply woven into Christian tradition. It informs the image of the Christian life as a pilgrimage towards our final home in heaven. It is also alluded to in Hebrews 11.13–16.

Supplementary Texts
These texts relate to both of the preceding rites, and should be used according to pastoral need.

Introductions
1 This form of words centres on two passages from the Epistle to the Hebrews – Hebrews 4.14, which speaks of Jesus as our great High Priest, and Hebrews 7.25, which carries the promise of salvation for all who come to God through him. This is an important twinning of images of Jesus in the context of the healing ministry, for it recalls both the priestly aspect of Christ and his concern for weaknesses that encompass far more than simply physical illness.
2 Based mainly on Romans 8, this Introduction concentrates on the painful coming to birth of a creation renewed and made whole in Christ. Its emphasis on struggle makes it suitable for integration into liturgies of healing in particular contexts.
3 Beginning with Jesus' command to the disciples to love one another (John 15.12, 17), this Introduction goes on to allude to the common life of the earliest Christian community described in Acts (e.g. Acts 2.42–47). The care of this body of Christians for its members continues to be an example in the contemporary world, and more substance is added by the reference to Matthew 25.40. The parable in which this verse falls illustrates how acts of charity and concern are done not only to others, but to Christ in others. This kind of ministry is therefore also a way of coming unexpectedly across the divine image, and it is with that understanding that the healing ministry might be practised.
4 This Introduction starts with a general summary of Jesus' ministry as recorded in the four Gospels, taking his actions as a mandate for present-day ministry to the sick. Further endorsement is provided from the fifth chapter of the Epistle of James, possibly the clearest single scriptural

injunction to the Christian community to continue the ministry of prayer and healing.

Bible Readings

These reflect the wide embrace of the notion of wholeness, and take into account the healing of the world, the healing of the effects of sin, the healing of bodily afflictions and the healing of those disturbed in mind or spirit. There is also an opportunity to reflect in an eschatological way on the resurrection and the bread of eternal life as part of the redemption of time itself.

Prayers over the Oil

Some attention to the non-responsive version of the first prayer has already been given above in the commentary on the Celebration of Wholeness and Healing. The use of a responsive form should be governed by local circumstances. Certainly, it moves the emphasis further away from the president and closer towards a pattern of communal intercession. While this makes the paragraph 'By the power of your Spirit . . .', look less like an epiclesis, for some the question remains: 'What happens to the oil, and how does this prayer encourage the people to think about it and receive it?' The short form refers to Mark 6.13, where the Apostles anointed those who were sick. It is specific in asking that God will bless the oil, though careful not be over-specific in its prayer for the functions that it may perform. Put plainly, it avoids any suggestion that application of oil will result directly in physical healing.

Prayer for Individuals in Public Worship

Although this section consists of Notes, it has the status of a third rite for those places which offer prayer with individuals on virtually every occasion. Points to stress are that this ministry should be properly integrated in the corporate prayer of the people and that it should not 'overshadow the gift and promise of communion' when offered in a eucharistic setting. At the same time, where such prayer is offered, the intention should be properly honoured. This may mean arranging to have an identifiable team of people who can pray with individuals, perhaps during the laying on of hands and anointing, or who can pray with those who so wish after the service. Practice cannot easily be prescribed, but those assisting individuals in prayer should be sensitive to their wishes when asking whether there is anything they would like prayed for explicitly. Prayer for individuals may also be part of any intercessions that are offered – in the familiar form of the 'list of the sick' in parish worship or in a form which names those who have particularly asked for prayer.

Ministry to the Sick

The Notes to this section pay close attention to the pastoral sensitivities of ministry to the sick and allow officiants to shape the rite in such a way as to avoid making undue physical and mental demands on a person who cannot concentrate or maintain a single position for long periods. Reception in one kind allows for difficulty in holding the chalice steady or in swallowing, and those too ill to receive at all are to be assured that they partake in faith in the benefits conveyed by the body and blood of Christ. The forms offered may be extended to use in residential homes.

The Celebration of Holy Communion at Home or in Hospital

Forms of this service according to Order One (contemporary and traditional language) and Order Two are provided. In Order One the Prayers of Penitence are introduced by optional texts from Matthew 11.28 and Romans 5.8 that emphasize Christ's willingness to bear the burdens of those who feel unable to continue in their own strength, and the unconditional nature of his love for the human creation. An optional prayer at the Preparation of the Table sets all weakness and inadequacy under God's transforming power. It is very suitably tied to the offering of gifts of bread and wine because it recognizes that all things are capable of being used by God for his purposes, even ill health and other forms of weakness. It was not newly drafted for this service but singled out from the existing texts in the *CW* main volume.

Although the debates preceding the appearance of *Ministry to the Sick* (1983) resulted in the provision of a shortened form of eucharistic prayer, no special provision, other than Proper Prefaces, is made here. This is because there is no way of prescribing when an authorized eucharistic prayer may or may not be used, and in the *ASB* era some parishes used the prayer for use with the sick at the Sunday Parish Eucharist, thus disturbing the balance of the liturgical action. *CW* now provides prayers short enough to be used with the sick. Prayer E is recommended, because the responsive forms D and H can be too demanding for sick people. On some occasions, familiarity will be more important than brevity, and that is why Order One (Traditional) instead recommends Prayer C with its Prayer Book wording. At the Giving of Communion the suggested invitation is 'Jesus is the Lamb of God who takes away the sin of the world. Blessed are those who are called to his supper', to which the response is 'Lord, I am not worthy to receive you, but only say the word and I shall be healed'/'Lord I am not worthy that thou shouldest come under my roof, but speak the word only, and my soul shall be healed.' The scriptural rooting of this text in the healing of the centurion's servant is an important resonance in the service, and the invitation and response illustrate the power of implicit as well as explicit teaching and association.

The Distribution of Holy Communion at Home or in Hospital

Two outline orders, for Order One and Order Two, are provided. The sequence of actions in the liturgy varies in conformity to these two *CW* eucharistic Orders, and pastoral sense will dictate which of them is used. The Notes indicate permitted ministers for the distribution and set out how and when they should receive the consecrated elements. Seasonal material may be included and there is a place allotted in each order for the laying on of hands and anointing. As in the case of the Celebration of Holy Communion at Home or in Hospital, variations in the form of reception are permitted.

Laying on of Hands with Prayer and Anointing

This is intended as part of a larger liturgical action. It could be used in place of intercessions and clearly has the capacity to be used when several people are joining the priest and the sick person in worship. The main prayer concentrates on petition for healing, strength, support and restoration of all the sick in the divine image. It presupposes that the oil of anointing will have been previously blessed, so that the focus of prayer becomes the sick person rather than the act of blessing. The words of administration are those used in the public setting of a celebration of healing, but the character of the act is significantly altered by the home setting.

Prayers for Protection and Peace

These prayers should never be confused with the ministry of deliverance proper, or 'exorcism' as it is commonly called. Guidance for the exercise of the latter is given in the Notes, with emphasis on episcopal authorization for any such ministry. The prayers were a late addition at the revision stage, and responded to requests from those who might arguably have been seeking something closer to a rite of exorcism. In that sense, they describe a limit to the kind of ministry that can be offered without direct episcopal supervision. The material offered is eclectic, mainly because it is a sample of the sort of material that could be used, leaving the burden of choice with the person offering ministry. It sets a stylistic pattern that moves firmly away from any form of prayer with characteristics of exorcism. It would be possible, for example, to find other forms of St Patrick's Breastplate, such as the metrical 'I bind unto myself this day'. Christaraksha (an Indian prayer) is beautiful in its own right and known to some through *Celebrating Common Prayer*, but is not as obvious a resource for this sort of need as other more familiar prayers might have been.

Further Reading

House of Bishops' Report, *A Time to Heal*, Church House Publishing, London, 2000.

Colin Buchanan, *Services for Wholeness and Healing*, Grove Worship Series 161, Grove Books, Cambridge, 2000.

Martin Dudley and Geoffrey Rowell (eds), *The Oil of Gladness: Anointing in the Christian Tradition*, SPCK, London, 1993.

Christopher Gower, *Speaking of Healing*, SPCK, London, 2003.

Charles W. Gusmer, *The Ministry of Healing in the Church of England*, Alcuin Club Collections 56, Mayhew-McCrimmon, Great Wakering, 1974.

Charles Harris, 'Visitation of the Sick' and 'Communion of the Sick' in W. K. Lowther Clarke (ed.), *Liturgy and Worship*, SPCK, London, 1932.

Carolyn Headley, *Home Communion: A Practical Guide*, Grove Worship Series 157, Grove Books, Cambridge, 2000.

Carolyn Headley, *The Laying on of Hands and Anointing*, Grove Worship Series 172, Grove Books, Cambridge, 2002.

Paul Roberts, 'Healing and Reconciliation' in Michael Perham (ed.), *Liturgy for a New Century*, SPCK/Alcuin Club, London, 1991, pp. 63–71.

Chapter 8

Reconciliation and Restoration

A. HISTORY

Old Testament

The system for reconciliation and dealing with human sin in the Old Testament is too complex to cover in detail in this chapter. Atonement was made primarily by the offering of sacrifice, and the intricate sacrificial system and Temple cult provided outward forms to enable God's people to admit sin and its uncleanness, turn to God and make recompense. But it was a consistent part of God's call to his people that reconciliation is a matter of the heart, not just outward action. Unless contrition is real, and repentance is a true turning to God and his ways, then even strict adherence to the restorative ritual is not acceptable to God who is holy and just (Isaiah 1.10–20). Psalm 51 epitomizes the right approach of a sinner with a sincere desire for mercy and forgiveness before God, coming with the sacrifice of a broken spirit and a broken and contrite heart (Psalm 51.17).

The New Testament and Early Church

Christ is portrayed in the Gospels as having authority over sin or evil and possessing the power to forgive. In some instances healing is a validation of this claim, as in Luke 5.18–26, the bringing in of the kingdom being the key factor in the link between the two. The early Christians emphasized that forgiveness of sin came through faith in Christ and was part of the turning away from the old life and beginning of a new life. It was thus primarily linked to baptism, which signified dying and rising with Christ to walk in newness of life (Romans 6.1–11; Colossians 2.6–15). However, the Church struggled to make sense of sin committed after baptism and began to wrestle with how it should react towards those Christians whose lives exhibited serious moral failings. Apostasy is described as a fearful prospect (Hebrews 10.26–31), and John also speaks of sin that leads to death, alongside encouragement to pray for those whose sins can be forgiven, to whom God can give life (1 John 5.16–17). Paul advocates excommunication for serious sinners in the hope of remedial discipline away from the haven and care of the church community (1 Corinthians 5; see also 1 Timothy 1.20). James gives hope of forgiveness of sin through the ministry of mutual confession and anointing, and again brings forgiveness and healing together (James 5.15–16). Christ's commission is to the whole Church to share in the heavenly calling of following Christ the apostle and high priest (Hebrews 3.1), and the New Testament is full of the mutuality of this ministry among the body of Christ. However, Christ was understood to have delegated his authority to his Apostles to bind and to loose (Matthew 18.18) and to forgive sins (John 20.23), and this initial and distinctive call along with the promise to Peter that he would be given the keys of the kingdom of heaven (Matthew 16.18–19) have formed the basis of the Church's practice of giving authority to forgive sins to designated church leaders.

The problem of post-baptismal sin greatly exercised the early Church. If sin was committed frequently, then it brought into question the person's regeneration, and if forgiveness was pronounced too readily, then the awfulness of sin was undervalued. An approach that only permitted penance and reconciliation once in a lifetime was seen to hold the tension between recognizing the seriousness of sin and showing mercy. This in turn made delaying confession until the point of death the safest option in terms of assurance of eternal life. Some of the earliest evidence comes from the *Shepherd of Hermas*, a text emanating from Rome some time in the second century. This allows for only one occasion of penance in a lifetime, and treats restitution through penance as a second baptism, a repetition of baptismal washing. This is one strand of thinking that develops through the centuries, removing the ministry of reconciliation to a preparation for death. Another strand of teaching allowed for repeated penance, with fasting and a variety of penalties for sin.

The evidence provided by Tertullian in North Africa is crucial to our knowledge of penitential practice in the late second and early third centuries. He introduces two categories – remissible and irremissible sin – and supplies a list of sins in each. This distinction became a pressing issue a generation later, when the Roman presbyter Novatian and the newly elected Pope Cornelius, proclaimed in 251, found themselves in opposition over the treatment of Christians who had denied their faith during times of persecution. While Cornelius favoured full acceptance of those who had fallen away at a time of extreme danger, Novatian, with other clergy who had remained faithful during the persecution, saw no case for restitution. This group went further in consecrating Novatian pope, so that a rival papacy came into existence. Cyprian of Carthage became the arbitrator in the dispute. His view was that salvation was impossible outside the communion of the Church, and urged that true penitents be received back as soon as possible. Eventually, Cornelius convened a synod at Rome, which ruled that the lapsed were to be restored to the church with the usual 'medicines of salvation'. Novatian and his party established a separate church, schismatic, but regarded as orthodox.

The Peace of the Church (or Peace of Constantine, 313) saw little difference in penitential practice from pre-Constantinian times. However, a flood of new converts entered the Church at this time. They had not been through an

exacting catechumenate, nor had the genuineness and depth of their conversion experience been rigorously tested, and so they could not be guaranteed to
avoid post-baptismal sin. This ought to have made a case for some relaxation
in the administration of penance. Yet all the surviving texts agree that the discipline of penance actually became stricter, to the point where it was an
impediment in the spiritual lives of Christians.

The process of penance typically began with the enrolment of those who
had committed serious sin as members of the order of penitents. A period of
expiation followed, supervised by the Church. At the end of this there was an
act of reconciliation, presided over by the bishop. The enrolment was public,
and accompanied by the laying on of hands by the bishop. The penitent was
then clothed in a garment of goatskin (the *cilicium*), which was worn during
the period of penance. Over this, the penitent wore sombre clothes, and did
not wash or trim hair or beard. After the enrolment, the penitents were sym-
bolically expelled from the Church. Penitents were still welcome to attend
church worship, but they were banned from receiving communion and from
offering oblations until their penance had been completed. During this time,
fasting, almsgiving and acts of mortification were imposed. Penitents knelt
through worship on feast days as a sign of mourning. It was their task to carry
the dead to the church and to bear them to the grave. The restrictions imposed
on penitents forbade them to work and committed them to celibacy, sometimes lifelong. The community meanwhile continued to pray for those
excommunicated. The length of the period of expiation was determined by the
bishop, and the early texts are silent about the possibility of permanent excommunication. Those who became ill while serving penance completed it when
they recovered. The dying were exempted from canonical penance, however,
and were reconciled quickly. Any who died during the period of expiation were
deemed to have been restored. From the fifth century, reconciliation of penitents probably took place on Maundy Thursday, so that they might participate
in the Easter festival and receive communion then. Restoration to the rights
and privileges of the Church was assumed to go hand in hand with restoration
to the grace of God. The bishop laid hands on the penitents and prayed over
them.

Towards the end of the sixth century a new penitential system appears. It
seems to have originated in Celtic and Anglo-Saxon monasteries and quickly
spread to Europe. It allowed all Christians – both clergy and laity – to seek a
confessor and ask to do penance and be reconciled each time they sinned, in
contrast to the old system in which only the bishop could reconcile a penitent,
and only once in a lifetime. (This finally disposed of the anxiety over post-
baptismal sin, which had often caused church leaders to encourage the young
to delay enrolling as penitents and had made a number of believers delay their
baptisms.) For the penance, small 'fees' were exacted in the shape of fasting,
almsgiving and days of mortification, and hence the term 'tariff penance'. Each
sin carried a distinctive penance, and manuals called Penitentials were issued

to guide the clergy in the administration of standard penances. English, Irish and Scottish monks brought their Penitentials to Europe in the eighth century and the number of books very soon escalated enormously. The completion of the penance was understood as pardon, although some manuals indicate a second visit to the confessor to receive absolution. Confession was made in private and the process was secret: there was no order of penitents, nor did penitents wear distinctive clothing, occupy special places in church or undergo rites of public restoration. Tariff penance is the direct antecedent of the form of sacramental confession still used today in the Western Church.

The Middle Ages

The Carolingian kings attempted to restore the ancient system of penance, but the ninth century was a great age of manuscript copying, and Penitentials flourished. Thus a dual system developed, with public penance for serious public sins and private penance according to the tariff system for serious secret sin. The rites of public penance were definitively fixed for the whole of the Middle Ages, and up to the modern period, in the Romano-Germanic Pontifical (c. 960) and the regulations of Réginon de Prum (915). In essentials, they preserved the ritual of the earlier Gelasian Sacramentary.

By the twelfth century the pattern of private penance had changed so that absolution followed immediately upon confession, and the penance itself was performed afterwards, with the result that it was no longer part of a preparation process. At the same time a declaratory absolution replaced prayer for forgiveness. The history of this becomes complicated by the developing doctrine of purgatory, understood to complete purification of the soul after death, the selling of indulgences, and the idea that penance could be done by proxy. Initially indulgences could offset the penance required, but then they began to be seen as a way of offsetting God's punishment, or shortening the period of purgatory for the purchaser or a relative. Proxy penance could be obtained by payment, with other people being able to undertake penance, or priests saying masses, on behalf of sinners. This loses the moral dimension of penance, and the system favoured the rich, who could afford to 'buy' masses. Another factor to be considered was the growing importance of absolution at the hour of death. By definition, this left no time for penance, which could therefore not be understood as having a causal value in the efficacy of the sacrament, although the Scholastics attempted to provide an account. These and other related practices were unacceptable to the Reformers, and the whole ministry of personal penance and reconciliation became a focus for criticism.

The Reformation

The systemized approach to penance had become a focus for abuse by the Church, according to the Reformers. As a sacrament it had become a solely priestly function. Auricular confession (confessing sins privately to the priest), and priestly authority to forgive sin, to determine the penance, have intimate knowledge of peoples' lives and power to direct them, had become an opportunity for clerical power. The Reformers wanted Scripture to be the foundation for hearing of God's holiness, judgement, mercy and forgiveness, and the challenge to change direction and walk in newness of life. Private confession may well be a useful pastoral ministry, offered to those in need, but was not the required norm to know assurance of forgiveness. So Luther advocated its use in the *Babylonian Captivity* (1520) and he and Melanchthon retained it as one of three sacraments, although Luther did so because it led back to baptism (as had Aquinas *c.* 1225–74). He saw its efficacy only as God enacting his promise, received by faith, and not dependent on the effort of the act. Calvin still saw value in it as preparation for communion (*Institutes* III.4.13) and as assurance of God's mercy and pardon when restored to the fellowship of the Church (III.4.14), but this was in addition to general confession within the context of corporate worship. He also saw the value of mutual confession and recognized the role of pastors as those especially designated by God to assure us of God's goodness (III.4.12).

In England Henry VIII defended the retention of the seven sacraments, but as opinion progressed towards regarding only baptism and the Eucharist as sacraments (with various sets of Articles reflecting different positions along the way), penance remained slow to relinquish its claim. Even Cranmer's *Catechism* of 1548 regarded it as one of three. However, the change came and baptism was seen as the Christ-ordained sacrament of repentance, with Holy Communion as a frequent reminder whereby assurance could be received of remission of sins and all the benefits of Christ's passion, because of his all-sufficient sacrifice for sin.

The exhortation in the 1548 *Order of Communion* encourages 'auricular and secret confession to the Priest' for those whose conscience is troubled and who lack comfort and counsel, and this is used again in the 1549 communion service. A form for private confession was included in the Visitation of the Sick in the 1549 *BCP*, which could be used for special confession at any time. The form of absolution, with the priest's authoritative 'I absolve you' formula, is of particular importance. With Christ's authority invested in the Church, its priests have his authority to forgive sin. This was based on the commission to the Apostles in John 20.22–23, the passage on binding and loosing in Matthew 18.18, and keys of the kingdom being given to Peter, on whom the Church is built, in Matthew 16.18–19.

The Reformers recognized the need to be true to this scriptural commission, and to the role of the Church, while wanting to redress any abuse of clerical power and barriers to personal access to the mercy of God. So this was an area of contention and difficulty for them, with a variety of views on the interpretation and application of those scriptural promises. For example Martin Bucer, in his critique of the Visitation of the Sick, made the absolution corporate: 'we absolve this our brother/sister'. Basically they saw the commission as being to the whole Church not just to those ordained priest, but also understood the Church as discharging that commission through its ministers.

In the 1552 Prayer Book, the exhortation in the communion service still offered a confessional ministry to those who needed it, but the vocabulary changes, offering counsel, advice and comfort by 'ministers of God's word'. The brief provision for the Communion of the Sick in 1552 does not include a penitential section, but after its special elements the communion service is to resume at 'Ye that do truly and earnestly repent of your sins . . .', so the same importance is attached to the attitude of approach as in the main communion service. The 1549 form for personal confession and priest's absolution remained in the 1552 Visitation of the Sick but the rubrics changed, removing the expectation of this being used on any other occasion. This is the same in 1662, apart from making the confession of sins something to be encouraged ('be moved to') rather than demanded, and the absolution to be given if the person 'desires it' and then it will be after this 'sort' (not this 'form'), thereby giving flexibility for wording. The prayer following it was from the Gelasian Sacramentary Maundy Thursday service for Reconciliation of Penitents, and was expanded to include 'strengthen him with thy blessed spirit; and when thou art pleased to take him hence, take him to thy favour'.

The importance of a general confession at Morning and Evening Prayer (from 1552 onwards) and at Holy Communion relates to this change of emphasis from auricular confession to general confession. In the communion service this must be seen in conjunction with the exhortations, which clearly spell out the need for heartfelt and true repentance, mindful of God's wrath, but grateful for the extent of his great mercy. Only then can we 'spiritually eat the flesh of Christ, and drink his blood; then we dwell in Christ and Christ in us'. The satisfaction for sins is complete in Christ, and therefore the transaction can be direct, not reliant on any action demanded by the Church. So in any service general confession, rightly and sincerely approached, can appropriate the promised forgiveness of the heavenly Father, declared to humankind in Christ, and can bring assurance of his mercy and forgiveness, and grace for a changed life that will show the fruit of true repentance – in amendment of life and love of neighbour. This remains the approach in 1662.

Services for public penance had some limited provision: 1549 included a service for 'The First Day of Lent: Commonly called Ash Wednesday'. At this point an annual service for penitents was envisaged, as had been common practice since the seventh century. It consisted of two exhortations, the second one being very lengthy, various versicles and responses, Psalm 51 and prayers. The service was based on existing provision, and some of the prayers come from the Gelasian and Gregorian Sacramentaries. It was to follow the saying of the litany. In 1552 it was renamed 'A Commination Against Sinners' and it could be used on occasions other than Ash Wednesday. This remained virtually unchanged in 1662.

After 1662

Private confession and absolution continued to be offered, mainly to the sick using the provision in the Visitation for the Sick, and as a pastoral necessity as outlined in the communion exhortation. But, influenced in part by contemporary Roman Catholic practice, calls for it to be more widely practised as part of personal spiritual discipline, and as an important part of a priest's care of the people in developing their personal holiness, came during the nineteenth century. Those who desired greater use of this ministry invoked the provision of the *BCP*: in the communion exhortation's offer of counsel and absolution after 'opening his grief' for the quietening of conscience; and in the authority given to priests in the Ordinal, with its clear commission to forgive sins at the laying on of hands, using the words of John 20.23. Fears of the re-emergence of medieval abuses or any theology that might suggest that confession and absolution were *necessary* then surfaced in several quarters; in response, various apologias for the practice appeared. For example, Edward Pusey preached and published his sermon *The Entire Absolution of the Penitent* in 1846, and a full treatment of the subject was written by Thomas Carter, *The Doctrine of Confession in the Church of England*, in 1864.

The issues related to the ministry of reconciliation and restoration at the turn of the century initially continued to be entwined with the ministry to the sick, but this link quickly became less firm and discussion on both strands became more focused. The Fulham Conference of Anglican theologians over the New Year 1901/02 was devoted to the subject of confession and absolution. Two main points of agreement were reached, that John 20.23 was not only addressed to the Apostles but to the whole Church and that existing provision (the Anglican Formularies) did allow for the ministry of confession and absolution. Consequently priests minister on behalf of the whole body of 'kings and priests' – the Church – through 'God's Word and Sacraments and godly discipline'. So the discipline of confession and absolution should be available to those who wish to make use of it. There remained disagreements as to the extent to which the ministry should be encouraged, whether it should be seen as beneficial in general spiritual and moral life or should be kept for exceptional circumstances. The proposed 1927/28 Prayer Book retained a form of confession in the Visitation of the Sick. However, it added words for introducing a confession that followed ancient practice: 'I confess to God . . . and especially I have sinned in these ways . . .' The absolution remained unchanged from 1662, but the prayer following it was simplified.

Towards Common Worship

As work on material leading to the *ASB* developed, it was envisaged that rites for initiation, healing and reconciliation would all be related. In 1980 *Services for the Sick* (GS 471) was published at the same time as *The Blessing of Oils and the Reconciliation of a Penitent* (GS 472). Both of them received General Approval in 1981, and *Services for the Sick* continued on to receive Final

Approval as *Ministry to the Sick* in 1983. It was decided to send Reconciliation of a Penitent and Blessing of Oils through the process separately, but they were both rejected by the House of Laity. A number of issues that have recurred in the history of the ministry of reconciliation were responsible for the failure of the former to gain approval, notably the absolution formula 'I absolve you from all your sins'. As previously seen, this is connected to the way in which a priest's authority is understood, and how exercising this ministry on behalf of the Church, in accordance with Christ's commission, assures a penitent that sins have been forgiven by God. Consequently the form that later appeared in *Lent, Holy Week and Easter* (1986) was worded, 'I declare that you are absolved from all your sins'. This wording found enough agreement to allow its commendation, but the debate and explanation were inadequate, causing further concern and problems for the subsequent journey of this provision. In 1988 David Silk (then Archdeacon of Leicester) included both the rejected form and the *Lent, Holy Week and Easter* form in a private publication, *In Penitence and Faith* (Mowbray). In his Introduction he said that he saw no incompatibility between the teaching of the 32nd Homily of the Church of England and the Council of Trent, on the components of penance – contrition, confession, absolution and satisfaction (amendment of life).

Although legal opinion at the time had been that the proposals required full synodical authorization, more recently that opinion has been reversed by the ecclesiastical lawyers: reconciliation rites are not now regarded as being alternatives to those in the *BCP*; and so after further revision, the rites were presented in 2004 simply for commendation by the House of Bishops. When the *CW* Initiation Services had first been brought to General Synod, it had been intended that Reconciliation and Restoration would to be brought together with them in an integrated collection that would include all the initiation material, supporting rites for those on the journey of faith, and rites to enable a renewal of the baptismal covenant after sin, so that they could be 'restored to the new life in Christ given in baptism' (see the report, *On the Way: Towards an Integrated Approach to Christian Initiation*, GS Misc 444, 1995). The current provision was therefore put to General Synod in 2004 along with Rites on the Way, as a rather belated supplement to fulfil the expectation expressed in the preliminary edition of the *CW* Initiation Services (although without the Blessing of Oils, which appear elsewhere – for the sick in Wholeness and Healing, and for catechumens and chrism in Times and Seasons). The underlying theology and much of the text was the work of Michael Vasey, and the report *Common Worship: Initiation Services – Rites on the Way and Reconciliation and Restoration* (GS 1546, 2003) paid tribute to him.

The rites themselves fall broadly into two categories: corporate penance and reconciliation of individual penitents. The category of individual reconciliation is subdivided, with one pattern following the traditional usage of the Western Church, while the other places the reconciliation of individual penitents in the context of personal renewal of the baptismal covenant.

The Service of Corporate Penance is envisaged as normally taking place within a church setting, either as an independent service or as the first part of a longer act of worship. The setting for the two rites for the Reconciliation of a Penitent is not so easily determined. Form 1, which is a general recognition of sin, is less formally constructed than Form 2, although this in itself is not an indication of place or context. Although confession often conjures up images of confessionals in which a screen or grating separates the priest from the penitent, this fixture is relatively recent and is thought to have originated with Charles Borromeo, who became Archbishop of Milan in 1565. Before this time, penitents confessed in the open church, either kneeling before the priest or sitting at his side, but this proximity had been abused. (It is worth noting, in this light, that modern concerns have seen the return of screens and gratings in some churches where confessions are regularly heard.) Borromeo believed firmly in the formative value of confession in the lives of the faithful, and took care that only specially licensed clergy generally heard confessions, except in cases of pastoral necessity. An immediate consequence of this measure of control was that orders of friars which had specialized as preachers and confessors, and which had resisted the authority of diocesan bishops, found themselves marginalized.

Modern practice varies widely. At the Anglo-Catholic end of the Anglican spectrum, there is a well-established tradition of regular individual confession, and confessionals may be part of church furniture. The ministry of spiritual direction, moreover, may also include opportunity for repentance and absolution. This could very well take place in the director's home or office. Forms 1 and 2 are careful not to use the word 'confession' in their titles, thereby avoiding language which suggests a particular churchmanship. The emphasis is on reconciliation and on welcoming the penitent back into the fullest possible participation in the life of the Church, and it is right that the setting chosen for this act should be one in which the penitent feels comfortable and secure. For some, this will be the church building, for others a more domestic setting will be helpful.

B. COMMENTARY

The Theological Introduction

The Theological Introduction to the texts very succinctly sets out the 'broader theological context', which aligns the rites with 'the renewal of the baptismal covenant and of the prayer of the Church for healing and restoration'. Baptismal restoration – the condition of reconciliation with God and with the Church – therefore describes the desire contained both within the rites of wholeness and healing and the rites of reconciliation and repentance. This applies equally to corporate and individual acts of penitence. As the introduction to the form for use with an individual notes, 'the reconciliation of a penitent, even when celebrated privately, is a corporate action of the Church, because sin affects the unity of the body'.

While the Introduction refers to the saving aspect of Jesus' healing miracles, the exhortations to Christians to confess their sins to one another and the response to serious public sin, it does not mention the assurance of forgiveness of sin that often accompanies Jesus' acts of healing. This may reflect a wish to discourage any simplistic causal association between sin and sickness, but it is worth remembering the positive resonances of freedom and health in body, mind and soul which are present in this pairing.

A Service of Corporate Penitence

This is an appropriate form to be used at a diocesan, deanery or parish occasion. The accompanying Notes suggest that it might be used in preparation for a penitential season; to mark the desire of a community to achieve reconciliation within itself; or in response to national events. As with the Reaffirmation of Baptismal Vows, it is not a rite that should be over-used.

Corporate penitence may be placed in the context of a celebration of the Eucharist or marked as a separate occasion. This has some structural consequences, particularly in the case of the position of the Peace. Following the Greeting, a series of scriptural sentences is read. These correspond exactly to what were known as the Comfortable Words in the *BCP*, uttered by the priest after the absolution and before the Prayer of Consecration. In the *CW* main volume they appear in the Form of Preparation for Sunday worship as an alternative to the Ten Commandments. The Collect is that for Lent 4 in the *CW* cycle. It is found in the *BCP* as the Collect for the Twenty-Fourth Sunday after Trinity, and derives from the Sarum Missal. A useful table of readings is provided, which takes account of both seasonal and thematic considerations. The final section of the rite is an extended Sending Out. It begins either with an act of Thanksgiving for Holy Baptism, using a form of words found in the Thanksgivings for use at Morning or Evening Prayer on Sundays in *CW*, or with a proclamation of the Gospel. The table of readings includes suggestions for short Dismissal Gospels. If the Holy Communion has not been celebrated, the president introduces the Peace before the Blessing and Dismissal. In a departure from familiar practice, however, the sign of Peace is exchanged *after* the Dismissal.

The Reconciliation of a Penitent

Both the traditional form of individual penitence and the form based on renewal of the baptismal covenant conform to a basic outline structure of Preparation, Gathering, Liturgy of the Word (including Readings and Confession and Counsel), Reconciliation (including an Act of Contrition, Absolution and Thanksgiving) and a Dismissal (which may include a blessing).

Form 1

The words of greeting, adopted from the Anglican *Prayer Book for Australia*, are designed to convey warmth and reassurance. The readings may be prefaced by an introduction derived from the *BCP* invitation to confession at Morning and Evening Prayer. It emphasizes the reassurance of Ezekiel 33.11 – that God does not desire the death of sinners, but rather that they should turn away from their sin and live.

A sentence found in the *Methodist Worship Book* (1999, p. 424) and before that in the Roman Catholic Rite of Penance (1976) invites the penitent to confess his or her sins, empowered by God. This frames the act of confession within the love of God, rather than distancing the penitent from God by suggesting that sin is an entirely alienating condition. Two forms of words are given for the act of confession, using a traditional introduction or a form based on the Form of Preparation for Sunday worship in the *CW* main volume. An act of contrition follows. After this the priest pronounces an authorized absolution (suggestions are offered in the Resources section of the rite).

The Thanksgiving that follows absolution is shared by priest and penitent, and this is elegantly reflected in the direction that the psalm of thanksgiving (Psalm 106) be recited half-verse by half-verse, with the two voices alternating. Thereafter, the priest may pray for the penitent, for his or her restoration to grace and for continuing fidelity to the promises of baptism. A blessing may follow, and the priest dismisses the penitent with the assurance of forgiveness and with the traditional request that he or she pray for the priest. This has great pastoral importance and the evidence of those who seek the ministry of reconciliation, and of clergy who regularly celebrate those rites, is that the priest's acknowledgement of fallibility adds a dimension of humanity and solidarity to a process which might otherwise seem coldly disciplinary. The notes of guidance allow for a penance to be set. This is to be seen not as punishment but as a device to assist the process of spiritual restoration.

Form 2

The priest greets the penitent informally and silent preparation for the rite follows. A brief reading (Romans 6.3–4) signals the baptismal intention of the rite, and after this priest and penitent join in reciting verses from Psalm 145, Psalm 103 or Psalm 51. In various ways, these texts reflect the longing of the penitent for God, God's compassion, mercy and faithfulness, and the washing away of uncleanness which is part of a restored relationship with God.

The priest introduces the act of confession by reminding the penitent that his or her first act of repentance took place at baptism, and that the present act expresses the desire to return again to baptismal 'newness of life' through the confession of sin. The penitent may use his or her own words or words adapted from the 1979 American *BCP*. The language of this form of confession is evocative, and alludes to the creation narrative of Genesis; redemption through the cross of Christ; the Catechetical Lectures of Cyril of Jerusalem ('the shining garment of righteousness', *Procatechesis* 4.5); and the parable of the Prodigal Son (Luke 16.11–32). After this, he or she may make the sign of the cross in water and may be encouraged by the priest to make some tangible sign of repentance – a prayer might be suitable. At this point, the priest may offer to pray for the penitent.

In the act of reconciliation that follows, the penitent makes a verbal act of contrition. Words from the *CW* main volume (p. 132) are offered, but other similar words are permissible. At the conclusion of this act, the priest lays hands on, or extends hands over, the penitent, or traces the sign of the cross on his or her forehead, while pronouncing an authorized absolution. A scriptural act of thanksgiving, shared by priest and penitent, follows, and together they say the Lord's Prayer. The priest may bless the penitent before the dismissal, which, as in Form 1, carries a confident note of forgiveness and a new beginning.

Resources

There is a rich provision of material, drawn from a number of sources across the mainstream Christian denominations, to be considered for use at points where only one suggestion appears in the main text. Three new compositions are noteworthy additions to the available possibilities: David Kennedy's prayer at the preparation of the table (GS 1546, p. 105) which alludes to the scattered bread of the *Didache*, but also draws on the Matthaean account of the gathered fragments after the feeding of the multitude (Matthew 14.20); and his formulae for blessing and dismissal, the latter based on 2 Corinthians 5.19 (GS 1546, p. 106).

Further Reading

James Dallen, *The Reconciling Community: The Rite of Penance*, The Liturgical Press, Collegeville, Minnesota, 1986.

Martin Dudley and Geoffrey Rowell (eds), *Confession and Absolution*, SPCK, London, 1990.

Joseph Favazza, *The Order of Penitents: Historical Roots and Pastoral Future*, The Liturgical Press, Collegeville, MN, 1988.

Monika K. Hellwig, *Sign of Reconciliation and Conversion: The Sacrament of Penance for our Times*, Michael Glazier, Wilmington, DE, 1982.

R. C. Mortimer, *The Origins of Private Penance in the Western Church*, Clarendon Press, Oxford, 1939.

Nicolas Stebbing, *Confessing our Sins*, Mirfield Publications, Mirfield, 2002.

Chapter 9

Marriage

A. HISTORY

It is uncomfortable for many Christians to accept, but what is commonly referred to as 'Christian marriage' is a relatively modern concept. For much of the first millennium of the Christian era marriage in itself was not regarded as a special part of the Church's domain, and while a nuptial blessing became important for Christians, other sorts of partnership or commitment might also be hallowed in some way. The sacramental theologians took a long time to place marriage among the sacraments, and certainly many regarded the conse-cration of virgins as being equally important in the High Middle Ages. The development of marriage law is outside our scope, but went alongside the development of marriage rites, and although marriage law developed fairly consistently, in marriage rites little uniformity is found before the Reformation.

Jewish Precedents
The Jewish Scriptures say little about marriage customs and nothing at all about wedding ceremonies, which should not surprise us since their view of marriage was as a civil contract, and there was no public religious marriage ceremony, though it might equally be said that their understanding of God sacralized all aspects of life. The Old Testament norm is polygamy, but it is plain that the post-exilic prophets developed a high theology of marriage as being the lifelong union of a man and one woman, with a shift in emphasis from fertility to fidelity. The features that we know about are among those seen by anthropologists in many cultures, such as processions and veils. By the time of Christ forms of blessing prayer for marriage were certainly in use, but had not yet become the set texts that they were once thought to have been. The Seven Marriage Blessings are a later Jewish development.

The Early Christian Centuries
There is no serious New Testament evidence of Christian marriage cere-monies, nor much direct evidence during the first three centuries. It still seems reasonable to believe that the origins of early Christian liturgical practice are to be found in Jewish rites, and so the supposition is that blessing prayers were

the central feature, while Ignatius of Antioch suggests that the bishop was involved in some way (though this may not mean liturgically). There is evidence of growing diversity of practice, which was to continue into the Middle Ages, as the domestic rites of betrothal and marriage metamorphosed into the 'church wedding', presided over by priest or bishop.

Diversity of practice is clear once literary evidence for the Christian solemnization of marriage appears in the fourth century; for instance, the veil is used in the West, wedding-crowns in the East. No liturgical texts survive earlier than the so-called 'Leonine Sacramentary'.

Later Eastern Practice

Tertullian had criticized the use of crowns at marriage as a pagan practice, but the crowning became a characteristic Eastern form, as early as the fourth century, and was defended by John Chrysostom as representing victory over unchastity. The eighth-century Byzantine texts have separate rites of betrothal and marriage. The betrothal involves no explicit expression of consent, but simply prayers of blessing for the couple. In the marriage itself there is a litany with three special petitions for the couple and a prayer of blessing, after which the couple are crowned and their hands joined, and then two more prayers of blessing. The centrality of the priest's role as minister of the sacrament is clear. By the tenth century the two rites were usually celebrated on the same day, and generally in a single service, which was becoming more elaborate. A ring appeared at the betrothal in the tenth century, which became two rings a century later; and explicit consent, at the very beginning of the rite, appeared in the twelfth century. In the Armenian rite readings multiplied, and the crowns were bound onto the couple's heads to be removed a week later. In the Coptic rite wedding costumes were blessed at the start, and the crowning was the great climax, colouring much of the symbolism of the prayers. The general tone of various Eastern rites is joyous, celebrating marriage as the creation of God, and expressing mutuality between the couple, but the central action is their blessing by the Church.

The Medieval West

As soon as liturgical texts appear, they establish that the norm in the West is for a nuptial Eucharist. The nuptial blessing was pronounced before the couple received communion, and there were proper readings, psalms and prayers. In the Roman tradition the nuptial blessing was exclusively of the bride, which seems to be an inheritance from pagan Roman practice. The Roman choice of readings sets a distinctly less joyful tone than the Eastern, with no use of Ephesians 5.22–33 or John 2.1–11, which are common in the East, but instead 1 Corinthians 6.15–20, with its warning against fornication, and Matthew 19.1–6, 'one flesh'. The betrothal involved consent, and the giving of a ring to the bride. There is enormous variety in Western rites, but as the lawyers emphasized the importance of the consent and the vows, so those came to be set down according to local patterns, and used at the church door before the nuptial Eucharist began. Away from Rome, the nuptial blessing often included the bridegroom, and a veil was often spread over the couple at that point in the rite. The ring was generally blessed during the betrothal.

The developed medieval Western forms featured elaborate ceremonial before the start of the Eucharist, and in England in particular a multiplication of blessings. If we are to generalize, this might include the expression of consent (usually in the vernacular), the giving away of the bride (first seen in Spain) and her handing over by the priest to the groom, the joining of hands and the blessing and giving of the ring (and other 'tokens of spousage') followed by prayers. The priest's joining the couple's hands (and wrapping his stole around) was a French feature, which did not appear in the Sarum rite, although this rite on the other hand did include a developed set of vows, in English.

The Reformation

Generally the continental Reformers detached marriage from the Eucharist and continued such customs and ceremonies as were locally current. Luther had the couple give their consent at the church door, and then give each other a ring (unblessed). The pastor joined their right hands using the words from Matthew 19.6 and pronounced them to be married. A procession moved into church, where Scripture was read, and finally the pastor blessed the couple with hands outstretched, using a blessing which summed up the biblical material just read.

In Calvin's rite, marriage was to take place during the normal worship of the Church, but not on occasions when the Eucharist was celebrated. He begins with an address about the origin and purpose of marriage, and then the minister asks whether there are any impediments. He says a prayer for the couple and asks them whether they consent and pledge themselves to each other. He then says another prayer for the gift of the Spirit for the couple, and reads Matthew 19. 3–6 and pronounces that God has joined them together, and finishes with a long prayer and a short blessing.

The Church of England

Archbishop Thomas Cranmer's rite of 1549 drew on Sarum and Reformed sources to produce a shape which is very familiar. The service was divided in two, the first part at the church door, where the priest gave a long address (in Reformed fashion) explaining the reasons for marriage, which ended with the opportunity for any impediment to be lodged (as in medieval rites it had often become usual to have the final reading of banns at this point). The couple themselves were asked if there existed any impediment to their marriage, and were then asked whether they consented, in a form combining Sarum and Luther. The giving away then followed, the priest asking, 'Who giveth this woman . . .', which was only to be found in the York use in medieval England.

The couple then joined hands and exchanged vows, following a form similar to both Sarum and York (though with a Reformed tinge). The ring was given, unblessed, but accompanied with the formula from Sarum, 'With this ring . . .' The couple then knelt, and the priest prayed a long new prayer over them, and then joined their hands while reciting Matthew 19.6 and declared them to be married, with a formula taken from the German Reformer Hermann von Wied. A blessing of the couple, based heavily on a Sarum blessing, concluded the first part of the service. The couple then went to the altar during the recitation of a psalm, and prayers followed, using fragments of the Sarum nuptial blessing reworked with other material. The Eucharist was to follow.

The 1552 rite changed little from 1549 other than deleting the 'tokens of spousage', and nothing altered either in 1559 or 1604 despite Puritan opposition to the ring. The rite of 1662 was of course the result of hard negotiation, but in the end virtually nothing altered, except that it was recognized that the Eucharist would not normally follow and so the rubric was altered, and a scriptural exhortation provided to finish the rite. The rite of 1928 provided readings for the Eucharist, should it happen, and made provision for Scripture to be read if it did not. The declarations and vows were made symmetrical, shorn of the bride's promise to obey. The groom said, 'With my body I thee honour', rather than 'worship', when the ring was given (a change desired by some since the seventeenth century), and most noticeably the Preface read by the minister at the beginning was altered to be much less negative about sexuality. A desire for equality between partners and a more positive view of sexuality were to be consistent themes throughout the revision processes of the twentieth century. Series 1 reproduced 1928, with the addition of the blessing of the ring and the option of retaining 'obey'.

Like the funeral rite, marriage was never part of the Series 2 Alternative Services, and jumped straight to the modern language of Series 3, which was produced in 1975, authorized in 1977 and incorporated into the *ASB* in 1980. The *ASB* provided for marriage to be celebrated within, rather than before, the Eucharist, on the pattern adopted for other offices. Readings were an integral part of the rite, but either right at the beginning or before the prayers at the end. A fairly wide choice of readings was provided (though only half were printed). A liturgical greeting and a modern form of the 1928 collect (which might both be omitted) preceded the Preface, which was still cast in traditional form, but with the reasons for marriage utterly changed, so now they were mutual comfort, sexual union and children (as opposed to 1662's children, remedy for sin and mutual society). The charges and declarations followed entirely traditional forms, and then came the giving away, only as a rubrical option, much debated and with no words. Two forms of the vows were printed, the first symmetrical ('to love and to cherish . . .'), and the second complementary ('to love, cherish and worship . . .' balancing 'to love, cherish and obey . . .'). The return of 'obey' was greatly desired by people citing Scripture, and resisted by those influenced by feminism. The return of 'worship' was also very contentious. Provision was made for two rings, but one remained the norm. The blessing of the ring, in a new form, became mandatory (it was optional in Series 1). After the exchange of rings came the proclamation of the marriage, and the hugely controversial abandoning of the traditional rendering of Matthew 19.6, in favour of 'That which God has joined together, let not man divide', a phrase which annoyed several different groups. There then came the composite blessing, as in 1662, but followed by an optional set of acclamations, based on the Jewish seven marriage blessings. Provision was made for the registration to take place at this point, or at the end. A psalm or hymn was to follow, and the couple were directed to kneel 'before the holy table' for the prayers, which might or might not include a nuptial blessing. The rite was quite unclear as to when the couple were blessed. Only the modern form of the Lord's Prayer was provided, and the final blessing of 'the couple and the congregation' was in the form proper for Trinity Sunday in the *ASB*.

When the Liturgical Commission set to work to produce *CW*, their task was to escape from the close dependence on 1662 that had lasted up to the *ASB*. In the event, their draft service was structurally distinct, but used a remarkably conservative set of texts. In the revision process, however, several more novel texts came into the rite. As in the *ASB*, only a modern-language version was provided, as the Series 1 text continues to be a lawful alternative for those desiring a traditional language form.

B. COMMENTARY

One of the innovations in *CW* is the provision in the Supplementary Texts of Prayers at the Calling of the Banns, an expression of the debate about banns and preliminaries for marriage at the time of writing. The attempt is made to escape from dry legalism by commending the couple to the prayers of the faithful. Two prayers are offered, but others may be used.

The rubrics refer throughout to 'the minister'. The *ASB* had followed Series 1 and 1928 in referring to 'the priest', whereas 1662 had variously referred to 'the Priest', 'the Curate' and 'the Minister'. Anglican custom had been to restrict the conducting of weddings to priests, while allowing that deacons were legally entitled to preside and might do so in emergencies. With the ordination of 'permanent' women deacons in the mid 1980s this changed, and the matter was widely discussed, with the result that a deacon's ability to preside at a wedding was firmly established. The *CW* rubrics reflect this.

The marriage service is prefaced by a worthy Pastoral Introduction, intended to be printed in local service books and directed to members of the congregation. It expounds in fairly simple language a traditional Christian understanding of marriage, without referring to it as a sacrament, and is adapted from a New Zealand text. The use of a quotation from 1 Corinthians 13 is understandable, but not a happy use of that text.

The great break from the Anglican past is to move the point in the service where it is divided into two: 'Introduction', containing the declarations of consent, and 'The Marriage', containing vows and blessing, replaces the division between the marriage ceremony and the prayers. Thus, the historic notion of the betrothal, which in Sarum took place at the church door, has been reasserted, and the consent separated firmly from the vows. There are no instructions as to conducting the two parts in different locations, however, because the layout of buildings varies so much, and so in practice the division may be somewhat obscure.

Introduction

The minister welcomes the people with the Trinitarian formula, 'The grace . . .', or, as is customary, 'other appropriate words'. The sentence from 1 John, as in the *ASB*, may then be used. A congregational prayer may follow. In the 1997 draft, this was the modern form of the Collect for Purity, headed 'The Prayer of Preparation', but in the final version these headings have disappeared, and the prayer is 'God of wonder and joy', borrowed from the Church of Scotland. It would undoubtedly be effective with a gathering of committed churchgoers, but it is to be doubted how comfortable the average wedding guest will feel about some of the phrasing. The New Zealand rite has an option for a congregational prayer (of quite different content) at this point, but its use here is unusual.

After the congregational prayer comes the first mandatory item (possibly preceded by a hymn), the Preface. This was called 'The Introduction' in the draft version, a more understandable title and the one used by the *ASB*, but that is now the name of the whole first half of the service, and so we revert to the historic title, but since it only appears in the 'Structure' list at the beginning of the rite it will probably not be seen by ordinary worshippers anyway. The Preface is even longer than that in the *ASB*, which remains, with some minor alterations, as an alternative. Those who disliked the expression in the *ASB*, 'they may know each other in love', may also cringe at 'the delight and tenderness of sexual union', but it is plain that the new rite expresses a desire to affirm sexuality in stark contrast to what is perceived as the 'brute beasts' approach of the past. This is the most distinctive feature of the new Preface, which seems to the user to be more different from its predecessor than in reality it is, as the content is actually largely similar.

We 'celebrate their love' at the very start of the Preface, which sets the mood. Subtle variations from the *ASB* create a new tone: we no longer hear that 'the scriptures teach us' or that 'it is God's purpose', although the content remains the same. Marriage is no longer a 'means of grace' or a 'holy mystery', which may be said to remove a sacramental interpretation, and the loss of 'man and woman become one flesh' surely reinforces that. 'One flesh' may be an obscure phrase, but its omission certainly weakens the sense of permanent change expressed by the rite. The parallel from Ephesians is, on the other hand, helped by the new rite's spelling out that the Church is the bride of Christ. The historic 'reasons' for marriage are given less emphasis, and for the first time sex comes first, followed by children and companionship, though children and companionship may be thought to be conflated in one 'foundation of family life'. It is important to observe that marriage is no longer said to have been created by God (or even 'instituted in the time of man's innocency') but merely to have been made holy, and blessed by Christ's presence at Cana (the ancient reference losing its prominence at the start, but perhaps gaining in intelligibility here), a realistic anthropological account, but a major departure for the Church of England. The new contention is made, that 'marriage is a sign of unity and loyalty' which 'enriches society and strengthens community', which is undoubtedly a happier phrase than that in the *ASB*, 'new life together in the community', and attempts to express succinctly a heavy burden of sociological thought. Husband and wife no longer 'belong' to one another, which is a piece of cautious post-feminism.

The injunction had one of the better pieces of prose rhythm in the *ASB*, 'carelessly, lightly, or selfishly, but reverently, responsibly, and after serious thought', and this is not improved by being changed to 'lightly or selfishly but reverently and responsibly in the sight of almighty God'. The threefold adverbs simply give a better rhythm, even given the clumsiness of 'after serious thought'. The final text is the result of amendment in the revision process, as the draft had 'lightly or selfishly but only after weighing the consequences in the sight of almighty God', so the contrasting adverbs were obviously popular. The 'sight of almighty God' (with its echoes of 1662) has made it from the draft, where it made more sense, into the final text, where it is at best incongruous and owes its place simply to the fact that the phrase has very strong resonance in the popular mind when it comes to church weddings. In a text which seeks otherwise to avoid obscure phrases this is a striking anomaly. It is curious that reference to the couple's joining hands has been omitted in the final paragraph, where the 'actions' of the rite are listed as in the *ASB*. In the draft the omission was much less striking. Since the joining of hands does in fact take place, the effect is to downgrade its significance, whether intentionally or not. We shall revisit this question later.

The draft of the rite had preferred an unaltered version of the *ASB* as the Preface, but the revision process produced the new text (as well as amending the *ASB* text). The differences from the *ASB* text to that which now appears in the Supplementary Texts are small and of little significance. Instead of the Scriptures teaching us, we have the Bible doing so. The ubiquity of two rings is recognized by '(each)' being inserted into 'they will give and receive a ring'. The downgrading of procreation as a reason for marriage is expressed in the alteration of the statement in the *ASB*, 'It is given that they may have children and be blessed in caring for them and bringing them up in accordance with God's will', to the new, 'It is given as the foundation of family life in which children may be born and nurtured in accordance with God's will'. Otherwise the various verbal infelicities of the *ASB* remain.

The Declarations are little changed from the *ASB*, although they are now made 'in the presence of God' rather than in the name of God, which suits the sense of the charge better. However, the small detail as to whether to retain 'forsaking all other' or change to 'forsaking all others' was the cause of great debate and inordinate delay in the revision process, before the latter was eventually approved. The Notes allow the 1662 texts of the Declarations to be used. The question to the bridegroom is printed first, but the Notes allow that the order may be reversed if desired. The novelty here is the question to the congregation, a concept borrowed from the Dedication of a Civil Marriage, where it has proved popular and successful. This is mandatory, and cements congregational participation in this rite, one of the striking weaknesses of the *ASB*, where the congregation might only say 'Amen' and the Lord's Prayer.

The Collect follows, a product of the revision process, and a much stronger composition than that in the *ASB*, which was a modernization of the 1928 collect from the nuptial Eucharist, and like all the collects at *ASB* occasional offices prayed for all those present. This collect prays explicitly for the couple.

At least one reading must be used. A selection is printed in the Supplementary Texts, but these do not pretend to be exhaustive. Twenty-two are offered, all printed out in full, rather than just eleven in the *ASB* (of which only five were printed). The sermon is also mandatory (unlike the *ASB*). The strongly preferred position is here, separating the Declarations from the Vows, but the Notes do allow the reading and sermon to follow the nuptial blessing. The 1662 rite had no readings, since the assumption was that the readings at the Eucharist would follow, but a sermon or homily was to end the marriage service. The 1928 rite essentially kept that position, but allowed a portion of Scripture as an alternative, with a proper dismissal after it. Series 1 followed 1928. In the *ASB* the alternatives were to have the readings after the marriage itself (between the Registration and the Prayers) or to have them right at the start, before the Preface. Neither position was very satisfactory, and *CW* certainly integrates Scripture into the rite better than its predecessors.

The Marriage

The marriage proper now begins, possibly after a hymn, with the couple standing before the minister, who introduces the section with an invitation to the couple. This is a necessary link, but also an alternative to the 'giving away', as the modern perception is plainly of the couple as free agents, independent of their families. There is no mention of 'giving away' in the main text, whereas the *ASB* had a rubric that permitted the action, but a long Note deals with the question. Since most clergy will still find that most brides want the 'traditional ceremony', the Note spells out how it is to be done (which the *ASB* did not). The disapproval of the *ASB* for the ceremony was evident in the suppression of the question, 'Who giveth . . . ?', but *CW* provides, in the Notes, a modern version, 'Who brings this woman . . . ?' The change of verb is obviously significant. The ceremony can clearly happen without this phrase. The Notes also provide an alternative format in a fourth question at the Declarations, addressed to parents, '. . . will you now entrust your son and daughter to one another as they come to be married?' This is ingeniously phrased, but could not cover every circumstance, and so is unlikely to find a regular place in the rite as used in most churches.

The Vows in the main text are symmetrical, and are substantially the same as the *ASB*. The sense and syntax is, however, improved. The *ASB* words, 'I take you . . . till death us do part, according to God's holy law; and this is my solemn vow', are replaced by 'I take you . . . till death us do part; according to God's holy law. In the presence of God I make this vow.' The *ASB* had, of course, simply followed its predecessors in the form of the Vows, whereas the *CW* revisers felt free to simplify the English, as in the Preface. The change of syntax will certainly emphasize the force of the vow as a personal commitment. Experience showed that symmetrical vows rather than complementary ones were what couples wanted, but some provision for the older form remains. The Notes allow the use of alternative vows, printed in the Supplementary Texts. Form 1 is the set of vows from the main text with 'obey' added to the bride's vow. Form 2 is the 1662 vows, with the provision for 'obey' to be omitted from the bride's vow if desired. The complementary vows of the *ASB* are no longer permitted; the bridegroom's 'worship' of his wife had always been a controversial synodical decision, and no trace of it remains.

The Giving of Rings is unchanged from the *ASB*, except that the norm is now the exchange of two rings, not the giving of one. This is simply reflecting experience. In the Supplementary Texts an alternative blessing of the rings is provided, carefully entitled 'Prayer at the Giving of the Ring(s)', to satisfy the consciences of those in the Church of England who reject the concept of blessing inanimate objects. It employs rich imagery from Song of Solomon 8 and 1 Corinthians 13, and deserves to be used.

The Proclamation repeats the presumption that two rings will be used, but otherwise simply reproduces the *ASB*. The omission of mention of the joining of hands from the Preface seems all the more odd since the Proclamation still says, 'They have declared their marriage by the joining of hands . . .' The minister then joins their hands, as in the *ASB*. This offers a conundrum: to what action does the Proclamation then refer? It is usually supposed that the Proclamation in 1662 refers to the priest joining their hands, which happens immediately before the Proclamation, and which was a new ceremony to England when Cranmer introduced it, but the Proclamation in the *ASB* (where it is called the Declaration) cannot mean that, as the order has been inverted. If the *ASB* Proclamation means anything it must mean the couple's joining of hands as they made their vows. The *ASB* was very emphatic in the Western view that the couple were the ministers of their own marriage, and this inversion of the order from 1662 was part of that emphasis. The order in which the *ASB* Preface enumerates the 'actions' of the rite suggests the same conclusion: consent, joining hands, exchanging vows, giving and receiving of rings. *A Companion to the Alternative Service Book* (by R. C. D. Jasper and Paul

F. Bradshaw, SPCK, London, 1986), however, appears to miss this point, and confusingly heads a section, 'The Declaration, the Joining of Hands and the Blessing' (p. 387). As far as the rites of the *ASB* and *CW* are concerned, the 'Joining of Hands' is an action performed by the couple as they make their vows, and the action of the minister at the Proclamation is simply a demonstration of what is being proclaimed.

One of the most disliked phrases in the *ASB* was 'That which God has joined together, let not man divide', and it has been replaced in *CW* with 'Those whom God has joined together let no one put asunder'. 'That which', a reference to the bond created by God in marriage, has rightly been said to be a triumph of biblical scholarship over common sense, and was an unnatural and ugly wording. A good deal of effort went into justifying the *ASB* phrase at the time, but with little success. It might be observed that the problem is with the Gospel quotation (Matthew 19.6/Mark 10.9) since 'joining together' does not mean 'creating', and is bound to be taken as referring to the couple, who are the two things available to be joined. *CW* bows to the ostensible meaning of the text, rather than its scholarly exegesis. At the same time many congregations and many clergy found themselves increasingly uncomfortable with 'man' at the end of the *ASB* phrase, now felt unacceptably exclusive by many. Both problems are resolved by *CW*, even if 'put asunder' is an archaism which may resonate more with clergy than laity.

One of the major criticisms of the *ASB* was that it relegated the true nuptial blessing to being just one of several 'Additional Prayers' which might be said at the end of the service. Hence it was often omitted entirely by the liturgically unlettered or careless. Cranmer had used the Sarum nuptial blessing as the foundation of a number of prayers, spreading it, as has justly been said, like butter over a whole intercessory section, and this plainly inspired the *ASB* to treat it as just another prayer in that section. It is described in *A Companion to the Alternative Service Book* (p. 390) as a replacement for the 1549/1662 prayer, 'O God, who by thy mighty power . . .', using phraseology 'from a similar prayer' in the modern Roman rite, which is of course one of the forms of nuptial blessing provided there. Although plainly this was the nuptial blessing, the *ASB* allowed it to be just an option as part of the intercessions. *CW* remedies this situation, firmly identifying 'The Blessing of the Marriage' as a section of the rite and using a substantial and recognizable nuptial blessing straight after the Proclamation, followed by the blessing, 'God the Father, God the Son . . .', taken directly from the *ASB*, where it was itself a composite descendant of two of Cranmer's blessings. It is worth noting, however, that only the 'God the Father . . .' blessing is actually mandatory in *CW*, to attempt to meet the desires of those who preferred the *ASB* arrangement. On the other hand, the layout of the text does not encourage it to be used alone.

An array of alternative forms for the nuptial blessing is printed in the Supplementary Texts. The nuptial blessing in the main text is a new composition, cast in the Jewish *berakah* prayer form, with a substantial borrowing from the

ECUSA rite (though this was slightly diluted at the revision stage). It follows ECUSA in using imagery of love as a seal on the heart from Song of Solomon 8.7 and as a crown on the head from Isaiah 61.10. Mention of the crown will recall Orthodox rites for the liturgically learned or well travelled. The final section improves on ECUSA by using 'banquet' rather than 'table' and makes a pleasing eucharistic and eschatological connection. In the alternatives, the first is a longer version of the blessing in the main text, beginning with a Trinitarian form, 'God of life and beginnings . . . God of love and forgiveness . . . God of grace and strength . . .'. The second is from the New Zealand rite, shorter, but notable for saying, 'God of love . . . you have created courtship and marriage', when the Preface pointedly avoids saying exactly that. The third alternative is divided into three short prayers. The fourth is an elaborate series of acclamations, to be said by minister, bridegroom and bride in turn, leading into a series of *berakoth* loosely derived from the acclamations in the *ASB*. Finally, a revised version of the *ASB* acclamations may be added to any of the preceding acclamations, or used on its own. This latter option would be similar to the *ASB*, but with the order inverted. In the acclamations, while the first is unchanged, the second and third are altered. Whereas the second read, 'You have brought new life to mankind', its replacement now reads, 'You bring life to the world', which is both a significant change in meaning, and also a small piece of inclusive language ('world' being suggested by the Liturgical Commission's report, *Making Women Visible*, 1988). The third read, 'You bring us together in love', in the *ASB*, and this has now become 'You bind us together in love', which is a second striking use in *CW* of quotation from popular evangelical hymnody.

After the Blessing of the Marriage the main text expects the Registration to take place, though a Note allows registration after the Proclamation, or at the end of the service. The Note is ambiguous, since it appears not to permit the normative option, so perhaps 'after the Proclamation' is meant to mean the normative position after the Blessing. Nevertheless, it is clear that after the Proclamation a marriage exists, which can be registered as well as blessed.

A hymn may precede the Prayers. The material in the main text is a new composition, in responsive form. The alternatives provided in the Supplementary Texts are numerous: 1, 2 and 3 are litanies; 1 is a new composition, 2 is from *A Prayer Book for Australia*, and 3 is from ECUSA, slightly altered; 4 is a long prayer, closely resembling a nuptial blessing, based on the Scottish *Book of Common Order* and incorporating portions from two prayers in the *ASB*: the prayer for children, derived from 1662, and a prayer for married life taken from the Church of South India marriage rite. The shorter prayers are gathered into sections reflecting a set of concerns spelt out in the headings: Thanksgiving; Spiritual Growth; Faithfulness, Joy, Love, Forgiveness and Healing; Children, other Family Members and Friends. These derive from many different sources. The most notable feature is the lack of emphasis on children, as compared with previous rites.

The Lord's Prayer concludes the prayers, with both modern-language and traditional forms printed in the main text, with different introductions as in the *CW* eucharistic rite. The final hymn may follow the Lord's Prayer, and then the final congregational blessing, as in the *ASB*, though the curious rubric in the *ASB* that 'The priest blesses the couple and the congregation' is omitted. The blessing is the *ASB* one for Trinity Sunday, echoing the Trinitarian form of the greeting at the start of the service, and perhaps distantly recalling the Sarum Rite's provision of a Mass of the Holy Trinity for the nuptial mass.

The Marriage Service within a Celebration of Holy Communion

CW gives for marriage, as for a funeral, a pattern for the rite to take place within the context of the Eucharist, and prints this as a whole service. This is in contrast to the *ASB*, where two alternative orders were outlined in rubrics and only a set of propers printed. The alternatives in the *ASB* were for the marriage to take place between the Liturgy of the Word and the Liturgy of the Sacrament (which was the standard *ASB* position for rites included within a Eucharist) or for the marriage to take the place of the Liturgy of the Word, which could be said to be reproducing Cranmer's intended structure.

CW interweaves the Marriage Service with the Eucharist and provides numerous alternatives for elements of the Eucharist, as well as propers. The order begins with The Welcome from the Marriage Service, using greeting, sentence and the prayer 'God of wonder and joy . . .'. Then Prayers of Penitence follow, with two proper forms of confession and absolution, one in the now popular *Kyrie* form. The 'lighter' nature of the latter was regarded as particularly suitable for the occasion of a wedding. Conventional forms from the Eucharist may also be used. The Preface to the Marriage Service follows, then the Declarations and then the Collect. As at the Eucharist, this is followed by readings, with provision for a psalm or canticle (four canticles are printed in the Supplementary Texts) and a choice of proper alleluias. After the sermon come the Vows, the Giving of Rings, the Proclamation and the Nuptial Blessing (though this may be deferred until the traditional place after the Lord's Prayer). The marriage is then registered (though the alternatives in the normal service are available, but not encouraged) and the Prayers follow, as the intercessions at the Eucharist. The rubrics accompanying the Prayers in the Marriage Service are repeated, and obviously other forms might be used. The Peace then follows, with two proper introductions: 'To crown all things . . .' from the *CW* Eucharist; and another derived from 1 Peter 5.14. Propers are provided for the Eucharist, with a prayer at the Taking of the Bread and Wine from the Roman Rite, a short preface from the *ASB*, a new extended preface, and a prayer after communion adapted from ECUSA. For the Dismissal there is provided a solemn version of the Aaronic blessing, 'The Lord bless you and keep you . . .' The traditional position for the nuptial blessing, after the Lord's Prayer, is signalled both in the text and in the Notes.

Ecumenical Provisions

CW refers to a form, published separately, which may be authorized by the bishop where a couple come from different Christian communions. This is a composition by the Joint Liturgical Group. In the Notes *CW* provides exhaustive guidance on which parts of the Anglican service a non-Anglican minister may take. Because it requires the consent of the bishop for its use, the text was not included within the collection of regular pastoral rites.

The Commended Services

It is not obvious from the text, but *CW* includes material which is technically only 'commended' by the House of Bishops, rather than authorized by General Synod, since that which is not an alternative to anything in the *BCP* need only be commended. The canticles already mentioned fall into this category, but so do two significant pastoral services.

The Order for Prayer and Dedication after a Civil Marriage is virtually unchanged from its previous publication, commended by the House of Bishops in 1985. A few alterations may be noted. The Preface is now the revised *ASB* form. The forms of Confession and Absolution are now those from the Marriage Service within a Celebration of Holy Communion. The Blessing of the Rings now assumes two rings. The Lord's Prayer is printed in the traditional as well as the modern form. Even the Notes are reproduced largely unchanged, stressing the difference of this rite from a wedding. If the service is to be used within the Eucharist, the order is to be equivalent to that for a wedding, but it is stressed that in that case prayers of penitence must be used.

Thanksgiving for Marriage is also provided, to cover a number of pastoral occasions for which the Dedication service may have been used somewhat uncomfortably in the past. An outline service is given, unlike the full marriage rite, which is required by law to be prescribed in detail. In the text as printed, the Welcome is the usual Trinitarian grace, followed by the sentence from 1 John. The Prayer of Preparation is the *ASB* marriage Collect, though with the couple's names inserted. The Preface is the revised version of that in the *ASB*, with optional variations for different circumstances, and a rubric that silence should follow for reflection. The Renewal of Vows has the couple saying in turn, 'I, *N*, took you, *N*, to be my wife/husband', then repeating the vows together following the *ASB* form ('this was our solemn vow') and then affirming their continuing commitment. The question to the congregation follows. If rings are to be blessed, the alternative form from the Marriage Service is used. Rings may be given with the words from the Marriage Service, or if not, the couple may touch each other's ring, saying, 'I gave you this ring . . .'. The composite blessing follows, with the Acclamations in the *ASB* form. The form of prayer prescribed is that which appears as 4 in the Prayers at the Marriage Service (based on the Scottish *Book of Common Order*). The Lord's Prayer is, as usual, printed in both forms, and the couple may use the prayer, 'Heavenly

Father, we offer you our souls and bodies . . .', from the Dedication service before the *ASB* Trinity blessing.

Further Reading

Stephen Lake, *Using Common Worship: Marriage*, Church House Publishing, London, 2000.

Philip Lyndon Reynolds, *Marriage in the Western Church*, Brill, Leiden, 1994.

Kenneth Stevenson, *Nuptial Blessing*, Alcuin Club/SPCK, London, 1982.

Chapter 10

Funeral

Just as the Christian faith seeks to speak of life and death, our rites of final passage elucidate the Christian faith. The Christian life inspires the praise of God, from baptism to burial. Today we find a mixture of attitudes towards death, producing a blend of hope, fear and denial. Death does not go away, but comes to us all, in various forms and stages of life (2 Samuel 14.14). Some have tried to create 'funerals' that barely acknowledge that a death has taken place, or that a life has really ended. The modern-day superstitious attitude towards death is much blander than some of the more exciting excesses of pagan and medieval practice, and we have swathed death in flowers and poetry that invites mourners to believe in ghosts. The inventiveness of some modern attempts to extend or preserve human life by freezing or genetic modification represents a genuine effort to prevent the inevitable. The Christian funeral has always acknowledged the reality of death, because of the pastoral need to do so, and because all Christian funerals attempt to help those present to look forward to eternal life, and to understand that death is not the end. Thus the gospel of eternal life can upset those who find talk of death offensive. Yet the funeral service is, and always has been, an act of worship: primarily a liturgical occasion, in which God is praised and the eternal promises made in Jesus Christ are rehearsed and depended upon.

A. HISTORY

From Jewish Background to the Middle Ages

There are no descriptions of anything like a funeral in either the Gospels or the New Testament as a whole, although there are accounts of Jesus raising the dead, notably Jairus' daughter; (Luke 8.40–42, 49–56), the widow of Nain's son (Luke 7.11–17) and Lazarus (John 11.1–44). In the first case, Jesus appears on the scene before any action has been taken, but when he visits Nain, the widow's son is already dead and is being 'carried out', presumably to his grave (Luke 7.12). A large crowd are present, and in their presence Jesus touches the bier and bids the young man rise. It is quite clear that Jesus is here interrupting a funeral procession. From the story of Lazarus, and from the accounts of Jesus' own death, we have a good idea of what happened next. In both cases the body is described as being bound with cloth and laid in a tomb, sealed with a stone.

It seems reasonable to suppose that Christian burial adopted the practices of the Jewish tradition. For Jews, the burial of a body was an important religious duty. Corpses were considered unclean and had to be disposed of as soon as possible. This necessity took priority over any other religious obligation, such as the reading of Scripture. The burial itself involved the reciting of the *Kaddish*, a prayer in which was enshrined both the coming of the kingdom and the hope of resurrection. Texts from the Jewish Bible were read, notably Job 1.21 and Psalm 16. Three days of weeping then followed, and four days without work; after this period came three weeks of official mourning.

Burial practice was also influenced by pagan customs in a similar way, for while the beliefs about death might have changed, the manner of disposal did not. Thus in Rome, in the necropolis beneath the Vatican, there is evidence of burials of both pagans and Christians, where the Christians are distinguished only by *chi-ro* symbols on their memorials. Roman pre-Christian practice involved a funeral meal at the graveside, and it may be from this practice that the idea of Mass for the dying or recently departed gained popularity when Rome became Christian. However, pagan practice contrasts with the early Christian reverence for the deceased: if someone died of plague, their bodies would simply be dumped, and not buried properly. Pagan funerals took place at night, and mourners wore black. Cremation was also widespread.

The earliest description of something like a Christian funeral is to be found in St Augustine's *Confessions*, in which he describes the death of his mother Monica. He admits grief, but feels it inappropriate to shed tears, because death is not to be seen as a cause of misery. Augustine is proud of his ability not to cry, and tells us that his mother had not wanted any lavish show, but wished only to be remembered at the altar (*Confessions*, 9). The *Apostolic Tradition* mentions the existence of Christian cemeteries and discusses the cost of funerals. Tertullian (*c.* 200) refers to a funeral Eucharist and an anniversary Eucharist, and the fourth-century Sacramentary of Serapion includes a prayer for the dead, to be used before burial. In all cases, burial rather than cremation is the norm. John Chrysostom tells us that hymns and psalms were sung at funerals, particularly Psalms 22, 23 and 116. Mourners gave food or money to the poor, and wore white rather than black. In this way, the understanding of death expressed at funerals was one of hope, brought about in the Easter promises of resurrection.

As time went by, there was a diversity of practice, but a common pattern. The funeral began at the house, where the deceased lay. Introductory prayers and responses were said followed by the singing or saying of psalms. A procession, either to the church or directly to the tomb, followed, while more psalms were chanted and palm leaves and lights were carried. On arrival, a service of prayers, hymns, psalms and readings took place, during which the final 'kiss of peace' was offered. A Eucharist was celebrated, either in the church or at the graveside, and the body would be buried with feet pointing towards the rising sun. Short prayers would be said at this point and earth would be sprinkled, very much as it is today.

In the medieval Western Church, the emphasis at funerals moved from affirmation of the hope of eternal life to the inspiration of fear of judgement. Hell and purgatory were very much in evidence. Funerals became a public event at which the Church attempted to discipline the people, and murals and altar paintings also expressed the torments of the damned and the rewards of the faithful. In 1533 Pope Clement VII asked Michelangelo to paint the *Last Judgement* on the wall behind the altar in the Sistine Chapel, commissioning one of the most vivid depictions of this kind of death-view. Similarly, mystery plays portrayed the souls of the damned being dragged into hell, and Dante emphasized this in his *Inferno*.

With the Office of the Dead, the medieval liturgy introduced the *Dies irae*, a Latin text which reflects this later emphasis on damnation, rather than the hope and salvation which the early Church had promoted. As there was a fear for the destination of the deceased's soul, via purgatory or not, absolution, sprinkling with holy water, and incense were introduced. Praying for the dead has its origin in 2 Maccabees 12.38–46, where Judas Maccabeus orders that sacrifices be offered in the Temple for slain soldiers, and perhaps in 2 Timothy 1.18, where the author prays for his friend Onesiphorus, who appears to have died. By 211 Tertullian writes of prayers being offered for the dead as part of public worship. At the Council of Trent in 1563, the doctrine of purgatory was reaffirmed and prayer for the deceased commended.

The Reformation

The Reformers eschewed purgatory and deplored prayers for the dead. Once a person had died, they were subject to judgement and they could not be helped, nor could God be influenced by human intercession. Luther, it seems, continued to advocate funeral services, so long as they were intended for the living, rather than the departed, and were positive and encouraging about eternal life. John Knox's Genevan Prayer Book of 1556 said that the body should be brought reverently to the grave, accompanied by mourners, but that a sermon should be preached in the church after the body had been simply buried.

Thomas Cranmer's Prayer Book of 1549 responded in a negative way to inherited medieval practice, and positively to the concerns of the continental Reformers. He stipulated a procession to church, or to the grave, during which scriptural sentences would be sung or said. Then the corpse was to be buried, to the accompaniment of more sentences and words of committal and commendation, and earth would be thrown onto the body in the grave. After this interment a non-eucharistic service (office) would be said in church, at which Psalms 116, 139 and 146 were used, together with a reading from 1 Corinthians 15.20–58, *Kyries*, the Lord's Prayer and responses. A final prayer involved intercession for the deceased. Sometimes this office would be said in church before the burial, rather than afterwards. After this, a Eucharist was celebrated.

In 1552 much of this content was abandoned. The procession to the grave still took place, but once the grave was reached, only the words of committal were used. From the Office of the Dead and the Eucharist only the concluding prayer and collect remained. The act of committal and the prayers were altered so as to avoid any commendation of the soul or intercession for the dead. Later, some Puritans would not trouble themselves with funerals at all, considering them to be perfunctory disposals of corpses, and the *Westminster Directory* of 1645 specified that the body be buried without any ceremony.

The Book of Common Prayer

The funeral service remained unchanged for a century, until the 1662 Prayer Book included some more material. Psalms 39 and 90 were added after the procession, to be used on arrival at the church. The reading from 1 Corinthians followed this. A rubric denying Christian burial to those excommunicated, suicides or the unbaptized was added, but in other senses the service was little changed.

By the time of the 1927/28 abortive revisions to the Prayer Book, the saying of Requiem Masses and praying for the dead were more widely acceptable, and the nation had had large-scale wars with which to contend. Many options were introduced at this time, such that the minister was, for the first time, faced with decisions concerning the content of the funeral service. More sentences were added for the opening procession, and the opportunity to say Psalms 6, 32, 38, 51, 102, 130 or 143 was provided. Once in church, the range of psalms was doubled, Psalms 23 and 130 were offered as alternatives to Psalm 39 or 90, and the option to replace the *Gloria Patri* at the end of psalms with 'rest eternal grant unto them . . .' was permitted. The anthem text 'O Saviour of the World' was also included as an option, to be used before or after the Psalm(s). Other readings were also suggested, expanding on the passage from 1 Corinthians 15. These were 2 Corinthians 4.16—5.10; Revelation 7.9–17; and Revelation 21.1–7.

When the body had been taken to the graveside, the use of Psalm 103.13–17 was allowed instead of the traditional sentences, and a new committal prayer, which was based on Cranmer's commendation from the 1549 Prayer Book, was offered as an alternative. Similarly, the versicles and responses from that period were restored as an option in the final prayers. Three further prayers were also added, all of which have become familiar by now, finding their way into the later *ASB* of 1980. Other prayers were suggested, such as the Collects of All Saints' Day or the Twelfth Sunday after Trinity, or indeed any from the Occasional Prayers in the book. Rubrics stated that the burial might precede or follow the service in church. A hymn could replace a psalm, and the reading from 1 Corinthians 15 could be divided up to make three short lessons. The rubrics also suggested that the service in church and the prayers together might well be used as a memorial service on another occasion. Special lections were included for a Eucharist 'on the day of the burial', with two options for a Gospel reading: John 6.37–41 or John 5.24–29. Other rubrics spell out what to do if the rite is used in the context of a cremation, or of a later burial of ashes, thereby acknowledging the first practice and encouraging the latter. Finally, there was a newly created Order for the Burial of a Child. This service followed the same pattern as the main service, but added different lections (Psalm 23 and Mark 10.13–16) and some sensitive prayers. It is significantly shorter, possibly for pastoral reasons.

The ASB

The services dating from the 1920s were never officially authorized, but were widely used for many years, eventually becoming part of the Series 1 provision in 1966. In 1964 the Liturgical Commission finished a new draft rite, which was published in Series 2 in 1965. In it, the Commission suggested that a funeral has five functions: to ensure that the body is disposed of reverently; to commend the deceased person to God; to proclaim the resurrection in Christ here and hereafter; to put the congregation in mind of their own mortality and judgement; and to proclaim the eternal unity of Christ's people, both living and departed, brought about through the death, resurrection and ascension of Jesus. There is no specific mention of 'consoling the bereaved', but it was felt that the pursuance of the other five aims would naturally lead to this desirable end. The Commission, in drawing up Series 2, effectively concluded that one service would suffice for all baptized people (including those who take their own life), but that special provision needed to be made for the burial of children. It was also made clear that there was no assumption to be made about the 'state' or 'place' of the deceased. A desire to involve the congregation more was expressed, and that as much of the service as possible should take place indoors. As with the 1928 provision, the Commission also expressed the desire that the service material could be used for memorial purposes.

These principles that were expressed in the mid 1960s also serve as a background to what followed in Series 3, and in the *ASB* of 1980. The whole process was stymied in the late 1960s by a rejection of Series 2 by the House of Laity, who voted against the inclusion of prayers for the departed, eventually causing the rites to be sent back to the Liturgical Commission in 1968. While they were still pondering this setback, the Doctrine Commission published a report, *Prayer and the Departed*, in 1971, in which a way through was suggested, and this ultimately helped to pave the way for optional prayers for the dead in later rites. Only then could Series 3 be prepared, in 1973, keeping much of the material that came through from 1928 and Series 2, but changing the title from 'Burial' to 'Funeral Services'.

The *ASB* Funeral Service omits any stipulation that the funeral service should be denied to those who had taken their own lives, or had died unbaptized. Since 1928 there had been a pastoral need for an altered service for the funeral of a child, but meanwhile baptism rates among children had been falling. Thus by 1980 it could not be assumed that every child was baptized. Another possibility was catered for: that of a stillborn or newly born child, where presumably baptism had not been possible. Furthermore, a tacit distinction is made with the advent of the *ASB*: that matters of policy on such issues were the concerns of canon law, not pastoral liturgy.

The *ASB* revised the provision of opening sentences, and put the collect from the 1928 service into modern speech, employing the 'you' form rather than 'thou'. In the psalmody, Psalm 121 was introduced, along with suggestions for alternatives, among them Psalms 27 and 42.1–7. The reading of John 16.1–6 was also introduced, and printed out in full as the first option. The traditionally used text from 1 Corinthians 15 was edited, so as to convey the basic meaning in shorter form. Many other readings were suggested as alternatives. An optional sermon followed the readings. Instead of a hymn following the sermon, verses from the *Te Deum* were recommended, although with hindsight the *Te Deum* might not have been used so frequently, with a hymn being preferred in many contexts. However, the appropriateness of the *Te Deum* is not in doubt, with its references to the 'sting of death', the 'opening of the kingdom of heaven' and 'glory everlasting' with the saints.

The prayers in the *ASB* began with the Lesser Litany and Lord's Prayer, just as 1928 had done, but there followed a freedom hitherto unknown. Prayers in a later section were indicated, but were not exclusively directed. This not only gave flexibility and permission to compose one's own prayers, but also avoided the debate about praying for the departed. The minister could do as he or she wished in this respect, and the supplementary prayers that were offered catered for both theological perspectives. There was a prayer printed in the next section which was explicitly for those remaining alive, seeking God's grace to 'use aright the time left to us on earth'. A composition first found in Series 3, this prayer was mandatory. The service manifests a tradition invented in Series 2 that separates commendation and committal. As there were other sentences from Scripture to end the funeral, it was felt right to begin the Committal with Revelation 14.13 ('Happy are the dead'), and the Committal itself was revised. It was similar to Cranmer's 1549 version, but since a commendation preceded it that described the whole person ('our brother/sister') as having been entrusted to God, it then proceeded to commit to earth or fire the person's body. Thus a subtle distinction is alluded to, which did not come too close to any separation of body and soul.

As with the 1928 rite, a separate service for a child's funeral was included in the *ASB*, and also, as already mentioned, a selection of prayers for the funeral of stillborn or newly born infants. Such a situation had hardly been envisaged in previous books, with only a prayer alluding to infant mortality at the end of the service for the Churching of Women being found in the 1928 Prayer Book.

A very brief service for the Interment of Ashes was also offered, being based upon the Committal. Similarly, a short service for the laying of a body in church prior to a funeral was included, using a reading from Romans 8.31–39, verses from Psalm 27 or 139 and prayers. The pastoral need to hold this service in the home before the funeral was acknowledged. The final provision of the *ASB* concerned a funeral in the context of Holy Communion. Rite A or B could be used, and the Propers dovetailed nicely with the eucharistic material offered elsewhere in the book.

The Transition to CW

For ministers taking funerals in 1980, the new *ASB* provided choice and freedom hitherto unknown. It was not considered perfect in its funeral provision, however, for in its renewed emphasis on the resurrection hope, it was felt by some to be a little weak in terms of the recognition of inevitable feelings of fear, doubt and sorrow that bereavement brings. Related to this was its apparent 'churchy' feel: for while the service spoke to those who attended church quite often, it was felt by some to be alien to the unchurched, more so than the *BCP* had been. It also lacked material for certain pastoral situations, but this was partly remedied by the appearance in the late 1980s of two further services, one originally intended for stillborn children that was ultimately broadened to become *Funeral Service for a Child Dying Near the Time of Birth*, and the other, *Ministry at the Time of Death*, intended to make better provision for situations of terminal illness than had the 1983 booklet, *Ministry to the Sick*. Both of these have subsequently been incorporated into the *CW* provision. *CW* has also attempted to respond to the other criticisms of the *ASB*, and has given even greater flexibility, evidently making a genuine attempt to meet the pastoral needs of particular situations with sensitivity, care and creativity. The 'liturgical' possibilities are increased, and yet, while there is more freedom of content, there is also a firmer thread holding together what Church of England funeral services should share *in common*.

Some of the material in *CW*, including the two services mentioned above, is 'commended' rather than 'authorized'. The distinction concerns the relationship between the new material and that found in the *BCP*. Services that are alternatives to ones in the *BCP* must be authorized by the General Synod, but those that have no counterpart in the *BCP* may simply be commended by the House of Bishops.

For those seeking a traditional-language service, however, both the *BCP* and Series 1 rites remain authorized. The life of the latter was renewed at five-yearly intervals until 2002 (although nearly failing to receive approval from the House of Laity in 1990), and then extended indefinitely.

B. MINISTRY AT THE TIME OF DEATH

Unusually but logically, the *CW* material does not begin with the 'main' service – the funeral – but with a service that might be used as a person lies at the point of death. The exact timing of such a service may be hard to judge, but the service is not so much intended to be an event the timing of which is crucial; rather it is intended to help the dying person to understand their death, to accept it and be aware of it. Thus, the ministry of reconciliation may be a major precursor to the more formal liturgy of this brief but moving service. It is also a service very much for those who sit and watch beside the dying, also helping them to come to terms with the inevitability and closeness of the death of their loved one. Thus with this service begins a liturgical journey, during which we say farewell to loved ones, comforting them at the beginning, and being comforted ourselves as they pass through death to the hope of eternal life. As indicated above, this material first appeared in a supplementary booklet, *Ministry at the Time of Death*, published in 1989.

A Note before the service explains that it should ideally follow the ministry of preparation and reconciliation. The Church of England has enshrined within its history a tradition of personal confession and absolution, a tradition best summed up as 'all may, none must and some do'. Ministry at the Time of Death is commended, not authorized, and so can helpfully and rightly recommend the ministry of reconciliation as an integral part of a bedside event.

Thus, with this service there are some practical issues which the officiating priest needs to resolve beforehand. First, the family and friends need to be absent where the ministry of reconciliation is used, but then need to enter the room for the rest of the service. Such details of explanation and arrangement are best dealt with outside the room, whether in a hospital, hospice or at home. If in a hospital, then care needs to be taken to create the right conditions of privacy, peace and security. The service is quite evidently intended for a bedside situation, but parts of it can be used on the occasion of a sudden death, and it may be possible and pastorally appropriate to use some of the material soon after someone has died, rather than beforehand.

Preparation

The Preparation precedes the ministry of reconciliation and is intended to be used with only the dying person present. Short sentences open the service, setting a tone of hope and comfort. The order of these texts appears random, but presumably expresses a priority of perceived relevance on the part of the compilers and a general progression from short sentences to brief passages from the Bible. After some of these sentences have been said, the minister says the Lord's Prayer, perhaps with the dying person joining in. As with all of *CW*, the modern translation of the Lord's Prayer appears first, but it may well be most appropriate to use the latter, traditional form, with which the person is more likely to be familiar.

Reconciliation

The minister 'may encourage some expression of penitence': the 'Jesus Prayer' is suggested, or a more lengthy prayer of confession, taken from the Eucharist, or a simple *Kyrie* form. Realistically, the person dying, even if alert, may not be able to follow a text in a book, so these texts are familiar, and in two cases, very simple. Two options for the absolution by the priest are offered, or if the officiant is not a priest, the second, briefer absolution is used. This part of the service provides the opportunity for a lengthy introduction and lucid 'confession' with an absolution that may include the laying on of hands. Yet it also accommodates a person lying almost unconscious, able to repeat barely a few words. Both allow the possibility of a sacred space being created, and although this part of the service takes up only five pages it could take many minutes.

Opening Prayer

When the ministry of reconciliation is complete, the family and friends can be invited into the room. There is no greeting as such, but there is an opening benediction eliciting an optional response. More space for silence is offered, at what may be a cathartic time. As the friends and family gather around, there may well be a realization that as all are gathered, the imminent death of their loved one becomes awesome to contemplate. In the newly created sacred space, time for spiritual adjustment and composure may be necessary. Thus the opening prayer includes the option to pray for 'us who surround *him/her* with our prayers'. The prayer seeks the words to say to one another, and to God, and speaks of the peace 'beyond understanding', given by God, through the Spirit. A *Kyrie* follows, with an allusion to Psalm 130.1.

The Word of God

Three readings are suggested. The first, Romans 8.35, 37–39 speaks of the lack of separation between us and God (and naturally omits verse 36, which speaks of 'being killed all the day long'). Psalm 23 ('The Lord is my shepherd') is paired with 139 ('O Lord, you have searched me and known me'). The third reading is John 6.35–40 ('I am the bread of life . . . and I will raise them up on the last day'), and there is an option of adding verses 53–58, which is particularly appropriate where communion is to be shared. Other readings are, of course, permitted and the service order refers readers to the section entitled Bible Readings and Psalms for Use at Funeral and Memorial Services. It is very likely to be appropriate for others present to do the reading(s).

The readings may be followed by an act of faith or commitment to Christ. For many this will be an act of renewal and an expression of trust in God, but for some it may represent a 'deathbed conversion'. In many cases, the person dying may not be able to say anything, but may assent non-verbally to what the minister says on his or her behalf. Four suggestions of suitable words are made for this, three of which come from Scripture: Luke 23.42; Mark 9.24; and Luke 23.46. All these passages use the first person singular, which may help those present to identify with the person dying, and give them a sense of their vicarious role, not only in praying for them, but praying *for* them, in their place, so to speak. There is also the sense in which, rather like parents and god-parents at baptism, these people speak for themselves and for the person dying. Where sons or daughters of the dying person are present, there can be a poignancy here; as they were spoken for soon after their birth, at their baptism by the person now dying, so now, they speak for their parents, soon before their death.

Prayers
Other prayers may follow, and while a litany is provided, other forms of prayer may be used. The litany begins in the usual Trinitarian form, and then, for brevity's sake, employs only petitions that are specifically relevant near to the time of death. There are overtones of the Prayer Book Litany ('that it may please you to deliver your servant *N* from all evil and eternal death'), and care has been taken not to make the litany too modern, for the sake of the person lying near to death who may be familiar with more traditional forms. If these prayers are to be used, however, the officiant needs to ensure in advance that there are plenty of copies of the *Pastoral Services* book or other leaflets from which people may read. Such formal prayer is not compulsory, and the minister is free to extemporize or use other prayers from *CW* or elsewhere. The key factor is to use material which is sensitive to the spiritual needs and experiences of those present.

Laying on of Hands and Anointing
The tradition of laying on of hands is pre-Christian (see Mark 5.23) and can be comforting at a time near to death, even if physical recovery is hardly to be expected. When oil is to be used, it is preferably that which has been conse-crated specially for the purpose, and which may have been collected at a chrism Eucharist presided over by the diocesan bishop in the cathedral. Many dioceses follow this tradition, and it is precisely for this kind of use that such oil is provided. If none is available, however, Note 3 provides an appropriate prayer of consecration. After the anointing, there is an optional prayer which is almost an absolution, and may be helpful where the dying person has remained silent throughout the service.

Holy Communion
It may not be possible for the dying person to receive communion, but it is certainly desirable that others present should receive, for in one sense they may be seen as receiving communion on behalf of their friend or relative. A Note says: 'Believers who cannot physically receive the sacrament are to be assured that they are partakers by faith of the body and blood of Christ and of the benefits he conveys to us by them.' The Notes also refer to the reception of communion in only one kind, which is also acceptable. A priest is

expected to use an authorized eucharistic prayer from *CW*, or if the leader is a lay person they should be appropriately authorized to administer the reserved sacrament. No specific material is provided at this point for this eventuality, but ministers can refer to the earlier section in the *Pastoral Services* volume entitled 'Ministry to the Sick'.

Commendation

This section begins with the Lord's Prayer, which may already have been said twice up to this point, first as part of the ministry of reconciliation and then as part of the celebration of communion. However, this may be no bad thing, especially if it is one of the few ways in which the dying person can participate verbally.

Three prayers precede the Commendation itself, and should be selected according to the circumstances. The first two are similar: the first is taken from *A New Zealand Prayer Book* and the second one derives from the Sarum Rite. Both are addressed to the dying person. Alternatively, or additionally, there is a third prayer, a new composition, which addresses God as the dying person is 'summoned out of this world', and is very much a prayer for them, near to death. The prayer has overtones of the *Magnificat* ('as you promised to Abraham and his children for ever'), Psalm 9.13 ('you are the one who lifts me up from the gates of death') and Psalm 107.30 ('grant *him/her* a haven of light and peace').

There are two prayers of commendation, which are deliberately different to the one used in the funeral itself. The first draws on Romans 8.38–39 ('nothing in death or life . . . can separate us from your love') and Luke 23.46 ('Jesus commended his spirit'). The second reminds us of Christ the Good Shepherd (John 10.1–18) and of the parable of the Lost Sheep returning to the fold (Luke 15.1–7). The *Nunc dimittis* may follow, in modern or *BCP* language, and two other canticles are also provided: a modern translation of the Russian *Contakion* of the Dead and the Song of St Anselm, the latter being specified as appropriate at or just after the point of death. The service ends with a blessing for all those present, and if led by a lay person, the first option, which employs the 'may' form, is appropriate. The second option comes from the *ASB* eucharistic provision for Saints' Days.

Prayer when Someone has just Died

It is rare for a priest to be in attendance when someone dies, but not unusual to be summoned immediately or soon afterwards. This brief section of the service is provided for that situation, and may also be led by a lay person, such as a family member. Opening words of consolation are said, drawing on 1 Corinthians 2.9 ('What no eye has seen, nor ear heard, nor the human heart conceived, what God has prepared for those who love him'), and then a new prayer, which is a form of committal, drawing on Revelation 21.1–4. Other appropriate prayers follow. No blessing or dismissal is provided for this brief section.

C. BEFORE THE FUNERAL

CW provides a handful of brief services which may be used before the funeral itself, accommodating the pastoral needs of those who wish to pray at home, those who cannot attend a funeral and those who wish to surround the immediate period of mourning with prayerful liturgy.

At Home before the Funeral

This service may be used at any point between the death and the funeral, but may be particularly appropriate in the context of a pastoral visit from the minister officiating at the funeral itself. The singing of hymns at this service is specifically encouraged. The liturgy opens with preparatory words of comfort, drawn from the Beatitudes and 2 Corinthians 1.3, and then there is a brief responsorial exchange drawing on words from 1 Corinthians 15.51–52. Readings of 1 Thessalonians 4.13–15, Psalm 121 and John 11.21–24 are suggested. An opportunity for sharing of thoughts or memories is provided, which is ended with a prayer adapted from one by Janet Morley. Other prayers follow (three are provided), the second of which comes from *Pastoral Prayers* (ed. Richard Deadman). The third prayer draws on Psalm 121. A final benediction, taken from Martin Luther King's 'I have a dream', concludes the service.

For those Unable to be Present at the Funeral

A two-page spread outlines how a service based very much on the funeral service itself may be used simultaneously in another location where others join in, in spirit. It is very likely that this service would be led by a member of the bereaved family, a friend or some other lay person. A special opening prayer makes this clear: 'we join with those in (*place*) in remembering our *brother/sister* . . .'. A second prayer abbreviates one found in the *Ministry to the Sick* (1983), and there is a third, new prayer. After these opening prayers, those present are encouraged to share memories, and then to refer to the Funeral Service material itself for Prayers of Penitence and the Collect. A reading should follow, from the wide provision found on pages 383–91, and it may be appropriate to ascertain what is being read at the funeral and to use it here too. Informal prayer may be more appropriate after the reading, or it may be helpful to use some of the prayers found in the *Pastoral Services* volume. Then the leader might say some connecting words, and then use the Commendation and Farewell from the Funeral Service. To end, the Lord's Prayer and a form of dismissal are proposed, but this is all left to the discretion of the leader.

Receiving the Coffin at Church before the Funeral

The practice of receiving the coffin in church prior to a funeral is hardly new, but this is the first time the Church of England has provided liturgical material for doing so in any official publication. The carrying into church of the deceased person is a kind of homecoming, and it may take place soon before the funeral or on the previous day. Of all the services provided in *CW* this one is most loaded with visual symbolism and with the potential for expressing Christian truths in non-verbal ways. Thus a candle, symbolizing the light of Christ overcoming the darkness of death and the Easter resurrection hope, may precede the coffin into church and remain with it until the funeral itself. A Bible or cross may lie on the coffin, and there is an opportunity to sprinkle baptismal water on the coffin when it is received at the door. Such sprinkling is appropriate for a baptized person, as a reminder that we are baptized into Christ's death, which leads us to eternal life. Placing a white pall over the coffin reminds us of the same truth, although these latter actions are best reserved until the coffin has been set down.

The opening words of the service are adapted from the 1979 ECUSA Prayer Book, and may be followed with the sprinkling, for which suitable words are provided, in short or longer form, the longer being a version of the traditional *BCP* Collect of Easter Eve. Then the coffin is led to its resting place accompanied by the saying of the usual sentences found in the Funeral Service. When the coffin is in place, the priest says a prayer from *A Prayer Book for Australia*, which reminds us of the resurrection hope, and seeks God's care for those who will come to the funeral and the assurance of the Spirit's presence, perhaps not only for those present, but also during the hours when the deceased person may lie unattended in the church. With the arrival of the coffin, the church becomes a place of vigil, even if empty of the living. When in place, the coffin may be draped with a pall, and words from 1 John 3.2 or Isaiah 25.7–8 may be read. The first of these texts has baptismal overtones and is the better choice for occasions when a white pall is used; the second for those where a darker-coloured one is employed. If either a Bible or a cross or both are placed on the coffin, suitable words are provided, and there is an opportunity to share memories as other symbols of life and faith are placed on or near the coffin. The keeping of silence is specifically mentioned at this point in the brief service.

Whether an extended vigil or a brief pause is envisaged, it is right to read Scripture and pray with the coffin in church. A prayer precedes these readings, and while John 14.1–6 is suggested, other readings may be used. The readings are also followed with a prayer. As the service ends, *CW* provides further prayers, and a rubric suggests that the mourners might want to touch the coffin in a private moment of farewell before the larger-scale liturgy of the funeral itself. The first prayer printed is one that enables everyone to leave if they wish to: 'As we leave *his/her* body here . . .'. Another prayer, adapted from *Ministry to the Sick*, follows, and a responsory which serves to draw those present back together before they depart.

A Funeral Vigil

The service or reception into church may be extended into a vigil, perhaps continuing through the night. Alternatively it may take place somewhere else, such as in the family home or in a chapel. If it forms part of another service, some adaptations need to be made, as the service provided in *CW* stands on its own, in which form it may be needed. The variety of circumstances for which the service is offered entails that it is not to be assumed that the coffin is present in the place of the vigil. If the coffin is present, candles may be lit, if they have not already been so.

The service begins with the invocation 'O Lord, open our lips' and opening prayers which draw on many themes that may be expanded during the vigil. A prayer, 'Christ yesterday and today' is a traditional component of the Easter Vigil, drawing on Revelation 21.6. The lighting of candles may follow, before a period of prayers and readings commences. These are grouped according to specific themes, and each group contains: an Old Testament or Apocrypha reading; a psalm and a prayer based upon it; a New Testament reading; a canticle; a Gospel reading; and an opportunity for prayer. Since these are outline services rather than full texts advance preparation is necessary before leading this kind of event. However long the vigil is, it should conclude with the Lord's Prayer and a 'suitable ending' – one example being provided.

On the Morning of the Funeral

This very brief service may meet a need when the minister is to leave for the funeral from the family home, or it may be conducted by a family member on the day. There is perhaps an assumption that 'morning' is the best or most likely time for this kind of event, but it would of course be appropriate to use this order in the afternoon if the service were later in the day. A journey theme is introduced at the outset, with penitential *Kyries* drawing on the themes of Christ showing the way to the Father (John 14.6–8), being a light to our path (Psalm 119.105) and the Good Shepherd (John 10.11–14). An edited reading from Lamentations 3 is provided, and a closing prayer, which is also used in the service for receiving the coffin. So surrounded in prayer, the family and friends may set off for the church or crematorium for the funeral itself.

D. THE FUNERAL SERVICE

Pastoral Introduction

The main funeral section begins with an introduction, which it is hoped that ministers may make available to congregations in some form. The Pastoral Introduction makes clear that every life is precious to God, and that there is hope and new life in Christ. The purpose of the Funeral Service is also alluded to: 'to express our faith and our feelings as we say farewell, to acknowledge our loss and our sorrow, and to reflect on our own mortality'. It is also stressed that the coming together of mourners for a funeral has a supportive function for those who mourn.

The Outline Order for Funerals

Before the full texts of the service are laid out, an outline order is given as the required 'core' of a much more freely adapted version, in order to indicate the permissible limits of any such flexibility – a new development in the Church of England. Similar outline orders are provided for the Funeral of a Child and for a Funeral Service within a Celebration of Holy Communion. In all three cases, the fuller material follows, but the outline is intended to show how that material may be used pastorally and creatively or quite different material be included within the required framework.

The Gathering

As is traditional, the first of the sentences suggested is John 11.25–26. Romans 8.38–39, 1 Timothy 6.7 with Job 1.21b, Lamentations 3.22–23 and John 3.16 have remained from the *ASB* provision, while Deuteronomy 33.27 has been replaced by 1 Thessalonians 4.14, 17b, 18. If the coffin has already been received into church, the service starts with these sentences, which are often read in procession. Other sentences are suggested on pp. 293–4 of the Pastoral Services volume of *Common Worship*. If the coffin is received at the door of the church or crematorium only at the beginning of the service, then it may be appropriate to use candles, a pall, the sprinkling of baptismal water and symbols of the deceased person's life, as suggested on pp. 242–3 and 295–6.

Introduction

When the coffin, congregation and the ministers are in place, the service formally opens with a greeting that requires no response. Further words of explanation are offered, but may be substituted according to pastoral need. Many ministers have inserted this kind of explanatory welcome in funerals before the Collect which opened the *ASB* service, but here the opportunity is acknowledged and encouraged. Two prayers are provided, both of which focus on the grief of the congregation. The first comes from *CCP* (and has hints of a prayer found in *Ministry to the Sick*) while the second is from *A New Zealand Prayer Book*. Neither of these prayers is compulsory, because under some circumstances such an acknowledgement of congregational grief may not be the best starting point. A hymn may be appropriate at this point, and also what has become known as a 'tribute'. The tribute is recommended at this early point so as not to interrupt the flow of readings and preaching, although the main points of a tribute may be woven into a sermon, thereby making this kind of contribution unnecessary. However, it is often appropriate for a member of the family or a friend to give a tribute or 'eulogy', and this is the point to do it. It should precede the Word of God and ministers should take care to ensure that it will not divert the service in any inappropriate way. The purpose of a tribute is to 'remember and honour' the deceased and to indicate 'evidence of God's grace and work in them' (p. 291).

Prayers of Penitence

Prayers of Penitence are new at this point. They take the pattern found in the *CW* eucharistic provision, except that here the main prayer is not a corporate one: the congregation are only expected to say 'Amen'. The prayer itself is new, and not found in the main *CW* volume. The alternative repetitive *Kyries* may be more satisfactory to a congregation familiar with such material. The absolution is also new, and picks up on 'dust and ashes'. Prayers of Penitence may not follow a tribute very well, and so may be moved into the main body of the prayers instead.

The Collect

An essential part of the service, the Collect, as in other liturgies, gathers the prayers of the people together before proceeding with the ministry of the word. The prayer is derived from the Roman Catholic liturgy. Another version that indicates how the name of the deceased may be inserted into the prayer is provided on p. 350 of the Pastoral Services volume of *Common Worship*, along with an alternative Collect.

Readings and Sermon

A psalm or hymn, a New Testament reading and a sermon are mandatory. These may be preceded by other readings from Old or New Testament. After the psalm, a related prayer may be said, and a series of these is to be found on pp. 380–2.

Prayers

Prayers are often led at funerals by the officiating minister, but another person (or people) may do so. Rather than provide pages of prayer material at this point, *CW* suggests a sequence of four subjects, and then gives just one a single example, while indicating an extensive section elsewhere containing other possibilities. This example concludes with a communal petition that speaks of 'entrusting into your hands', which may seem to pre-empt the prayer of Commendation which soon follows. The Lord's Prayer may conclude the Prayers or may be deferred until the Dismissal. A prayerful hymn may also be appropriate at this point.

Commendation and Farewell

The distinction between commendation and committal, established in the Series 2 provision, is maintained. Reflecting a practice that is already widespread, the minister is instructed to go to the coffin and stand by it. Others may join him or her. In some crematoria, the catafalque is positioned off-centre, thus conveying the impression that the deceased is placed 'out of the way', or to one side. Thus, for the Commendation, the minister can move to the coffin, and make the deceased the centre of attention at least for this part of the service. The introductory sentence is unchanged from the *ASB*, but a new rubric encouraging silence is added. One prayer of 'entrusting and commending' is included, although others are permitted (pp. 373–7). The prayer formerly used in the *ASB* does not appear in this selection. The prayer itself avoids distinctions between body and soul, entrusting the whole person to God, creator and redeemer. It 'claims' the promises made in Christ, and speaks confidently of eternal life. In some contexts, such as in church before an immediate cremation elsewhere, this section leads directly to the Dismissal.

The Committal

The Committal may begin with sentences of Scripture. In the *ASB* Revelation 14.13 was recommended, but there is greater flexibility here in those suggested. Two familiar texts are provided for use before the prayer. The first is Psalm 10.8, 13–17, and the second is the famous tenth-century anthem by Notker, 'Man that is born of a woman', which, like the first text, has been rendered in modern, inclusive language. Both have survived from the 1662 and *ASB* provision. The second of these texts has a long history and has become well known, hence its inclusion. It is quite a lugubrious text and some feel that its sentiments are rather downbeat and desperate and do not integrate well with the note of eternal hope that a funeral should convey. The opening verse comes from Job 14.1–2. The reference to 'Lord most holy, Lord most mighty' is derived from a response that used to be part of the text, and which is reminiscent of the *Trisagion*, still used in litanies. The final lines have come to us via a Lutheran addition which Miles Coverdale translated, finding their way into the 1549 Prayer Book. In that context, the burial of the body was at the beginning of the service, which means that it has only retained its relative position in the service. Notker, who is reputed to have composed it, was a monk at St Gall in Switzerland who died *c.* 912. His text found its way into the Sarum Rite, being used as the antiphons for the *Nunc dimittis* at Compline in mid Lent. With much of *CW* being new, it is good to see some traditional material holding a place in the funeral liturgy. Understandably, this text is optional, and many will prefer to use the words from Psalm 103.

Three Committal prayers are provided, for different contexts. At a burial we find the familiar 'ashes to ashes' formula, but expanded to include 'who will transform our frail bodies that they may be conformed to his glorious body' from Philippians 3.21. Originally in the Sarum Rite the formula was simply followed by a reference to the Holy Trinity (now absent). Cranmer was responsible for adding the specific reference to the ground (and in his day there was hardly any alternative form of disposal) as well as the passage beginning 'in sure and certain hope . . .'. An introduction, 'Forasmuch as it hath pleased Almighty God of his great mercy to take unto himself the soul of our dear brother here departed', was also added by Cranmer, but this was omitted at the time of the *ASB*. With it came a difficulty over whether the soul or body or both are being committed. Cranmer's phrase implied that God had already received the soul, and that the body was being committed. With the *ASB* provision and now with *CW*, the Commendation speaks of the whole person by name, and so it is appropriate to refer to the person while burying the body.

Where there is a cremation and a burial of ashes will follow soon afterwards, this is reflected in the prayer. The body is 'given' to be cremated, a word which acknowledges the functional, practical business of cremation, and accommodates the handing back of ashes for later interment. In this context, the sentiments of 'ashes to ashes' are delayed, because this is not the final Committal, but rather the first part of a two-stage process. Thus there is a reference to our waiting and looking for the resurrection.

If no interment of ashes is planned for the near future, then the third prayer, which includes the traditional words of committal, should be used. It is, of course, basically the same as the first prayer, save for a replacement of 'to the ground' by 'to be cremated'. The Series 1 rite uses the phrase 'to the fire', which, although strictly accurate, is perhaps evocative of a spiritual destination not hoped for by mourners nor ministers, nor deceased. *CW* has avoided this pitfall.

The Dismissal

In stipulating that there must be a clear ending to the service, *CW* also allows a great deal of flexibility. The *ASB* had no real dismissal, but only a scriptural passage (Psalm 16.11) and a closing doxology. Many ministers found this to be unsatisfactory, as there was not even the hint of a blessing.

The Lord's Prayer

The Lord's Prayer may have been said earlier, concluding the prayers, in which case it should not be used again. It is desirable that it should be said once during the Funeral Service.

The Nunc dimittis

Simeon's song (Luke 2.29–32) is well known, and its theme of departure in response to the revelation of salvation is eminently appropriate for funeral use. A tradition of saying it at funerals has arisen over the years, especially upon departure from the church to a graveyard.

Prayers

Three concluding prayers are offered, again with the option to select others from elsewhere. The first two are said corporately, the third by the minister alone. The first resonates with the 'sure and certain hope' of the Committal and the 'communion of saints, the forgiveness of sins and the resurrection to eternal life' of the Apostles' Creed. It has been modernized from a prayer in the 1928 Prayer Book. The second option is 'God be in my head', a text derived from the Sarum Rite provision for feasts of the Blessed Virgin Mary (published in London in 1514). It is thought to be originally of French origin. It may be said by all, or sung, perhaps by a choir, to settings such as those by H. Walford Davies or John Rutter. Some versions do not add 'Amen' at the end, but *CW* does, offering the text as a prayer. The third prayer, 'Support us, O Lord', has long had a place at the conclusion of funerals, and is taken from the additional prayers in the *ASB*.

Ending

The ending may be a blessing, where a priest is present, but as so many funerals are not conducted by a priest, three of the four suggested endings are not blessings. The first is derived from an older, extended form of ending, which contained references to the Queen and the Commonwealth, which has been adapted for funeral use. The second option is a blessing, simple yet effective in its reference to comfort, peace, light and joy. The third option is a phrase dependent on Psalm 16.11, which presents a vision of paradise 'at God's right hand', and does not require a response of 'Amen'. The fourth is a doxology, praising God for keeping us from falling so that we may be presented faultless before his glory.

E. THE FUNERAL SERVICE WITHIN A CELEBRATION OF HOLY COMMUNION

It is only right that *CW* should provide structure and content for the celebration of Holy Communion in connection with a funeral service. The structure that is offered echoes the broad structure of the *CW* eucharistic rites, with both necessary and optional insertions. The latter include a quotation from John 14.27 as an introduction to the Peace, and a brief prayer for the Preparation of the Table that resonates with the idea of an eternal banquet in heaven. Both short Proper Prefaces and an extended Proper Preface are provided for the eucharistic prayer. The first short preface comes from the *ASB*. The second is new, with a strong Easter feel to it, reminding the congregation that it is through Christ's resurrection that the sting of death is overcome and hope of eternal life promised. The extended preface, with the option of a response, is also new. Particularly apposite forms for the breaking of the bread, the invitation to communion, and words of distribution are suggested from among the standard *CW* options. The first of the two prayers after communion is taken from the 1979 ECUSA Prayer Book, and makes reference to the 'foretaste of the heavenly banquet' and to the comfort and fuller joy of those who grieve; the second is one found at the end of the Funeral Service. The Commendation and Farewell and the Committal are identical to those of the Funeral Service. The Dismissal is slightly different, consisting only of an optional use of the *Nunc dimittis* and of a blessing, because the Lord's Prayer will have been said already, as may the other prayers.

F. SUPPLEMENTARY TEXTS

Sentences

With the now expanded range of introductory sentences, we have a manifestation of *CW*'s trend towards choice and variety. Twenty sentences are suggested for funerals, and an extra one (John 6.54) for use with Holy Communion. The *BCP* originally offered only three and the *ASB* expanded these to eight. The new suggestions include selections from the previously unused Apocrypha, and sentences taken from the readings that might recur later in the service. This provides an opportunity for resonance between the opening of the service and the texts used later on. The tradition of beginning a funeral with sentences such as these is so ingrained that it would be foolish to try to supplant it. Instead, *CW* has enhanced it.

Some Texts which may be Used by the Minister

This section repeats the texts provided earlier for Receiving the Coffin at Church before the Funeral, in case it is desired to use them instead in the Funeral Service itself. These words may be helpful to some, but to others they will seem an intrusion. Where 'actions speak louder than words', the words can be omitted, as they are indeed only suggestions for those who wish to say something while performing a symbolic action. Such words do have a didactic purpose, and may be very effective in situations where the majority of mourners are not churchgoers, as so often happens, even if the deceased was a practising Christian. Thus these words can be helpful where non-Christians attend a Christian's funeral.

The Blessing of a Grave

Praying over a grave can be a simple yet powerful way of hallowing the ground before a burial. It can be done either immediately before burial or a few hours or days beforehand. Even though the ground may be already consecrated, there is no harm, and sometimes some good, in praying over the grave. The prayer itself reminds us that Jesus himself was laid in a tomb, but also reminds us of his resurrection.

G. THE FUNERAL OF A CHILD

The content of a child's funeral must and will be adapted to the circumstances, over which particular sensitivity and care must be exercised. The Notes mention the possible presence of children at the funeral, who must be welcomed and cared for. Note 3 is telling and relevant, for it is a reminder of an increased tendency, especially under tragic and public circumstances, to try to accommodate varying kinds of input and participation in the service. A wide range of readings, music and other spoken material can overcrowd the service which is always primarily an act of prayer and thanksgiving. It is therefore important that a distinctive leader of the service be apparent.

Resources for the Funeral of a Child

Every child, like every adult, is different, but there are certain contexts which the compilers of these resources had in mind. Thus at the beginning of the service, two passages of words of introduction are offered: the first of these (which comes from the Church of Scotland's *Book of Common Order*, 1994) might suit a funeral of a baby, whereas the second may be better for an older child or teenager.

In the suggested introductory sentences, three new ones occur, chosen for their gentle reference to the love of God for children and our relationship to God as Father: 1 John 3.2; Mark 10.14; and Isaiah 66.13. The first opening prayer is adapted from one found in the *ASB*, in the section of prayers for still-born or newborn babies. There it read: 'Almighty God, you make nothing in vain . . . Comfort this woman (and her husband) . . .'. Now the prayer is for 'us' and conveniently avoids any difficulties over whether the mother is married and whether the husband is the father of the child. The second prayer is a familiar one by Janet Morley, and makes an appropriate link between birth and death, and hints at a God who comforts his children. The third prayer reminds us of the bonds among those who suffer and the need for courage in facing grief.

A selection of readings is offered. Psalm 84.1–4; Isaiah 49.15–16; Jeremiah 1.4–8; Matthew 18.1–5, 10; and Mark 10.13–16 have been chosen with children specifically in mind.

In the midst of prayer are the best opportunities for pastoral care to be found. Thus twenty-three prayers are offered. First, there is a litany form. The use of this may be appropriate only in a few circumstances. Prayer 7 is also responsive in structure. The other prayers are in collect form. Seven of them address God as Father. Prayer 2 is adapted from one found in the Scottish *Book of Common Order*, 1994. Others are drawn from other sources or are specially written. Prayers 8–15 are meant to be said by the parents, if at all appropriate or possible. They could also be adapted for use by a third person. In prayers 14–15 there is sense of having been caught up in the divine gift of creation ('we acknowledge that our child is your child'), and for the presence of love, even in death. Prayers 16–18 are for the parents, to be prayed by the minister or other intercessor. Prayer 17 is specifically for the mother, who is described as a daughter of God. Prayer 18 has overtones of the *Stabat mater*, with Mary weeping at the cross. Prayers 19–20 are for other children in the family. Prayer 20 has a memorial feel, resonating with the mood of Remembrance Sunday, with a recurring ending: 'we will remember *him/her*'. Prayer 22 is for a stillborn child, and its being printed here moves that sad event very much into a funeral realm, emphasizing that even such a brief life had a beginning and an end, and that with any short life, hopes die too. The final prayer has a particular poignancy as it refers to the name of the baby.

The Commendation and Farewell also demands special material, and most scenarios are catered for. The more usual commendation is printed, but also special commendations for an older child, a young child, a baby, a stillborn child and a miscarriage. The commendation for an older child comes from the Anglican handbook, *Ministry to the Sick*, 1983. The commendations for a baby, a stillbirth and for a miscarriage are derived from prayers in Bishop Stephen Oliver's collection, *Pastoral Prayers*. The commendation for a stillbirth comes from *A New Zealand Prayer Book*, 1989.

Theological Note on the Funeral of a Child Dying near the Time of Birth

Professor Oliver O'Donovan of Christ Church, Oxford, wrote these two pages of theological reflection for an earlier version of this material published in the 1980s. In them he discusses the modern recognition of the needs of those affected by stillbirth and miscarriage. The inclusion of such a theological note is unprecedented and indicates just how careful the compilers of the *CW* funeral material have been with the questions that inevitably arise from some of the pastoral provisions they have offered.

H. SERVICES AFTER THE FUNERAL

At Home after the Funeral

This brief service need not be conducted by a minister, but may be provided by him or her for use by the family alone. The key theme is of peace to the house and to those who must return to an empty, new life without the deceased. The opening greeting speaks of peace and comfort, and of opening the door to a different life. For many the return to the home is particularly painful, especially if the deceased died in the house. This is not a house blessing nor an exorcism, but there are hints of both in this brief service. It is to be noticed that the members of the family (the congregation as it were) are required to say no more than 'Amen' during this service. Prayers follow, which may be informal, open prayer, or at the minister's discretion may be more formal. One prayer is printed here and is particularly suitable if there is to be some kind of reception in the home, where food and drink are served. This is common practice, and so ministers might prefer to use this prayer as a 'grace' even if the whole service is not used. Psalm 121 is provided as a possible way of ending the service, and it sets a suitably gentle attitude of hope and protection for the future.

The Burial of Ashes

During the pre-Christian, Hellenistic period, in Asia Minor, cremated remains were often interred in urns, in a manner not unlike modern practice. Christian practice has traditionally favoured the burial of the body, in anticipation of a bodily resurrection, but today roughly 60 per cent of funerals in the United Kingdom involve cremation. In recent years the pastoral need and theological value of the burial of ashes in consecrated ground has been recognized and has consequently become more popular. Many churches and cemeteries allow or encourage this practice. There is also an obvious practical advantage in burying ashes, as far less space is needed than for a body. Local custom and rules will determine the details of such an interment, as to whether an urn is to be used and whether it should be biodegradable in manufacture. The burial of ashes is to be preferred over scattering, as it makes the Christian hope in bodily resurrection more coherent if the remains lie in a grave. A grave, however small, has a location, and a memorial function which can be of great comfort to the relatives. *CW* provides no service for the scattering of ashes, but where scattering above ground is to take place, this service can be adapted.

CW improves and extends the provision of the *ASB*, in which there was a brief, half-page service involving a sentence, committal, a prayer and the Grace. The various editions of the *BCP* had previously provided no service for the burial of ashes whatsoever. It is suggested that the service might begin in the church or chapel (rather than at the graveside), and if it does so, the first part of the service may be conducted indoors. The minister opens with a greeting and an introduction in which the congregation are reminded that the burial of ashes constitutes the committal. There is no commendation in this brief service, the one at the funeral being deemed to suffice. Sentences of Scripture may be said, and one or more readings follow. Then comes the Committal, before which a small procession to the grave may be necessary. The Committal is in the traditional form, except that the phrase 'mortal remains' has replaced the clearly inappropriate word 'body'. The phrase 'earth to earth, ashes to ashes, dust to dust' has been reserved up until this point (it should not have been used at the crematorium), and this lends a poignant resonance of finality to the proceedings. As an alternative, a new committal is offered, perhaps for use where the traditional resonances of 'ashes to ashes' are not desired. This new prayer speaks of 'claiming God's love', and of 'returning' the ashes to the ground. There is an optional response for all to say together, from 1 Corinthians 15.57. The Lord's Prayer follows, and then two other prayers, with the option to insert others between them. A dismissal concludes the service.

An Outline Order for a Memorial Service

CW provides an outline order for a service, together with one within a celebration of the Eucharist, and then one sample form. These, while giving a structure, also permit a great deal of freedom over content. More could hardly be offered, for the service, while intended to take place some time after the funeral, may be for someone famous, with a large congregation expected, possibly in a cathedral or large civic church, or it may be a smaller, more private occasion, but nevertheless valued and desired by the relatives of the deceased. A memorial service is able to engage with and offer a different perspective on the death of a person, if only because of the passage of time since the funeral. The *CW* outlines can also be used to accommodate those rare and unfortunate situations where a funeral did not or could not take place. A word of warning is to be found in the Notes. As in the case of a funeral of a child, it is emphasized that a clear leader or president of the service should be evident. In order to ensure that continuity of potentially disparate elements, someone should begin and end the service, and should be seen to be holding it all together as a liturgical event, focused on Christian prayer and thanksgiving. For a more detailed study of memorial services, their theology and practice, Donald Gray's *Memorial Services* should be consulted.

A Sample Memorial Service

The Introduction refers to the unseen and the transient, drawing on imagery from 2 Corinthians 4.18. Two options for an opening prayer are provided, the first of which moves us through creation to gratitude, to an awareness that all gifts from God. The alternative prayer is perhaps more appropriate for someone of faith, but it also acknowledges sadness more overtly. A canticle, based on Isaiah 35, is suggested. Readings follow, either Old Testament and New Testament, or Old or New Testament and Gospel, being recommended. There may then be other readings, tributes, psalms or hymns, but *CW* is clear in its stipulation that a sermon should be preached. The next main section is an Affirmation of Faith, but a choice of two prayers can be used to provide a link. The Affirmation of Faith consists of a communal statement which is derived from 1 Corinthians 15.3–7. Prayers follow, with Prayers of Penitence first. These are introduced with words that resonate with 2 Corinthians 4.6–7. An optional response, which emphasizes the hope of resurrection, is provided for the intercessory prayers that follow. The prayers of thanksgiving include a section of the *Te Deum* and a responsive form based on Revelation 5.9–13. The Commendation tells the story of creation, rebellion against God, Christ's redeeming sacrifice, his resurrection and its significance for all people, and concludes with a vision of mutual communion with the saints in glory and a final doxology. The Lord's Prayer follows, and then the Dismissal, which consists of the greeting of Peace, introduced by a phrase from John 14.27, the Conclusion, introduced by familiar words from Romans 8.38–39, and a typical Easter blessing.

I. RESOURCES

The extensive section of prayers is tremendously valuable, providing prayers for use in many contexts. Their sources are indicated on pp. 406–10 of the *Pastoral Services* volume. A wide selection of appropriate readings and canticles are also provided. Most of the canticles come from the *CW* main volume. The new additions are: 'A Song of the Redeemer', from Isaiah 61; two from the Apocrypha, 'The Song of Manasseh' and 'A Song of the Righteous' (from Wisdom 3); 'A Song of the Justified', from Romans 4, 5 and 8; 'A Song of the Redeemed', from Revelation 7; and 'A Song of St Anselm', which is a tender piece, drawing on a mixture of Christian imagery.

Further Reading

Gilbert Cope (ed.), *Dying, Death and Disposal*, SPCK, London, 1970.

Richard Deadman (ed.), *Pastoral Prayers*, Cassell, London, 1996.

Donald Gray, *Memorial Services,* Alcuin Liturgy Guides 1, SPCK, London, 2002.

R. Anne Horton, *Using Common Worship: Funerals*, PRAXIS/Church House Publishing, London, 2000.

Stephen Oliver (ed.), *Pastoral Prayers*, Mowbray, London, 1996.

Michael Perham, *A New Handbook of Pastoral Liturgy*, SPCK, London, 2000.

Geoffrey Rowell, *The Liturgy of Christian Burial*, Alcuin/SPCK, London, 1977.

Richard Rutherford with Tony Barr, *The Death of a Christian: The Order of Christian Funerals*, rev. edn, Pueblo, Collegeville, MN, 1980.

Chapter 11

Ordination Services

A. HISTORY

Early Practice

Although the New Testament and other early Christian writings do not provide any details of the process by which Christian ministers were chosen, what evidence there is suggests that election by the local Christian community soon became the usual method of appointment to office. Among our earliest sources are *Didache* 15.1: 'elect for yourselves therefore bishops and deacons worthy of the Lord . . .'; and *1 Clement* 44.3: 'we judge therefore that it is not right to remove from the ministry those appointed by them [the Apostles] or afterwards by other eminent men with the consent of the whole church . . .'. While prayer is not explicitly mentioned in either of these accounts, it is reasonable to assume that it was part of the process, and in all later sources election and prayer constitute the two fundamental elements of the act of ordination: the community chooses those who are to be its ministers and then prays that God will equip them with the gifts needed to fulfil that particular ministry.

The election was not a mere preliminary to the ordination, but was an integral part of it, just as the catechumenate was of Christian initiation. The importance accorded to it, however, should not be understood as pointing to some notion of the ideal of democracy in early Christianity, nor necessarily to the principle that a congregation had the right to choose its own ministers. Nor was it seen as in any way opposed to the divine calling of the candidate, but on the contrary it was understood as the means by which God's choice of a person for that office was discerned and made manifest. In the case of a bishop, a candidate was not only selected by the local church but eventually also required to have the approval of other bishops, and it was this requirement, rather than any theory of sacramental transmission, which led to the presence and involvement of the latter in the rite of episcopal ordination. In the case of the presbyterate and diaconate, the right of nomination seems generally to have rested with the bishop, but he did not normally act without the consent of the clergy and people. Vestiges of this can still be seen in the later rites of East and West, where the congregation are invited to acclaim the ordinands as worthy, or (in the Roman tradition) are given opportunity to express any objections to them.

The local Christian community played a major part not only in the choice of its ministers, but also in the prayer for them. Thus, later ordination rites included a period of prayer by the congregation, either in silence or in the form of a litany and generally preceded by a bidding. This supplication culminated in a solemn oration recited by the presiding minister. The oldest texts of such prayers tend to focus chiefly on asking for the bestowal of the personal qualities necessary for the effective exercise of the office. As the understanding of ordination began to change, however, and the ritual of prayer and the imposition of the hand came to be thought of as the *real* act of ordination which made a person a minister, and election merely as a preliminary to this, the character of the prayers also reflected this development: later prayers tend to seek the bestowal of the gift of the office itself and of its powers.

It is interesting that the imposition of the hand is only rarely mentioned in the earliest references to the process of ministerial appointment. This may indicate that the gesture was not regarded as especially significant at this time, and was perhaps no more than the normal action which accompanied all solemn prayer and indicated its object. Certainly, the more ancient sources all agree that the imposition of the hand (usually the right hand) was originally performed during the time that prayer was being offered for the ordinand. The increased importance given to it as ordination rites evolved may be due at least in part to the ambivalence of the Greek term *cheirotonia*, 'the lifting up of hands'. In classical Greek usage this signified the act of election, but early Christianity extended it to designate not just the first half of the process of ministerial appointment but the whole ordination – both election and prayer with the laying on of the hand. By the late fourth century, however, the word seems to have been understood as referring primarily to the lifting up/laying on of hands in prayer rather than to the election, and so gave that gesture greater prominence.

Rites from the fourth century onwards indicate that ordinations concluded with the exchange of a kiss between the assembly and the new minister. This does not appear merely to be the kiss of peace which would normally occur within the eucharistic rite, but rather seems to have been intended to express the acceptance by the community of their new relationship with the ordained. Although the kiss continues to be practised in the later rites of East and West, it tends to become clericalized and to exclude the participation of the laity.

Ordinations in the early Church were conducted within the congregation in which the ministry was to be exercised, not simply so that the people might witness the proceedings, but because ordination was understood as an action which involved the active participation of the whole local church. 'Absolute' ordinations were originally unknown: a person could not be ordained simply as a bishop, presbyter or deacon in the universal Church, but had to be appointed to a specific, vacant ministerial role by and within a particular Christian congregation. It is for the same reason that the ordination normally took place on Sunday, the day of the community's regular assembly for worship, and the ordinand usually exercised the liturgical role of his new order in the Eucharist which followed.

Later Developments in the East

Later ordination rites in both East and West tend to become very elaborate, but perhaps surprisingly, the Byzantine Rite – still used in the Eastern Orthodox Church today – remains much simpler than those of most other traditions. In our earliest manuscript, from the eighth century, the rites for bishop, presbyter and deacon consist chiefly of a proclamation/bidding formula, a first ordination prayer, a litany, a second ordination prayer, vesting, the kiss and the seating of the newly ordained in his place. Later texts add only very minor embellishments to this pattern. There are reasons to suppose that the first prayer is a later insertion into the original sequence of proclamation/bidding – litany – ordination prayer, a structure which can also be detected underlying the other Eastern rites. Ordinations take place within the Sunday Eucharist, and not more than one candidate for any particular office may be ordained on the same occasion. A bishop is ordained at the very beginning of the eucharistic rite, so that he may then preside over the whole liturgy, a presbyter after the entrance of the gifts, so that he may participate in the eucharistic action, and a deacon at the end of the eucharistic prayer, so that he may assist in the distribution of communion.

Except for the names of the particular offices, the proclamation/bidding formulary is virtually identical for each order. For a bishop it reads as follows:

The divine grace, which always heals that which is infirm and supplies what is lacking, appoints the presbyter *N.*, beloved by God, as bishop. Let us pray therefore that the grace of the Holy Spirit may come upon him.

Its original function seems to have been as a sort of bridge between the two parts of the ordination process, proclaiming the result of the election of the ordinand and inviting the congregation to pray for him; and there is evidence to suggest that an early version of it was already current in Antioch before the end of the fourth century. Later, however, the imposition of the hand became attached to it, with the result that it tends to be regarded by many as the vital formulary which effects the ordination. Versions of it, elaborated to greater or lesser degrees, have also found their way into all other Eastern ordination rites.

The imposition of the hand is performed by the presiding bishop alone at ordinations to all of the orders, a practice that is reflected in virtually every other Eastern tradition. In addition, ordinations to the episcopate include the imposition of the Gospel book on the ordinand, a custom which is found also in the other Eastern rites and can be traced back to the fourth century, although its original meaning is not clear. It seems most likely that it was intended to represent the action of Christ himself ordaining the bishop.

The substance of the second of the prayers for a bishop is also found in most other Eastern rites for bishops, suggesting that again it derives from fourth-century Antiochene use. The two images of the episcopal office which constitute part of its original nucleus are those of the imitator of Christ the true shepherd and the teacher/guardian of the truth, utilizing a quotation from Romans 2.19–20. Cultic/liturgical imagery seems to have had no place at all in the earliest stratum. The second prayer for a presbyter in the Byzantine rite asks that the ordinand may be worthy to stand at the altar, to proclaim the gospel and exercise the sacred ministry of the Word, to offer gifts and spiritual sacrifices, and to renew the people by the bath of regeneration. The substance of this prayer recurs in some other Eastern rites, while others which have independent prayers also tend to give a prominent place to the ministry of the Word in their description of the presbyteral office. Some later versions, however, modify the references to that ministry (since it later ceased to be a function normally exercised by presbyters) and introduce the term 'priest' or 'priesthood' into the prayers. The Byzantine prayers for a deacon, both of which are also found in some other Eastern rites, say nothing about any functions which belong to the order apart from assistance at the celebration of the Eucharist, but they speak instead of the virtues which God is being asked to bestow upon the ordinand. While one of them draws upon the image of St Stephen to define the office, the other does not. This same variation, and also a similar tendency to reticence with regard to the actual functions of the diaconate, can also be seen in the independent prayers of other Eastern traditions.

Later Developments in the West

The early Roman tradition, known to us mainly through liturgical sources dating from around the eighth century, in theory maintained the ancient custom of ordinations taking place on a Sunday, but because they were preceded by a period of communal fasting, generally brought them forward to Saturday evening, which was regarded as the beginning of Sunday, so that the fasting might not have to be unduly prolonged. There was also a preference for holding ordinations at the end of a time when the Church was already fasting for some other reason – one of the Ember seasons, or even the Easter Vigil itself.

Candidates arrived already vested in the robes of the new order to which they had been appointed and the rites comprised a bidding, a litany with a concluding collect, an ordination prayer and the kiss. In contrast to the content of the Eastern ordination prayers, the Roman orations make strong use of Old Testament cultic imagery. The bishop is described as the spiritual counterpart of the Old Testament high priest. In a text that lays great stress on the subordinate position of their office to the episcopate, presbyters are viewed as the equivalent of priests in relation to the high priest and the sons of Aaron in relation to their father, as well as fulfilling the more common images of the seventy elders appointed to assist Moses and of teachers to assist the apostles. Deacons are defined as the equivalents of the Levites.

By the eighth century in Gaul and other parts of the West, however, this Roman material was being imported and used in combination with the native ordination rites of those regions. Thus, in the case of the diaconate and presbyterate, the Roman bidding, collect and ordination prayer immediately preceded the Gallican bidding and ordination prayer, so that in effect the candidate was ordained twice (the litany now apparently being sung earlier in the service so that it need not be repeated when both deacons and presbyters were ordained at the same time). In the case of the episcopate, the Roman material dominated rather more: the lengthy Gallican bidding rapidly disappeared and part of the Gallican ordination prayer was simply interpolated within the Roman prayer. The Gallican texts had also included directions requiring other bishops to assist in the imposition of hands on a bishop and other presbyters to share in the imposition of hands on a presbyter, but the bishop alone to lay his hand on a deacon. These 'rubrics' came to be placed at the head of the formularies for the relevant ordination in some of the combined collections of prayers, which led in the course of time to the imposition of hands itself being performed separately in silence before any of the prayers were said, rather than during the ordination prayer as in former times.

By this time the Gallican tradition included the custom of anointing the hands of a new presbyter, and soon afterwards those of a new bishop also. Furthermore, although the Roman prayer for a bishop had originally been intended to be understood in a mystical and metaphorical sense, the reference in it to 'the dew of heavenly unction' was now taken more literally and thought to refer to a physical anointing. Hence, the anointing of the head of a new bishop was soon added, the action being inserted into the very middle of the ordination prayer itself. The ceremonial vesting of the newly ordained in the robes of their office also began to follow the act of ordination.

The details of later ordination rites varied from place to place and there was much experimentation and interchange of practice before standardization was achieved in the sixteenth century. Nevertheless, this basic composite pattern crystallized into what is called the 'Romano-German Pontifical of the tenth century', and became normal throughout Western Christendom, displacing all other local rites. By the eleventh century it was also largely accepted in Rome itself, and was the immediate source of the Roman Pontificals of the twelfth and thirteenth centuries, which were widely disseminated in the West. These were eventually superseded by a revised version compiled by William Durandus in the Diocese of Mende in the thirteenth century, which became the model for the first printed pontifical of 1485.

The later texts reveal a number of additions to the earlier pattern. Chief among these is the *traditio instrumentorum* – the ceremonial handing over to the newly ordained of objects which symbolized his new office, accompanied by an appropriate imperative formula expressing the conferral of powers belonging to the order. This custom was derived from the minor orders, where it was already the principal ritual action in the ordination process, and it was also practised in the bestowal of office in civil life. Thus, in addition to the robes of his office, the deacon received the book of the Gospels, the presbyter the chalice and paten, and the bishop the pastoral staff, ring and Gospel book. The imposition of hands, performed in silence in the older texts, also eventually tended to be accompanied by an imperative formula similar to those now accompanying the *traditio instrumentorum*, and a second imposition of hands on presbyters towards the end of the ordination Mass, accompanied by the formula, 'Receive the Holy Spirit, whosoever sins you remit . . .' (Christ's commission to the Apostles in John 20.22–23), originated in certain French churches in the twelfth century, and then spread widely. In the thirteenth century newly ordained presbyters also began to concelebrate the ordination Mass with the bishop.

In the course of the Middle Ages the nature of the ordained ministry had changed dramatically from the situation in the first few centuries of the Church's history. Ordinands were no longer leading Christians whom the local community had chosen from among its number to exercise the ministry of leadership there, but rather men who had embarked upon an ecclesiastical career, who had served some form of apprenticeship in the lower orders, and who were chosen for advancement to higher office by ecclesiastical or civil superiors. Hence, influenced by the feudal system of the contemporary world around, both the rites of ordination themselves and theological reflection upon them became increasingly concerned with the conferral of powers, and almost entirely unrelated to ministry within a specific congregation. As a result, ordinations were now usually performed far away from the local Christian community, in a cathedral or even in the privacy of a bishop's chapel.

Because of the proliferation of minor orders and other ecclesiastical offices, there was uncertainty among medieval theologians as to how many different 'orders' there really were. Seven was the most commonly accepted number, but some spoke of eight or even nine. Some dealt with the multiplicity of ecclesiastical ranks by distinguishing between an order as such and a 'dignity within an order' (e.g. an archdeacon), and this became standard in later medieval theology. The same distinction was also often used to explain the nature of the episcopate. Because ordained ministry came to be defined in the medieval West almost exclusively in terms of the image of priesthood, it then appeared that both bishops and presbyters shared in a single order: both possessed what was regarded as the highest power of priesthood, that of celebrating the Eucharist. Therefore, while some medieval theologians maintained that the episcopate was a separate order, most concluded that it was only a dignity within the order of priesthood, and hence tended to speak of bishops being 'consecrated' rather than 'ordained'.

Since the medieval ordination rites had become extremely complex and their central features obscured by a wealth of secondary accretions, this posed problems for theologians in their attempts to define what constituted the principal elements of the sacrament. Some scholars believed that the essential ritual action and the words which effected the ordination – its 'matter' and 'form' in Scholastic terminology – had been instituted by Christ himself, while others thought that the Church had been left to determine what they should be. While some argued that the imposition of hands must be essential, because it went back to apostolic times, others, including Thomas Aquinas, inclined to the view that the *traditio instrumentorum* and its accompanying formula were the indispensable elements, because they more clearly signified the transmission of power, while still others thought that the priestly anointing must constitute at least part of what was vital.

The Reformation

All this uncertainty was swept away by the Reformers, who turned to the New Testament for authoritative guidance. They believed that it taught that appointment to Christian ministry should include the election or 'calling' of the candidate by a local church and his commendation to that ministry by prayer in a public assembly. Some, like Johannes Bugenhagen, thought that ordinations ought to take place in the congregation which had called the person, but Martin Luther, though sympathetic to this idea, preferred a more centralized practice, at least as a temporary expedient, since he believed that something was needed to replace the ecclesiastical hierarchy in supervision and legitimation of the actions of local churches. There was also some reluctance among certain Reformers to use of the imposition of hands in ordination, because of the existence of what they regarded as superstitious views about its meaning. John Calvin in Geneva omitted it altogether, and John Knox in Scotland substituted the giving of the right hand of fellowship.

Thus, ordinations in Reformation Churches were held during public worship on a Sunday and generally included: (a) election by the local congregation, or at least a period of time prior to the ordination in which they might make enquiries about the candidate and lodge objections; (b) preaching on the qualities and duties required of a minister; (c) a series of questions put to the candidate about his beliefs, etc.; (d) congregational prayer; and (e) prayer by the presiding minister, in most cases accompanied by an imposition of hands.

The first Anglican Ordinal, drawn up in 1550 by Thomas Cranmer, provided for the ordination of deacons, priests and bishops, and was based primarily upon an ordination rite composed by the Continental Reformer Martin Bucer, although supplemented with quite a number of features adapted from the former medieval practice. The rites were preceded by a preface, which stated that ministers should be admitted 'by public prayer with imposition of hands'. The main elements in the rite for deacons, which was the simplest of the three, were: a sermon, the presentation of the candidates, the litany, the eucharistic ministry of the Word up to the end of the Epistle, an examination of the ordinands, the imposition of hands by the bishop with an appropriate formula, and the giving of the New Testament (rather than the Gospel book, as in medieval times). The Eucharist then continued from the Gospel onwards (which one of the new deacons read), and concluded with a special collect before the blessing. It is clear from this that the litany (which included a special petition and concluding collect for the ordinands) was understood to be the requisite 'public prayer', which preceded and was distinct from the formal commissioning for ministry with imposition of hands.

The rite for priests was similar, except that it came after the Gospel and included the hymn 'Come, Holy Ghost' from the medieval rite, a lengthy exhortation to the ordinands, a period of silent congregational prayer, and another substantial prayer before the laying on of hands. In Bucer's rite this prayer contained a petition for those being ordained, but Cranmer removed it, so that once again the 'public prayer' for them was principally the litany. As in the medieval rite, the priests joined with the bishop in performing the imposition of hands. This was accompanied by a formula beginning with the words from John 20.22–23, 'Receive the Holy Ghost', which had been used at the second imposition of hands in the medieval rite, and the newly ordained then received a Bible as well as the chalice and paten formerly given.

Following medieval precedent, the rite for bishops was described as the form of 'consecrating' a bishop, instead of 'ordering', as in the other two rites. It was rather more elaborate than the others and did include a complete prayer for the ordinand before the laying on of hands which drew upon material from the medieval service. In accordance with tradition, the imposition of hands was performed by all the bishops present, after which the Gospel book was laid upon the ordinand's neck. He then received the pastoral staff.

When these rites were revised in 1552, all directions about how the candidates were to be vested were removed from them, and the *traditio instrumentorum* was modified: priests now received the Bible alone, and bishops did not have the Bible laid on their necks but given to them, and no longer were presented with the pastoral staff. No major changes were made to the rites at subsequent revisions of the *Book of Common Prayer*, with which the Ordinal was now bound up, apart from an alteration to the wording of the Preface to the Ordinal in 1662 to make episcopal ordination explicitly a sine qua non for admission to ministry in the Church of England. At the same time, opportunity was taken to make it clear by a number of minor changes that bishops and priests constituted separate orders of ministry and not merely different degrees within the same ministry. Candidates for the diaconate and the priesthood were now to be 'decently habited' and a candidate for the episcopate was to be 'vested in his rochet' and 'put on the rest of the episcopal habit' before the hymn 'Come, Holy Ghost'.

Modern Revisions

Both Anglican ordination rites and also those of many other Churches were revised during the twentieth century, and in virtually every case a classical style of ordination prayer closely accompanied by the imposition of hands was restored as their central feature. Chiefly because of the difficulty encountered when several candidates are to be ordained at the same service, however, the imposition of hands did not always take place during the prayer itself. In some cases, notably the Roman Catholic rite, it is still done in silence before the prayer (even when only one person is to be ordained!); in a few cases it follows the prayer and has its own formula; while in others, including the *ASB* and the rites in many other Anglican provinces, the precedent adopted in the Church of South India was followed, with the central petition of the prayer being repeated while hands were laid on each candidate in turn, before the prayer was then concluded. Most ecclesiastical traditions have also experienced an enrichment in the symbolism used in the service, and especially in the bestowal of symbols of office, and in the involvement of lay people, though in some cases they are still treated as little more than spectators at an essentially clerical act. But above all, it is ecumenical dialogue between Churches, including consultations initiated by the World Council of Churches and bilateral conversations such as those of the Anglican–Roman Catholic International Commission, which has done most to bring about a renewed and shared understanding of the meaning of ordination and ministry and is reflected in the character of recent revisions of rites.

The Ordinal in the *ASB* was the first authorized alternative to the 1662 Ordinal in England, and was based to a considerable extent on the Ordinal published in 1968 as part of the abortive Anglican–Methodist unity scheme. The rites for deacons, priests and bishops all shared a common pattern, and at many points used the same words. Like other rites in the *ASB* that involved the celebration of the Eucharist, the whole of the ordination was located in the middle of the eucharistic rite, between the ministry of the Word and the exchange of the Peace.

In 2000 minor amendments to the *ASB* Ordinal were approved. Most were designed to facilitate its use with the *CW* Order for the Celebration of Holy Communion, but an additional Note permitted (but did not require) 'dispersal' of elements of the rite, so that the presentation to the archbishop or bishop could occur after the Greeting, the Presentation to the people after the Declaration, and the Giving of the Bible and the giving of symbols of office as part of the concluding rite. Authorization of the *ASB* Ordinal in this amended form was extended until 31 December 2005, in order to allow time for the preparation of a *CW* Ordinal.

B. COMMENTARY

In preparing the text of the *CW* Ordinal, the Liturgical Commission took note of the International Anglican Liturgical Consultation's statement on ordination and ministry, *To Equip the Saints* (known as the Berkeley Statement), and of recent academic studies, including that of John Collins. The views of interested parties within the Church of England (including the Faith and Order Advisory Group, the Ministry Division and the Principals of Colleges, Courses and Schemes) were sought. The Commission also sought comments from the other Anglican Churches of Britain and Ireland, the Porvoo Churches, the Roman Catholic Church and ecumenical partners in England on an earlier draft.

The starting point for the new rites was the *ASB* Ordinal. In addition to enriching its texts, however, the structure of the rites has also been modified in two principal ways. First, building on the optional Note added to the *ASB* Ordinal in 2000, the ordination material was spread more widely throughout the rite than is the case in the *ASB* itself, where it is almost entirely concentrated in the middle. In that Ordinal the eucharistic celebration proceeds right through the ministry of the Word before the ordinands are explicitly mentioned and presented, as though the community has gathered for a normal Sunday Eucharist and are just happening to do an ordination in the middle, much as they might decide to dedicate a piece of ecclesiastical furniture in their regular act of worship. However, the congregation at an ordination will very rarely comprise a regular eucharistic community but will usually consist of individuals and groups who have not previously worshipped with one another and so need to be more consciously formed into a community at the outset. Similarly, in the *ASB* rites once the ordination is over and the Eucharist continues from the Peace onwards, there is again little further reference to what has just taken place. In the new rites, therefore, the presentation of the ordinands comes near the beginning, as is the case in the 1662 rites, thus revealing the purpose of the assembly and setting the tone for the whole celebration, and there is also the option of a more substantial sending out of the newly ordained to minister in their communities at the end. However, Note 7 (Note 8 in the rite for a bishop) permits the Bishop to defer the Presentation until immediately before the Liturgy of Ordination.

The second major difference from the *ASB* rites is that more material that is specific to each order has been included. The three rites for deacons, priests and bishop in the *ASB* not only share a common structure but also for the most part use the same texts, only varying them when absolutely necessary to indicate the character of the particular order being conferred. Here, on the other hand, many more parts of the service introduce variations so as to give greater emphasis to the distinctive character of each order of ministry rather than simply to what they share in common. However, just because a particular aspect of ministry is mentioned explicitly in relation to one order and not the others, it should not automatically be assumed to be an indication that it is seen as exclusive to that order. In some cases the intention is merely to highlight a dimension that seems especially appropriate to that particular office but may also be shared, at least to some measure, by the others as well. It is simply not possible, let alone desirable, to give equal emphasis to every aspect of ministry in all three rites.

In the commentary that follows, as each part of the service is described, what is common to all three rites will be depicted first, and then any variations that apply to the individual orders will follow. It should be noted that, as in the *ASB* Ordinal, the 'default' text for the Ordination of a Bishop is designed for use at the ordination of one bishop, and italics are used to indicate where a change would be required when more than one bishop is to be ordained.

The Gathering and Presentation

The Greeting

As in all the *CW* eucharistic rites, the service begins with a greeting of the congregation by the president. Here the bishop or archbishop (hereafter in this commentary for the sake of simplicity usually called the president) greets the people using a form taken from the *CW* confirmation service that emphasizes the unity of the Church. It is important that ordination is always viewed within its wider ecclesiological context, because otherwise the variety of ministries exercised by all the baptized may be undervalued or overlooked and the ordained ministry seen as constituting the totality of the Church's ministry, or, worse still, the process of ordination seen in largely individualistic terms and so unrelated to the Church which the ordained are intended to serve and to the whole ministry to which they bring order.

For the same reason, the first two paragraphs of the president's introduction focus on the whole Church and its diversity of ministries, and only in the third paragraph does it move on to the specific role of the ordained within that rich diversity. The first paragraph speaks of the calling of all the baptized, drawing in particular upon 1 Peter 2.9, while the second paragraph describes the Church by means of several New Testament images. The third paragraph is specific to each rite:

- The office of a deacon is defined primarily in terms of representing the servanthood of Christ, following a constant tradition that goes back at least to Ignatius of Antioch at the beginning of the second century.
- For priests, emphasis is placed on the biblical image of the Good Shepherd, on the collegial character of their ministry in association with other priests and the oversight of the bishop, and on their role as leader of their Christian community through word and sacrament so that it may grow into Christ and become a living sacrifice (alluding to Ephesians 4.13 and Romans 12.1). The image of the minister delighting in the beauty of the Church is

drawn from the seventeenth-century divine Richard Baxter, who wrote: 'No man is fit to be a minister of Christ that is not of a public spirit as to the Church and delighteth not in its beauty and longeth not for its felicity . . . so that he must rejoice in its welfare and be willing to spend and be spent for its sake' (*Reformed Pastor* 1.1).

• For bishops, it is their responsibility for the guardianship of the apostolic faith, for the proclamation of the gospel and for the unity and catholicity of the Church that is particularly emphasized.

Prayers of penitence normally follow, and Note 6 (Note 7 in the rite for a bishop) provides a suitable form of invitation to confession that may be used.

The Presentation

Each ordinand is then presented in turn. Not only are they announced by name, but the place in which they are to minister is also stated. This is because ordained ministry is always essentially rooted in a specific place or community. A person is not simply made a bishop in the Church of God, but first and foremost the bishop of a particular see which has need of episcopal ministry. Similarly, no one can be a made a priest or deacon in the abstract. From ancient times the Church has always refused to allow 'absolute' ordinations, as they are technically called, and insisted that each new deacon or priest must have a 'title', a particular Christian community which needs their ministry and in which they will serve.

In the 1662 and *ASB* Ordinals, following medieval tradition, candidates for the diaconate and presbyterate are presented by the archdeacon, who then answers questions as to their suitability for ordination. Frequently, however, the archdeacon may never have met the ordinands before the occasion, may have had no responsibility for their selection or training, and may therefore have no personal knowledge but only the word of others on which to base his or her answers. At the ordination of a bishop in those Ordinals, the candidate is presented by two bishops; this may perhaps convey the impression that the individual is being proposed for admission to a club by two existing members rather than being sought by a diocese to meet their need. Because the act of presentation is a very important element in the rite, setting before the assembled congregation both the need for an ordained person to fill a specific vacancy and reflecting all that has gone before in selecting this particular person to fill it, it is desirable that persons who truly represent that latter process should be publicly involved in it.

Thus, as Note 7 in each service (Note 8 in the rite for a bishop) indicates, it is advantageous if the questions about each ordinand's call and preparation are answered by persons most qualified to do so – the diocesan director of ordinands or someone who has been closely involved in a candidate's formation and training, perhaps a theological college or course principal in the case of a deacon; the training incumbent in the case of a priest; and the diocesan representatives on the Crown Nominations Commission in the case of a diocesan bishop. At the ordination of a diocesan bishop, the presentation may also be made by representatives of the diocese, and in the case of a suffragan bishop, by the diocesan bishop himself.

After testimony to the external call of the candidates has thus been given, the candidates themselves are then asked to testify to their own sense of vocation, rather than this question being deferred until the later questions and answers in the service, as it was in the *ASB*. The question has been rephrased, including being put in the present tense to emphasize God's calling as a continuing process and not merely a past event.

Finally, in the case of deacons and priests, the archdeacon or registrar confirms that the necessary oaths have been taken and the Declaration of Assent has been made. Canon C 15.1(3) requires those who are to be consecrated bishop to make the Declaration publicly and openly on the occasion of their consecration in the presence of the congregation as well as the archbishop.

It has been the custom at most ordinations for the ordinands to come in as part of the general entrance procession of ordained ministers and others at the beginning of the service. Note 5 in each service (Note 6 in the rite for a bishop), however, allows an alternative practice, in which the ordinands are seated in the congregation, together with those who will present them, before the service begins, and only come forward with their presenters at this time. If this is done, there will be a clearer symbolic expression of the fact that candidates for ordination arise out of the body of the faithful and are brought forward by the people who need their ministry, rather than simply appearing out of nowhere, as it were, to be sent to minister.

The Collect

These necessary preliminaries are concluded, as is the Gathering at all celebrations of the Eucharist, by a period of prayer and the Collect (Note 9 specifies that the *Gloria in excelsis* may be sung before the Collect). The Collect may be either the normal Collect of the day or the fourth of the *CW* Collects for Ministry, which was that used for ordinations in the *ASB* and is printed in the text of the rites.

The Liturgy of the Word

The 1662 and *ASB* Ordinals provided special readings for each order, and the new services continue this practice in Note 10, although permitting the readings of the day to be used instead, especially on a Principal Feast or a Festival, as there is much to be said for a Christian community pondering on the application of other parts of Scripture to the ordination of its ministers. The recommended readings seek to bring out appropriate aspects of the particular ministry being conferred. Thus:

- For the ordination of deacons, the Old Testament readings all concentrate on the theme of 'call', only one of which (Isaiah 6.1–8) was provided in the *ASB* rite. The New Testament options continue to include the readings from Acts 6 and 1 Timothy used in the 1662 rite, and the reading from Romans used in the *ASB* rite, but passages from 2 Corinthians (on being 'fools for Christ's sake') and from Philippians, on the humility of Christ, are added. The Gospels add to the *ASB* passage from Mark on servanthood readings from each of the other Gospels: Matthew, the parable of the Sheep and Goats; Luke, on servants being ready for the return of their master (as in the 1662 rite); and John, the account of Jesus' foot-washing.

- For the ordination of priests, the Old Testament readings add to the Isaiah 61 passage from the *ASB* rite another text from Isaiah, on the bringing of good tidings, and one from Jeremiah, on the new covenant. The New Testament options treat of the ministry of reconciliation (2 Corinthians 5.17—6.2, overlapping slightly with the *ASB* reading, 5.14–19); of the variety of gifts of ministry (Ephesians 4.7–16, used in the 1662 rite); of advice to ministers (1 Timothy 4.6–16); and of the qualities required of elders and bishops (Titus 1.5–9). Of the Gospels, the Matthew 9 reading was used in a shorter form in 1662, without the call of the Twelve, the Matthew 28 commission to make disciples of all nations is a new addition, the John 10 reading was used in the 1662 rite, and the John 20 reading was used in the *ASB* rite.

- For the ordination of a bishop, three options are provided for Old Testament readings: one of the 'servant songs' from Isaiah 42, the 'Spirit of the Lord' passage from Isaiah 61, and the image of God as shepherd from Ezekiel 34. The New Testament readings comprise the Acts 20 address to the elders of Ephesus and the 1 Timothy 3 passage about bishops, both used in the 1662 rite, as well as 2 Timothy 3.14—4.5, on preaching the word, and 1 Peter 5.1–11, an exhortation to elders. In addition to the Matthew 28 passage (used in a shorter form in the 1662 rite) and the reading from John 21 (used in both the 1662 and *ASB* rites), two other alternatives are provided: Matthew 18.1–7, on the greatest in the kingdom of heaven, and parts of John 17, the 'high-priestly' prayer of Jesus.

The Nicene Creed is mandatory for ordinations of deacons and priests that take place on Sundays and Holy Days, but optional on other days. However, the Creed is to be said at all ordinations of bishops, whenever they occur, because bishops have a particular responsibility for sound teaching.

The Liturgy of Ordination

Now that the ordinands have been introduced to the congregation, and the assembly has heard and pondered on the word of God, the ordination proper begins. The way an ordination is celebrated can sometimes make it look as if the bishop is setting some persons apart from the community of faith and transmitting to them a distinct 'power'. But an ordination is the act of the whole community presided over by the bishop. First, therefore, the ordinands must make before the people certain declarations about their faith and intentions so that the people may be able to give their consent to the ordination. Then the whole assembly will offer their prayers to God for the needs of the Church and the world, including petition for the ordinands, before the president, acting in the name of the Church, says the ordination prayer accompanied by the laying on of hands.

The Declarations

The *ASB* provided a substantial address to be said by the president to candidates for the priesthood, modelled on that in the 1662 rite, and somewhat shorter versions for deacons and bishops. As parts of these addresses were thought to be less than satisfactory, they have all been entirely rewritten in the new rites, although echoes of the older versions can still be heard in places, particularly in the rite for priests. Some of the material in the *ASB* addresses has also been adapted for use elsewhere in the rites, especially in the words of the bishop at the end of the series of questions to the ordinands that follow the address.

The *ASB* posed a series of near-identical questions to the candidates for episcopal, presbyteral and diaconal ordination; and ordinands repeated substantially the same promises on each occasion. In the 1662 rites, however, several of the questions vary from one order to another, and ordinands make promises appropriate to the particular order into which they are about to be ordained. The present draft draws on both the *ASB* and 1662 rites. It retains many of the words of the *ASB*, but it reverts to the 1662 tradition of varying the interrogations according to each order, and adapts a number of the 1662 rite's actual questions.

Three questions – about acceptance of Scripture, commitment to continuing prayer and study, and willingness to engage in collaborative ministry – are regarded as so fundamental that they are repeated on each occasion. Other questions are asked on each occasion, but in a form appropriate to the order. Thus, the theme of the Church's mission features with minor differences in the third question in the rites for priests and bishops, and in a somewhat different form in the fourth question in the rite for deacons. Similarly, the question about authority is asked in one form of the deacon, who is in most (though not all) settings in the Church of England a minister more particularly 'under authority' within the Church; in another form of the priest, who is both under authority and increasingly exercises authority as increasing responsibilities arrive; and in a third form of the bishop, who has a particular call to exercise authority in the government of the Church. The final question, about 'stirring up the gift of God that is in you', begins identically for all three orders, but ends with a purposive clause adapted to each.

Still other questions are asked on one occasion only, and the responses to these are intended to be cumulative: as the ordinand is called to new roles within the Church, the answers given at earlier ordinations are not forgotten. A deacon ordained to the priesthood remains also a deacon, and there is therefore no implication that a deacon's commitment to have a 'care for those who are in need' comes to an end if that deacon is ordained to the priesthood. There is an emphasis in the bishop's form of the 'household question' on hospitality (Titus 1.8 says that a bishop should be hospitable), but this is not intended to imply that deacons or priests should not also be hospitable! It is to be noted that 'household' may refer to a domestic establishment rather than the occupants of a house, and a 'householder' is defined as 'one who occupies house as his own dwelling' (*Concise Oxford Dictionary*); a household may therefore be a single-person household. After much discussion, the term 'household' has been retained in the appropriate question in the deacons' and priests' rites, in preference to others which would imply that deacons and priests always live in homes shared with others.

In general, the questions to deacons emphasize their role in carrying the Church's loving care to the wider community; the questions to priests emphasize their share in Christ's ministry of reconciliation; and the questions to bishops their service to the unity of the Church, their role in the articulation of authority within it, and their responsibility to ordain and commission other ministers.

When all the questions have been answered, the president then asks the congregation to express their consent to the candidates being ordained and their commitment to continuing support for them in their ministry. The practice of seeking the consent of the laity has been traditional at ordinations since the earliest times and is one of the ways in which expression is given to the concept of ordination as the action of the whole Church and not just of the bishop or archbishop who presides. In the 1662 and *ASB* rites it comes immediately after the presentation, but it is more appropriate for it to be done here, when the congregation has had opportunity to hear the responses of the ordinands.

After this, the president reminds the ordinands of the greatness of the ministry that is about to be entrusted to them and that they will not be able to perform it without the grace and power of God, for which they will need to pray constantly. The whole assembly then turns to prayer, first in silence, next in the case of the ordination of priests and bishops (and optionally in the rite for deacons) by invoking the Holy Spirit in the hymn 'Come, Holy Ghost', and finally in all three rites through participation in a litany. It is in accordance with ancient tradition that the hymn is not used at the ordination of a deacon, and it appears that it may have been omitted from the 1549 and subsequent Anglican Ordinals also because candidates for the diaconate were expected already to be, like St Stephen, 'full of the Spirit' (Acts 6.2; note also the first question put to the candidates and the absence of reference to the Holy Spirit at the laying on of hands in the 1549/1662 rites). However, Note 11 in the rite for deacons allows its use, if desired.

The Litany

The first three and last five of the biddings in the Litany are common to all three rites; the others are specific to the individual rites. The penultimate bidding supplies the penitential element otherwise omitted from the rites. The first two biddings are taken from the *CW* Form of Intercession No. 5 (pp. 286–7 in the main volume), and some others are adapted from *New Patterns for Worship*, Litany F39. As Note 11 indicates, another litany may be used here.

The Ordination Prayer

The *ASB* restored the ancient practice of the Church in having an ordination prayer for each order that gave thanks to God for his mighty acts, and especially for ensuring that his Church never lacked suitable ministers, and then asked for the necessary gifts of grace to be bestowed on those now chosen to serve in the particular order, comparable to the eucharistic prayer in the service of Holy Communion. It also returned to the ancient tradition of hands being laid on the ordinand while this petition was being made. The large number of candidates being ordained at the same time had been a principal factor in causing the medieval rites in the West to separate this laying on of hands from the prayer (that difficulty did not arise in the East because there only one person is ever ordained to any order on any single occasion). The *ASB* solved this particular problem by adopting an arrangement from the Church of South India: when the central petition in the prayer is reached, that petition is repeated for each ordinand accompanied by an individual laying on of hands, and then once they have all been prayed for in this way, the rest of the prayer is said over them collectively.

This solution, however, produces a problem of its own. It can appear that the ordination prayer is actually two independent prayers – a prayer of thanksgiving at the beginning and a prayer of petition at the end – separated by an ordination formula said over each candidate, rather than a continuous whole. Furthermore, it can also lead to the conclusion that the essential words of ordination, the vital words that actually make someone a deacon/priest/bishop are just the ones said while hands are being laid on the ordinand, and that all the rest is merely ancillary. In other words, it can seem as though the Church of England believes that ordination is conferred by a specific formula of words rather than by prayer – exactly the opposite impression that the *ASB* rites were attempting to convey. A second weakness of the *ASB* pattern is that it can all too easily appear to be essentially an action performed by the clergy to which the congregation are no more than spectators, rather than prayer by the whole Church for the ordinands, even though articulated on its behalf by the president.

As one way of trying to ameliorate this problem, the option of a congregational invocation of the Holy Spirit punctuating the prayer at points and following each laying on of hands has been provided (see Note 12). This responsive form would not only give the whole action a more corporate sense but also help to bind together the various parts of the prayer and give it a more unified feel. Any suitable invocation may be used. Some may wish to have it sung by the congregation continuously in a quiet manner all the time that the prayer is being said or sung by the president, rather than merely at the points indicated. It would also help to bring out the integral link between the prayer of the people and the ordination prayer if the music used for the latter cohered with that of the hymn 'Come, Holy Ghost' and of the litany.

The ordination prayers are modelled on those in the *ASB*, but with modifications and with enrichments drawn from other sources. All three prayers begin with four acts of thanks and praise.

The first, which is common to all three rites, praises God for his gift of the Church itself, using images taken from 1 Peter 2.9, thus once more setting the ordained ministry within a proper ecclesiological context.

The second affirms the christological foundation of all ministry. In the rite for deacons it praises God for Christ's acceptance of the form of a slave, drawing on the imagery of Philippians 2.7–8 (where the Greek word is *doulos*, 'slave', and not *diakonos*, 'servant'); and in the rites for priests and a bishop the thanksgiving is the same in both cases, describing Christ as the firstborn of all creation and head of the Church, language taken from Colossians 1.15 and 18 and already used in this way in the ordination prayer for priests in the 1979 Prayer Book of ECUSA.

The third praises God for the diverse gifts of ministry distributed to all members of the Church. The rite for deacons here adapts part of the 1984 Scottish Ordinal, which itself was influenced partly by Ephesians 4.12, to recall the gifts of the Spirit in every age; in the rite for priests Ephesians 4.11–12 is drawn on rather more fully, recalling also the death and glorification of Christ; while in the rite for a bishop this is adapted further to allude instead to the gift of the Spirit at Pentecost.

The fourth thanks God for calling the candidates to the specific ministry of the gospel to which they are now to be ordained, the general pattern being the same in each rite and differing only in the definition of the particular ministry, that for deacons drawing on Mark 10.45, that for priests and bishops incorporating the threefold image of Christ as Apostle, High Priest and Shepherd.

Once these four thanksgivings are over, the prayer moves on to pray directly for the ordinands in its second half, using the phrase 'Therefore, Father, though Christ our Lord we pray' in order to make this transition clear and also to include a christological reference in proximity to the invocation of the Spirit that is about to follow so that the Trinitarian character of prayer will stand out.

Note 12 not only indicates who should take part in the laying on of hands in each case in accordance with ancient Western tradition and the Canons of the Church of England, but also insists that any movement at this point should not detract from the unity of the whole prayer. Where more than one person is being ordained, this is probably best achieved if the president, who in any case is directed to stand (and not sit in his chair) throughout this whole section because it is a prayer, moves in turn to each of the ordinands already kneeling before him rather than having the ordinands come to him.

After hands have been laid on each one, petition for them all resumes in the rest of the prayer.

- The rite for deacons is influenced in part by the corresponding prayer in the Scottish Ordinal, and focuses on the gift of faithful service and perseverance in the proclamation of the gospel, on the deacons' humble service of others exemplified in Christ's washing of his disciples' feet, and on the example of holy living they are called to set as a model to be followed by all the faithful in readiness for the coming of Christ in glory, thus including in the prayer an appropriate eschatological note.
- The material in the rite for priests has also been influenced in part by the equivalent prayer in the 1984 Scottish Ordinal and prays that the newly ordained may have grace and power to proclaim the gospel and minister the sacraments, and for the gift of the qualities of holiness, wisdom, and discipline required for a fruitful collaborative ministry, and asks that the priestly functions of reconciling, healing, blessing and absolving may be used so that a priestly people may be formed, worthy to offer spiritual sacrifices to God (alluding to 1 Peter 2.5).
- In the rite for a bishop, the prayer remains close to the text in the *ASB*, praying that the newly ordained may have the apostolic grace and power to lead the people like a shepherd in their proclamation of the gospel before the world, for his steadfastness, wisdom and faithfulness, for the increase, renewal and union of the Church through his ministry exercised in collaboration with others, and for humility in the exercise of authority, so that he will be presented together with all God's household blameless before God (see 1 Corinthians 1.8; Ephesians 5.27; 1 Thessalonians 5.23; 1 Timothy 3.2).

The Giving of the Bible

The Giving of the Bible has always been an important feature of Anglican ordination rites, providing a vivid liturgical expression of the truth that all Christian ministry is grounded in the Scriptures and receives its only authority from the Word of God. However, the question of where it was to be located in the rite proved to be one of the most contentious issues in the revision process in General Synod. In the 1662 and *ASB* Ordinals, it is placed immediately after prayer and the laying on of hands, and many desired that to be its sole location in the new rites, so as to emphasize its importance. Because in this position, however, it was possible for the action to be misunderstood as being somehow part of the central rite of ordination itself or alternatively viewed as just one of several secondary symbolic acts that may take place at this point in the service – especially in the rite for priests (anointing, vesting, presentation with bread and wine) – rather than as the fundamental sign of ministerial authority, others desired to include the option of deferring it until later in the service, at the beginning of the Sending Out. In this position, it was argued, the action would be even more prominent and more closely associated with the sending out of the newly ordained to participate in the evangelistic mission of the Church. In the end, the possibility of opting for either position was allowed, but with the use of the formulae from the *ASB* Ordinal rather than the new forms of words that had been proposed by the Liturgical Commission.

In some dioceses a large Bible is presented to each of the newly ordained in turn; in others, individual copies of the Scriptures are handed over to them. The symbolism of the act may perhaps be more clearly seen when the first of these two practices is followed, especially if the same Bible has been carried prominently in the entrance procession at the beginning of the service and used in the Liturgy of the Word. Note 13 indicates that if the use of a single Bible is adopted, the Giving of the Bible should take place in the earlier position, and then individual copies should also be given, without words, at the Sending Out. If the Giving of the Bible takes place at the Sending Out, however, then individual copies should always be used for it, so that in both cases the newly ordained can proceed to carry them away with them at that point.

(Anointing and Foot-washing)

Although it is very important that the central ritual act of ordination – prayer accompanied by the laying on of hands – should not be obscured by a wealth of secondary symbolism surrounding it, as has so often happened in its earlier history, yet provision is made for one such optional act to take place at this point that may help to bring out the particular character of the order that has just been conferred.

In the case of bishops and priests, anointing with oil became an established feature of their ordination rites in the medieval West, is continued in the Roman Catholic Church today, is already officially provided for in some Churches within the Anglican Communion, and is increasingly practised in the Church of England. Both priests and bishops traditionally had the palms of their hands anointed, since they were about to handle holy things in their liturgical ministry, while bishops also had their heads anointed, following the Old Testament tradition of the anointing of rulers and high priests in this way (modern Roman Catholic practice is to anoint the head but not the hands of bishops). In these rites, therefore, Note 14 gives the option of anointing the palms of the hands in the case of priests and the head in the case of a bishop.

In the case of deacons, the bishop may wash the feet of the newly ordained, following the example of Christ in John 13 (Note 14). This liturgical ceremony was originally part of the baptismal rite in a number of centres of ancient Christianity, on the basis of Jesus' saying that 'If I do not wash you, you have no part in me' (John 13.8), but was later transferred to become an element in the liturgy of Maundy Thursday, where the emphasis of the rite moved away from those who were having their feet washed to the humility of the monarch, abbot or bishop stooping to perform this act of humble service. As only those who have had their feet washed can then be in a position to wash the feet of others (see John 13.14–15), this ceremony might be thought particularly suitable at the beginning of the ministry of deacons, who are called to model Christlike service to the Church.

The Welcome

Ancient ordination rites always concluded with an exchange of a kiss between the president and the newly ordained, and often also between the newly ordained and other members of their order who were present and the people as well. This was the climax of the rite and gave vivid liturgical expression of their acceptance into their office and into a new relationship with the rest of the body of Christ. (In modern Roman Catholic practice, the exchange of the kiss of peace between the bishop and the newly ordained priests and deacons is retained, together with the option of including other members of their order if circumstances permit; at the ordination of a bishop, all bishops present participate.) In these rites there is a dialogue with the congregation, which is intended to give expression to this changed relationship. As the exchange of the Peace within the eucharistic rite happens immediately afterwards, this offers an opportunity for the newly ordained to be greeted individually by the president, members of their order and congregation.

(Vesting)

The vesting of the newly ordained in robes appropriate to their new order has often become a very prominent feature in current ordination practice and, like the presentation of symbols of office, can be in danger of overshadowing the centrality of the prayer with laying on of hands. For that reason, Note 15 suggests two alternative practices for ordinations at which it is desired to vest the newly ordained. The first, that the ordinands should enter at the beginning of the service already wearing the robes of the order to which they are to be admitted, was the ancient practice of the church at Rome. The second is that the vesting should take place after the Welcome and before the Peace. In this case, it will not only be clearly separated from the ordination proper but also be done at the point in the service at which the newly ordained may be about to exercise the liturgical dimension of their new ministries in the Eucharist (as provided for in Note 16) and thus rightly be seen as preparatory for that action.

The Liturgy of the Eucharist

(Presentation of Eucharistic Vessels)

It was part of the Western medieval tradition for priests to be given a chalice and paten at their ordination as symbols of the eucharistic ministry they were to exercise as priests. This custom was explicitly provided for in the *ASB* Ordinal. In current Roman Catholic practice it is the chalice and paten that are about to be used in the ordination Eucharist which are presented to the newly ordained priests. The Revision Committee of General Synod determined that if there were to be any presentation, it should only be of the bread on a paten and the wine in a chalice that were to be used in the ordination Eucharist itself. The Committee, therefore, deleted from the Ordinal the Note that had been drafted by the Liturgical Commission permitting individual eucharistic vessels to be presented, and asserted that 'if individual chalices and patens are given to the newly ordained as presents, this does not form part of the rite'.

Proper Prefaces

While use of the preface of the day is encouraged for Eucharistic Prayers A, B and C, the *CW* Short Preface for Ministry is also provided for optional use in those prayers in the rites for priests and bishops, together with another that picks up images appropriate to the specific order. Because the first of these prefaces, with its reference to celebrating the sacraments of the new covenant, was not considered suitable for the rite for deacons, only one preface is included in this case. An extended preface that develops themes specific to each particular order is also provided as an option for prayers A, B and E in all three rites.

Prayer after Communion

Either the post communion of the day or the post communion that is printed in each rite is said, the latter being different in each case. The prayer after communion which follows is identical in all three rites, and is optional. As Note 17 indicates, one of the regular prayers after communion from the *Common Worship* main volume may be used in its place.

The Sending Out

If the Giving of the Bible has not already taken place, it is done here, immediately before the blessing. The same form of solemn, threefold blessing occurs in all three services, and Note 18 permits it to be preceded by the set of versicles and responses that may be attached to an episcopal blessing at the *CW* initiation services.

At the ordination of a bishop, because the new bishop will carry the pastoral staff on leaving the service, the giving of it is appropriately the last action prior to the dismissal itself. It too is provided with a congregational response.

Note 18 also suggests that the sending out of the newly ordained would be considerably strengthened as a liturgical action if the president were to lead them through the building at the end of the service and hand them over to representatives of the community in which they are to serve.

Further Reading

Paul F. Bradshaw, *Ancient Ordination Rites of East and West*, Pueblo, New York, 1990.

J. N. Collins, *Diakonia: Re-interpreting the Ancient Sources*, Oxford University Press, Oxford, 1990.

P. Gibson (ed.), *Anglican Ordination Rites. The Berkeley Statement: 'To Equip the Saints'. Findings of the Sixth International Anglican Liturgical Consultation, Berkeley, California, 2001*, Grove Worship Series 168, Grove Books, Cambridge, 2002.

Chapter 12

Public Worship with Communion by Extension

A. HISTORY

The Wider Context

The publication of *Public Worship with Communion by Extension* by the Church of England in 2001 was a part of a wider process both in Anglicanism and in the worldwide Church. Extended communion may be defined as the taking of consecrated elements from a Eucharist to a service of the Word, where they are distributed by a deacon or lay person to the congregation. Although there are ancient and medieval precedents, extended communion became a more regular practice in the latter part of the twentieth century. This period saw the development of the centrality of the Eucharist and of receiving communion, as the fruit of the Liturgical Movement. However, this did not go hand in hand with an increase in presbyters; indeed some Churches are suffering from a severe shortage. In light of this, Churches have begun authorizing rites of extended communion under the argument of pastoral necessity, but not without some controversy. It has been a development in the Roman Catholic Church and in some Free Churches, for example English Methodism in *The Methodist Worship Book* (Methodist Publishing House, Peterborough, 1999). As the latter can allow lay presidency, it is not a matter of either lay presidency or extended communion, but maybe of 'both . . . and' in the same church.

The Roman Catholic Church has particularly encouraged communion from the reserved sacrament in the absence of a priest. In 1988 the Congregation for Divine Worship gave instructions as to what was to happen in the *Directory on Sunday Celebrations in the Absence of a Priest*. This document enables bishops to train and authorize lay persons to preside at celebrations of Word and Communion. While the Directory gives only a simple form of the ministry of the Word and the ministry of Communion, various dioceses have elaborated the liturgy to include a set of thanksgivings in the place of the canon of the Mass. This can be seen in the liturgies of the Archdiocese of Regina in Canada (*Ritual for Lay Presiders*, St Peter's Press, Saskatchewan, 1984) and of the Diocese of Northampton in England (*Celebrations of Word and Communion,* Diocese of Northampton Liturgy Commission, 2001). Many Roman Catholic commentators do not welcome this move because they envisage the Mass as a whole rite and receiving communion as integral to the rite. They see a danger in this development of undermining the centrality of eucharistic worship.

The Orthodox Churches have a somewhat similar traditional rite known as the Liturgy of the Presanctified. However, the rationale for these ancient services is somewhat different in that they are conducted by a priest and held on days in Lent when church law does not permit the celebration of a full Eucharist. The Roman Catholic Church traditionally followed this practice only on Good Friday, and the Church of England authorized an equivalent service for Good Friday in *Lent, Holy Week and Easter* (1984, 1986). It is probably helpful to think of extended communion in a different category from all these services.

The Anglican Communion
The oldest example of extended communion in Anglicanism was in the Scottish Episcopal Church in 1764. At this time the Church was under Penal Laws and not allowed to gather in groups larger than five. Thus extended communion was used to take the sacrament to small groups of members. However, the practice was discontinued after the repeal of the laws.

There were some examples of extended communion in Central Africa in the 1960s because, while there were a number of permanent deacons, there was a shortage of priests. Similar reasons led to an 'Order for Communion with the Reserved Sacrament' in the Church of India, Pakistan, Burma and Ceylon. However, it was not until the 1970s and 1980s that many Provinces produced official orders, and now about half of the Provinces of the worldwide Anglican Communion have some sort of official provision. Both Wales and Scotland have authorized rites. The Welsh rite was produced in 2000 (*An Order for Holy Communion outside the Eucharist*) and the present Scottish rite goes back to 1992 (*Administration of Holy Communion by a Deacon or Lay Person*).

Extended communion was also debated in the Anglican Consultative Council (1984, 1987), which noted this growing trend within the Communion. It finally reached the agenda of the Lambeth Conference in 1988. This seems to have given it a certain amount of credibility, particularly as a temporary strategy in light of a shortage of priests. The conference (section 205) observed that this was a practice that had found acceptance in some parts of the Communion.

The Church of England
David Smethurst was an early advocate of extended communion. He was the Rector of Ulverston in Cumbria, a rural benefice, which soon became five congregations with one priest. As there had been many more priests in living memory, there was a high expectation of frequent services of Holy Communion. With one priest this was not possible, and so drawing on the laity, Smethurst developed the idea of extended communion and introduced it in

1979. This was not without controversy, and both Colin Buchanan and Bishop Richard Hanson expressed their concerns about the practice. The advocacy of extended communion in rural situations is also seen in the report of the Archbishop's Commission on Rural Areas, *Faith in the Countryside* (Churchman, Worthing, 1990), which asked for official provision. But this is not the only factor of note. The Church of England's services *Ministry to the Sick* (1983) allowed for previously consecrated elements to be taken to people's homes. Laity now led many parts of the services of the Church, and this included the distribution of Holy Communion. These factors came together to change the climate to make extended communion a possibility.

One factor that is perhaps in danger of being forgotten is the development of women's ministry. In 1987 women were ordained as deacons in the Church of England. It was not until 1994 that they were ordained priest. This left a seven-year period when there were numbers of stipendiary deacons in parishes. Extended communion was used in some places to cover emergencies, but there were also teams in which women deacons were put in the rota (alongside the priests) to preside at extended communion services. This made extended communion a regular event, but the practice ceased when they did become priests, and extended communion began to fade into the background.

Carlisle in 1979 seems to have been the first diocese in England to authorize a local rite. This was then to be followed in at least eight other dioceses in the next two decades and also in some Anglican religious communities. The House of Bishops produced a report *Extended Communion* in 1993 (GS 1082). This got a cool reception in General Synod, many members being unsupportive of extended communion, and some in favour of lay presidency. This led to the report *Eucharistic Presidency* (GS 1248, 1997), which rejected lay presidency. The House of Bishops produced further reports on extended communion in 1995 (GS Misc 452) and 1996 (GS 1230), the latter going through five versions before the final text was agreed. It was not obvious that General Synod would approve this rite. When the votes were taken to allow it to move forward in the synodical process, they passed with a straight majority, but often they did not get a two-thirds majority, which would be required for the final vote. The final voting only just got that two-thirds majority, being very close in the House of Laity.

Liturgical Issues

The House of Bishops makes a categorical distinction between communion of the sick and extended communion. The differences need to be noted, as the policy is different in each case and it is easy for the two to be confused. Communion of the sick takes consecrated elements to sick individuals from the Sunday Eucharist. These are members of the congregation who are not able to be present. There is a consensus that this is appropriate even in churches that have been traditionally against reservation. Extended communion takes consecrated elements to another assembly, owing to the shortage of priests. It is not for the purpose of an absent member but because of the absence of a ministerial priest. Clearly it is not the only strategy for such circumstances, one of which would be to have Morning Prayer or a Service of the Word. There is less agreement about the appropriateness of extended communion, a concern that is not located in any one tradition in the Church of England. Some would reject extended communion as a primary violation of the eucharistic action. Taking, thanking, breaking and receiving are one action. A number of scholars have argued that you cannot divide them and still have a Eucharist.

The service is very clear that it is not a Eucharist and that it is to be used in exceptional circumstances. How then is such a liturgy to be ordered? One way is to take the road of omission: simply leave out all the material in the Eucharist that is consecratory. In Order One this would be clearly seen as being the eucharistic prayer. Some rites in the Anglican Communion have taken this approach, for example the Anglican Church of Canada (*Public Distribution of Holy Communion by Deacons and Lay People*, Anglican Book Centre, Toronto, 1987). The House of Bishops wanted to include rather more than that. They have insisted that some reference is made to the parent Eucharist, as was also the position of Carlisle in 1979. So both Orders at various points introduce material to say something about where the elements were consecrated.

A more difficult issue is about the possibility of some thanksgiving in the service. This is found in a minimal form in both Orders. Other Churches have let this aspect of the rite flourish. This is particularly true of the Roman Catholic texts, where long thanksgiving prayers are included, even with seasonal variations. It has also happened in a few examples within Anglicanism, but most Provinces have been quite coy about developing this type of prayer. If consecration is by thanksgiving, as is the theory of *CW*, then the liturgy has to be very careful not to give the impression of some sort of reconsecration.

In some places there is an offertory procession with bread and wine at the Eucharist alongside the collection of money. This again could be a problem area if the pre-consecrated elements were also brought forward in at this point. To avoid this happening the rubrics direct that the consecrated elements should be on the holy table for the whole service.

While the House of Bishops states that this rite is a temporary provision in the case of pastoral necessity, it awaits to be seen what will happen in the parishes. The danger is that one year's pastoral necessity is next year's tradition. A too easy approach towards authorizing the use of the service could lead to it becoming a norm rather than an exception. This could then lead to confusion in the minds of the laity as to when a service is a Eucharist and when it is reception of communion. Terms like 'deacon's Mass' or 'sister's Mass' in the Roman Catholic Church are warning signs that this confusion can easily occur.

B. COMMENTARY

The name of the service has changed over the years. It began as 'extended communion', the title given to the first House of Bishops' report. In 1988 this was changed to 'Sunday Worship with Holy Communion in the Absence of a Priest'. While this followed the Roman Catholic title, it was felt that it was too negative. There is plenty of worship that goes on in the absence of a priest, for example Matins, Evensong and Services of the Word led by Readers and other lay people. 'Public Worship with Communion by Extension' appeared as a title in 2000 and was the one that was to stick. However, 'extended communion' is still used in the Church as another name for the service.

The Orders provided in *Public Worship with Communion by Extension* are derived from the eucharistic material in *CW*. As this is the distribution of previously consecrated elements, various sections are omitted: the eucharistic prayer in Order One and the prayer of consecration in Order Two. Adjustments are made for lay leadership to the absolution and the blessing, by turning them into prayers. New material is included in each service to clarify the nature of the rite.

Notes

It made clear that this is an exceptional service (Note 1) and thus explicit permission must be obtained from the bishop. The service was not put in the main volume of *CW* in order to clarify this. It is not a normal rite of the Church of England but only happens in exceptional circumstances. It is to be hoped that bishops will exercise their authority with great wisdom.

Care needs to be taken in a benefice so that the Eucharist is celebrated around the churches and that one church does not become a place with only extended communion (Note 2). The bishop not only gives permission for communion by extension to happen but he also authorizes particular people to lead the service. The note specifically says that they should receive some training. This appears to be neglected in some places and might be an appropriate task for a diocesan liturgical committee to undertake. The note also distinguishes those who usually share in giving communion in church from the leaders of this service. While the former may also administer communion in this service, their authorization does not automatically include permission to lead extended communion.

A number of the notes are concerned that the service be seemly and dignified in dress, transportation of the elements and conducting the service. The last note (Note 7) warns of the danger of insufficient amounts of the elements. If this does happen, then there is no way that there can be further consecration. If the wine is insufficient, it would be possible to continue with communion in one kind. It is normally possible to divide the bread into smaller pieces; however, in a severe miscalculation people would have to be told that the elements have run out and so they cannot receive. It might have been appropriate here to make a statement about spiritual communion. This might be an aspect to think through at the training session.

Order One

Order One follows the same named order as in the *CW* main volume and is thus in modern language. There are a number of departures from the text of the parent order and these will be concentrated on in this commentary.

Before the Prayer of Preparation the minister gives an introduction. This contains a Gospel reading (Luke 22.17–19), to set the scene of the Last Supper, and an introduction along the lines used in Morning and Evening Prayer. This specifically includes information on where the Eucharist was celebrated. The absolution is written for lay people to use, who will by definition be leading this service. The ministry of the Word otherwise continues as in the *CW* main volume.

The Peace has an introduction that also includes a statement about where the Eucharist was celebrated. The eucharistic prayer is then omitted and replaced with a reading, from a choice of five lessons from the New Testament (Mark 10.32–34, 42–45; Luke 24.30–34; John 6.53–58; Revelation 19.6–9a; 1 Peter 2.21–25), and a prayer said by the whole congregation. Neither of these two elements, the reading and the prayer, is directly about the Eucharist. In some traditions a reading of the narrative of institution from the New Testament and a prayer of thanksgiving form the heart of the Eucharist. The Church of England has been careful at this point not to confuse the issue, by adding a reading about the Last Supper and a thanksgiving prayer, as this might have looked to some like a Eucharist. There were suggestions in the past of a number of these thanksgiving prayers, but this was not accepted by all and so only one mandatory prayer is now given. This reading and prayer are to be said from the lectern or stall. Location here is also of symbolic importance, again indicating that this service is different from the Eucharist and the prayer is not a eucharistic prayer.

For communion the minister moves to the holy table. Again there are introductory words that go back to *Ministry to the Sick* (1983). This order then follows that in the *CW* main volume, save to replace the Blessing with the Grace.

It is important that those who lead the service understand the differences from the Eucharist and the rationale for the way the present order is created. It would be easy for someone ill prepared to be caught doing something that is of dubious theology. Leaders also need to be trained in the general issues of leading worship, preparation, choosing hymns, lectionaries, use of body and voice.

Order Two

This is shaped as in the *BCP* and is in traditional language. It also follows its parent order in the *CW* main volume. As in Order One, there is an introduction with a reading from Luke and some statements of the nature of the service. This is set in a form based on the introduction to Morning and Evening Prayer in the *BCP*. The service then continues as the *CW* eucharistic rite to the Comfortable Words.

The Prayer Book divided up the medieval eucharistic prayer into various parts. The preface with its thanksgiving was separated from the prayer of consecration, and so it is arguable that the preface might have been retained in this order. However, it is replaced by the General Thanksgiving. This is then followed by one of the five readings, as found in Order One, read at the lectern or minister's stall. There seems to be no reason why the order of thanksgiving and reading is reversed in this order from Order One, except that it does follow the Prayer Book flow of thanksgiving followed by Humble Access. The same words of introduction as Order One are used in the giving of communion. This is followed by reception, and the service continues as in *CW* Order Two, finishing with the Grace.

Guidelines Issued by the House of Bishops

The guidelines are an important part of the booklet and need to be read and studied by all leading this service. The first note shows the background to the service as being in the needs of the rural church. Benefices in the countryside have continued to get larger with pastoral reorganization and the situation has become more pressing than it was in the 1970s when Smethurst first began to experiment with extended communion.

The bishops note that there are affinities with communion for the sick, which is increasingly done by teams of lay people in parishes. However, the bishops acknowledge that extended communion is a step further and specific authorization is needed by those to lead the service. The bishops make plain that this is 'not in itself a celebration of Holy Communion' and is 'regarded as exceptional and provisional'. That it remain so will depend on the provision of either non-stipendiary or ordained local priests, particularly for these country parishes.

A Form of Preparation

The form of preparation is as in the *CW* main volume, except that the absolution is written in a form for use by lay people. This material is of a penitential nature and put as a separate preparation so as not to overwhelm the penitential section of the Sunday Eucharist. It can be used individually or as a corporate service, which might be appropriate in penitential seasons.

Further Reading

James Dallen, *The Dilemma of Priestless Sundays*, Liturgy Training Publications, Chicago, 1994.

A. Hughes, *Public Worship and Communion by Extension: Some Pastoral and Theological Issues*, Alcuin/GROW Joint Liturgical Study 53, Grove Books, Cambridge, 2002.

David Smethurst, *Extended Communion: An Experiment in Cumbria*, Grove Worship Series 96, Grove Books, Bramcote, 1986.

Phillip Tovey, *Communion outside the Eucharist*, Alcuin/GROW Joint Liturgical Study 26, Grove Books, Bramcote, 1993.

Phillip Tovey, 'The Development of Extended Communion in Anglicanism', *Studia Liturgica* 30 (2000), pp. 226–38.

Phillip Tovey, *Public Worship with Communion by Extension: A Commentary*, Grove Worship Series 167, Grove Books, Cambridge, 2001.

Index